Gender Work

Gender Work

Feminism after Neoliberalism

Robin Truth Goodman

GENDER WORK
Copyright © Robin Truth Goodman, 2013.

Softcover reprint of the hardcover 1st edition 2013 978-1-137-38119-4

All rights reserved.

A version of chapter 2 was originally published in Philosophy Today.

First published in 2013 by
PALGRAVE MACMILLAN®
in the United States—a division of St. Martin's Press LLC,
175 Fifth Avenue, New York, NY 10010.

Where this book is distributed in the UK, Europe and the rest of the world,
this is by Palgrave Macmillan, a division of Macmillan Publishers Limited,
registered in England, company number 785998, of Houndmills,
Basingstoke, Hampshire RG21 6XS.

Palgrave Macmillan is the global academic imprint of the above companies
and has companies and representatives throughout the world.

Palgrave® and Macmillan® are registered trademarks in the United States,
the United Kingdom, Europe and other countries.

ISBN 978-1-349-47960-3   ISBN 978-1-137-38120-0 (eBook)
DOI 10.1057/9781137381200

Library of Congress Cataloging-in-Publication Data is available from the
Library of Congress

A catalogue record of the book is available from the British Library.

Design by Newgen Knowledge Works (P) Ltd., Chennai, India.

First edition: December 2013

10 9 8 7 6 5 4 3 2 1

Contents

Contents

Introduction

In June of 2012, the US Congress rejected a bill that would have given working women rights to information about differential pay. The 2012 Paycheck Fairness Act would have required employers in the United States to prove that pay inequality was based on qualifications, performance, levels of education, or other considerations unrelated to gender, and it would have opened workplace gender discrimination, based on this newly available information, to litigation. The vote in the Senate was mainly along party lines, 52 to 47, short of the 60 votes the Democrats would have needed to avoid a filibuster. The consensus in the media was that the vote was an election-year spectacle that the Democrats knew had no chance of winning even as they appealed to the media for coverage, as the Democrats were aiming to woo women voters and force Republicans to explain at the polls why they supported gender pay inequality. A similar bill in 2010 had a similar fate, with the Democrats falling two votes short of passage, as Ben Nelson, Democrat from Nebraska, switched ranks and joined the Republicans. In 2012, in face of the Democrats' accusation that the Republicans were "waging a war on women," the Republicans cited two rationales: that in a time of unemployment at over 8 percent, the Democrats were trying to pass a "job killing" bill; and that the Democrats' bill would be a boon for trial lawyers. In such a climate, treating women unfairly, then, must be acceptable, such rationales assume, because anybody should be grateful for a job regardless of the conditions or discrimination.

Meanwhile, the Institute for Women's Policy Research published a report showing that the gendered wage gap is growing in all major race and ethnic groups, and that women's gains on the labor market have been slowing since the rapid increase evident in the 1980s and early 1990s. In 2012, the overall ratio of women's to men's median full-time weekly earnings was 80.9 percent, a decline by one point since 2011, and the overall ratio of women's to men's median annual full-time earnings was 77 percent in 2011. As women have come back faster than men to their pre-recession unemployment levels, they are placed in jobs that men were forced to leave during the crisis, meaning that the overall employment costs during the recovery are lower for the same number of employees: the recession transferred jobs to women at lower pay. What is more: "Both earnings ratios (for weekly full-time workers and for year-round full-time workers) reflect gender differences in both hourly wages and the number of hours worked each year (among full-time workers). If part-time and part-year workers were included, the ratios of women's to men's earning would be much lower" (Hegewisch, Williams, and Edwards). Both the US Department of Labor and the National Women's Law Center (NWLC) continue to document that women make 77 cents to a man's dollar at comparable jobs and performance levels (the percentage is even greater for women of color, down to 54 cents on the white male dollar for African-American women), and average $10,784 less per year, according to Naomi Wolf in *The Guardian*. In fact, Wolf goes on, an equitable pay-level for women would mean a 12 percent hike in labor costs that would be cut from corporate profits. "An unspoken driver of profits for corporate America is," Wolf concludes, "the ability to pay women less with impunity."

Gender Work: Feminism after Neoliberalism argues that feminist theory needs to reconsider the relationship between labor and gender because labor currently has acquired a reemergent public relevance.[1] The book considers ways that neoliberal ideological forces depend on the production of femininity, and how femininity clears a symbolic space through which the "free reproductive labor" of actions, traits, sensibilities, and affects linked to gender can be reconceived in capitalizable form: under neoliberalism, femininity has become the ground of an ongoing primitive accumulation that continues to separate workers from their production. If, for example, sociability and emotions could be the prior gesturings of private life, identified through the domestic as "women's work," now they have become an industry, produced and sold as profitable commodities in privatized processes of self-invention. "Women's work" is the territory on which capital captures reproductive time.

Gender Work poses, in fact, that economic demands have taken up some of the role which second-wave feminism, following Freudian and Lacanian psychoanalysis, attributed to the Symbolic or to symbolic exchange. In his famous essay on "Femininity," Freud set up an ideal category of the "normal woman" toward which women were supposed to develop but made that category nearly impossible for the developing individual to identify with. "A comparison," Freud observes, "with what happened with boys tells us that the development of a little girl into a normal woman is more difficult and complicated" (117). If the "normal woman" ideal does not destine the little girl, then Freud offers no suggestion of where it might come from, how it works, or what it has to do with the failures of development that he describes. Lacan reads in Freud's symbolic a fictional "ego-Ideal"—through which we project ourselves into social life—that is alienated from inner life. Jacqueline Rose reads Freud as saying that Freud's "femininity" assumes an acknowledgement that "there is a resistance to identity at the very heart of psychic life" (91), in other words, that there is a deep and irreconcilable division between the symbolic content of social life and the individuals who are called to embody that symbolic content.

Gender Work is concerned with addressing the relationship between the rise of corporate power under neoliberalism and the femininity that continues to misrecognize those who are called to be subjects in its image. For example, Ann Gray shows how "consumer skills and knowledges" embedded in the construction of the identity "femininity" "are being actively transformed into marketable commodities (especially, but not exclusively, by women)" (503). In other words, "the enterprising subject" and "the feminine subject" are being articulated together as a product and a value for management: "While these characteristics (flexibility, valuable skills, informal knowledges) would easily inhabit the discourses of enterprise, 'new' management, and postmodernity, they are also strikingly present in critiques of 'the feminine.' For example, flexibility is arguably a constant dimension of feminine subjectivity, especially, but not only, in relation to the labour market and the workplace. Now in the post-Fordist economy, this is a necessary 'attitude' for all workers, from manual to professional occupational groups. Similarly, those skills more often attributed to the feminine (listening, supporting and facilitating, caring and encouraging, emotional intelligence, and intuition) are now endorsed within management literature" (493). According to Gray, who celebrates this trend, entrepreneurial women are selling femininity as a "competency" that can enhance managerial employability. Such "femininity" is created or built through self-help, shopping, advertising, editorials, marketing, and training. Professional femininity—or the "ideal self"—is the "outcome, of…selecting and purchasing the right commodities" (495):

> Women are encouraged to see themselves as a project, their bodies and their selves as a site of production. 'New regimes' are the practical vehicle whereby the dedicated follower can achieve the transformation of body size, diet, face and hair, while fashion, cookery, interior decoration and sexual tips promise the same magical resolutions to the dilemmas of modern living. We might add to print media the more recent televisual versions for daytime and increasingly…evening viewing and their obsession with the 'makeover'. Thus, within these popular genres, the constituted feminine subject is a self in the process of transformation with

the expectation, or at least the possibility, of achieving an ideal self. Self-management is required in order to be successful in this enterprise, and underpinning transformativity is the possibility of the plastic body, the flexible subject, and of becoming a more desirable [read, more employable] self. (496)

The ideal self (for work) is feminine, a self that can be sold and, as such, is produced: "feminine" desire has become an apparatus that makes the productive laboring body, or calls it into being as a commodity.

Gender Work argues that the Freudian disjuncture between the Symbolic and the person it is meant to classify is inside and necessary to corporate "common sense": the idea that women must masquerade as "women" in the image of the corporation. Though Gray's ethnography shows the feminization of middle-management in service sectors, *Gender Work* indicates that this happens in different ways at different economic levels: though femininity appears differently for regimes of domestic labor, for example, than it does in Gray's examples, what counts as femininity is being invented and manufactured for profit throughout neoliberalism's economic hierarchies. This book poses two main theoretical challenges to thinking on the relationship between gender and the contemporary economy: (1) even as feminist theory has criticized Marx and Marxism for its reliance on the masculinity of the subject of labor, what does it mean that the subject of labor is now becoming increasingly feminized, and what would such a feminized subject look like as it is increasingly universalized? The gendered wage differential creates a new source of surplus labor: if women's work gets paid on average 77 cents on the white male dollar, then employing women gives the employer an extra 23 cents of pure profit. As a result, one can discern tendencies of the "feminization of work" where capital is expanding the economic applications of femininity in order to expand pure surplus, no matter what kinds of bodies end up answering the call to feminized work. In such instances, femininity has less to do with bodies than with the way capital is calling subjects into "feminine" positions from which it can extract profit. It is even possible to say that Marx foresaw the expandability of surplus as reliant on the expandability of a symbolic of femininity and gendered time.

This means that: (2) capital is creating and must create enclaves of femininity as a source of new profits. For Marx, "primitive accumulation" was when capital, in its ever-present need for expansion, would find places outside of capital to turn into capitalizable form. Marx's classic example is when the factory system drove the peasants off the land, not only dispossessing the peasants of their commons but also alienating the peasants from their means of production so they had nothing left to sell but their labor power.

Some contemporary Marxist theorists, like David Harvey for example, have argued that primitive accumulation is ongoing, and that capital needs continually to create new objects of accumulation once the existing ones deplete: in neoliberalism, says Harvey,

> Accumlation by dispossession has been more and more internalized within the core regions of capitalism even as it has widened and deepened through the global system. We should not regard primitive accumulation…as simply being about the prehistory of capitalism. It is ongoing and in recent times has been revived as an increasingly significant element in the way global capitalism is working to consolidate class power. And it can encompass everything—from the taking away of rights of access to land and livelihoods to the retrenchment of rights (to pensions, education and healthcare, for example) hard-won in the past through fierce class struggles by working class movements. (2010: 310),

As Harvey is concerned with addressing this surplus in relation to urbanization and construction, his insight is that areas of reproduction that have been considered "outside" to capital are now being reconceptualized as accommodating to and appropriable in capital's terms. Harvey, however, does not consider how capital can create new "outsides" by producing gender as a cultural symbol of outsidedness that can then become "reproduction" or "surplus" and therefore a target of accumulation. Feminist political economists have subsequently observed that within the process of primitive accumulation in neoliberalism, gender is "articulating a specific relationship between wealth and command" (Keating et al., 2010: 154). *Gender Work* shows how femininity has become a focus for capital's production of a symbolic of surplus. Capital needs gender, and creates gender, so that it can eat up the surplus of 23 cents on the dollar.

Because capitalist expansion now depends so fundamentally on the cultural production of gendered value, it has become urgent to analyze not only the traditions of feminist theory and political economy in relation to women's work but also the cultural texts, narratives, and literature promoting capital's new deployment of the gendered division of labor. Jennifer Bair has shown how feminist international political economy has moved from thinking through the large symbolic structures of capitalism and the international gender divisions of labor as underlying patriarchy (in writers like Maria Mies), to, more recently, foregrounding local, autonomous, diverse, and observable practices as openings for women's economic resistance. Inspiring a generation of feminist researchers, J. K. Gibson-Graham, for example, has labeled local markets as "nonhegemonic" and "noncapitalist" because they "did not line up and fit in with industrial change" (vii) and "must take place in the social interstices, in the realm of experiment, or in a visionary space of revolutionary social replacement" (3). For Gibson-Graham, such practices occur at the periphery of capitalism, an ill-defined category-space whose predominant concrete form is the female-centered household: "the before or the after of capitalism" (7). Such a vision would actually leave capitalist exploitative relations as they are and move into the spaces that capital seems to leave aside, despite the widespread evidence of capital's abilities to absorb whatever it encounters. Defining the female-centered household as somehow devoid or outside of capitalism, in fact, contradicts fervent, nonaccomodationist currents within feminism that have never understood reproductive labor as beside or beyond capital but rather, inextricably, at its very center, insisting, with Silvia Federici, that "We have never been outside of [capitalist relations]. We struggle to break capital's plan for women, which is an essential moment of that division of labor" (2012: 19).

As Bair continues, rather than to focus on local instances, a more satisfactory perspective "must look to how gender as a set of context-specific meanings and practices, intersects the structure of global capitalism and its systemic logic of value extraction and capital accumulation" (205). In other words, the symbolic structure of gender necessarily influences the production of value in work. Capital can extract value by producing and revising the connection between the symbolic and the economic relationships it fosters. Feminism should not lose sight of gender as a construction in process and a source of value. Gender assumes value or power in relation to broad social and symbolic needs in response to which capital produces bodies. *Gender Work* challenges political economy not to marginalize its correspondences with cultural narratives through which capital, moving through the symbolic, grasps at the social.

Neoliberalism and the War on Women

The intense focus on labor in political debate includes legislation over cuts to pensions, health care, and other benefits; an attack on teachers and teachers' unions (involving as well the charter school movement that redesigns teacher labor by excluding rights to collective bargaining); unmanageable levels of unemployment; a growing public awareness of growing economic inequalities and polarization (partly corralled into social movements like Occupy Wall Street); increased policy drives toward "flexibilization"; heated pronouncements (usually without evidence) about who are the "job creators" and how to treat them better (mostly, quite ironically, at the expense of working people); vilification of the underemployed, and even the semiemployed in low-waged industries like fast-food; heated vilification of those who "send jobs overseas" (even as incentives for "sending jobs overseas" are strengthened); and—most centrally—a "financialization" of the global economy that makes labor less essential for capital to profit.

At the same time, news reports have identified a set of rhetorical and political trends as what they are calling "the war on women," consisting, in part, of a whittling away at the few remaining abortion and welfare protections; a defunding of women's health care services (Planned Parenthood, most notably); a slashing of insurance coverage for certain areas of women's health; multiple state-level bills mandating ultrasounds for women seeking abortion; limitations on access to contraception; severe cuts to Medicaid (where women make up 70 percent (or 19 million) of its beneficiaries) and Medicare, where women constitute the majority of recipients (Covert); increasing controls on abortions for teenage girls; extensions of waiting periods for receiving abortions as well as reductions in the length of the "first trimester" during which *Roe v. Wade* protects the legality of abortions and access; a subprime mortgage crisis that disproportionally hit women and women of color in particular; a series of collapses of factory buildings in Bangladesh (currently up to four) where the workforce is composed of 80 percent women, employed in the production of cheap clothing for Western outlets (the latest of these collapses in April 2013 killed over 1000 and injured over 1000 workers); cuts to funding for battered women's shelters (including requiring drug testing and proof of citizenship before battered women can receive medical treatment); cuts to public sector employment which affect women more than men workers; cuts to public education at all levels; a disparagement of labor sectors and labor organizing initiatives that are identified with "women's work" (including teaching but not limited to that); restricting women's access to legal recourse for workplace abuse and discrimination by supporting barriers to class action law suits filed due to the vast and diverse mistreatment of working women (under a 5–4 Supreme Court decision on a lawsuit filed pursuant to Title VII of the 1964 Civil Rights Act:[2] Walmart v. Dukes (2012)); and a moralistic public nervousness about criminality, attention deficit, mental health, learning aptitudes, obesity, deviance, and general bad behavior in children that is usually connected, by those engaged in such allegations, to some kind of damaging parenting practiced predominantly by mothers (most often, working mothers). Despite all this, and despite how the attack on labor and the "war on women" intersect in multiple areas, feminist theory disassociated women's experience from theories of class in ways that *Gender Work* considers unnecessary and detrimental.

Gender Work foregrounds how changes in global economic structures understood as "neoliberalism" are foregrounding "women's work" in order to produce new fields of exploitation. "Neoliberalism" here is identified as a historical stage starting roughly in the early 1970s, distinguished by a set of economic and political transformations including: an attack on the welfare state (often related to a conscious decision on the part of those in power to shut down the activism in civil society in the sixties and early seventies); the financialization of the economy; the end of development as defining economic policies between nation-states; the end of the gold standard; the Bretton Woods agreement (particularly after 1971 when currencies were tied to the US dollar); the stagnation of wages in developed economies; the increase in access to debt (and an escalation in the amount of debt) for workers to make up for stagnated salaries; the movement of retirement savings into securities investments; the acceleration of economic polarization; the accelerated movement of manufacturing jobs into developing nations; the increasing "informationalization" of developed economies; the federal government's bail-out of New York City as it was on the verge of bankruptcy; the crack-down and depoliticization of labor related to the "flexibilization" of work; the privatization of public functions (particularly welfare state functions); an intensification of consumerism; an increasing consensus that all value is market value (economism) and related developments.

I would also add to this list of neoliberal practices the "feminization" of the economy: the growing dominance of service, caring, and affective jobs related to expanded markets in socialization processes. Many of the transformative features attributable to "neoliberalism" increase emphatically the ways that "women's work" has become exploitable as well as the ways that gender has been reconstructed inside the development of new labor regimes. For instance, cuts to public spending affect women disproportionally in various guises including forcing women into low-paid and deskilled "flexible" jobs with few benefits and virtually no security for individuals or families, and worker debt is used to lure "Third World" women into the financial circle—as David Harvey says, a politics that responds to capital's "perpetual need to find profitable terrains" (2012: 5), or to create them; microlending institutions search out such women because of their reputation for submission, reliability, and the tightness of community surveillance possibilities. In fact, women and the public sector—or, women *as* the public sector, *as* workers—can be understood as the few remaining spheres that are still in the process of being transformed into identification with capital. Marx describes as "primitive accumulation" "the expropriation and expulsion of the agricultural population, intermittent but renewed again and again, [which] supplied, as we saw, the town industries with a mass of prole-terians" (*Capital,* Vol. 1: 697). While Marx hones in on the historical force, backed by police and armies, applied to compel workers in agricultural and domestic industries into factories, where the means of production would no longer belong to them, today, there are few regions left that have not already become coterminous with capital, that are still independent. Though still partially unconnected and autonomous (at least on a symbolic level), "wom-en's work" and the public sphere are in the course of being molded to con-form to "neoliberal" models of appropriation under development, but the direction of such development has not yet been settled.

Gender Work looks at ways in which feminism has used the private sphere to create a conceptual zone of separation for women, apart from paid produc-tion. This separation between private life and paid production—where "pri-vate life" constitutes the "reproduction," preparing the laborer for the next day of work and socializing the next generation of workers—has informed other types of symbolic separation essential for industrial relations of capi-tal, like the separation between mental and manual labor, between ideol-ogy and base materialism, between use value and exchange value, between institutional regulation (law) and free markets, between unpaid (or surplus) and paid (or necessary) labor. Gender can be read as inside such divisions. Work that is specifically identified as "women's work" creates surplus value for neoliberal capital.

Gender Work examines how, within Second-Wave theories of femininity, the break from class analysis assumed new features within femininity that seemed disconnected from the contemporary economy and its institutions, concentrating more fundamentally on elements of gender construction like language, consumption, desire, socialization, symbolic exchange, domes-tic life, and the production of subjectivities. These elements, though, still maintained shadow correlations with a history associated with principles of labor and production, with Marxism and the new left, correlations that, with the consolidation of neoliberal economic relations, have become much more visible. Scrutinizing the configurations of work within innovations in feminist theoretical research, *Gender Work* then shows how literature and critical theory can reread women's unpaid work time as central to the global economy and interpret unpaid labor time as foregrounded within contem-porary constructions of gender. Finally, *Gender Work* brings class and class struggle back into communications with gender theory in order to empha-size not only how labor is becoming newly visible within political discourse but also how gender is becoming, on the one hand, the premise of a new organization of exploitable free time and, on the other, increasingly integral to retheorizing transformative social action and reclaiming time.

The Early Second-Wave and Its Discourse on "Women's Work"

Second-Wave feminist theory can be understood as rooted in a discourse about work. Betty Friedan's famous declaration—that the problem of women's isolation lay buried in the American psyche and could be solved by women's entry into the workforce—seemed to apply only to white elites of the suburban professional classes in industrialized countries (women in other in classes, races, geographical locations, and historical moments were often already at work). However, the idea that women's position in the private sphere meant that they were defined differently as workers provided a framework for politicizing women as a group even before 1963 when Friedan made her intervention, and the idea that "women's work" in industrialization influenced the historical formation of domesticity formed part of a discourse on women's oppression.[3] For Maria Dalla Costa in the early seventies, for example, "the housewife [is] central" (21) to understanding contemporary forms of capitalist exploitation because the housewife as a figure results from the destruction of community life precipitated by capitalist expansion and primitive accumulation, the separation of workers from their means of production, and capital's purchasing monopoly over labor power. The housewife's disengagement from productive labor makes it necessary for labor power to be bought and sold in markets, as the only property the laborer has left to sell.[4] Delineating geographies of reproduction outside of the direct control of productive technologies, the wage, she says, is not only a method for exploitation of the waged worker but also organizes the exploitation of nonwaged work for profit. The aim of a women's politics cannot then be to advance from the home to the workplace as a site of liberation but rather to "immediately break the whole structure of domestic work" (36), what she calls the "social factory" of reproduction (22) that sustains the growth of capital, and, in destroying the nuclear family, also to refuse work, to refuse liberation through work, that is, to build up autonomous creativity that does not offer the alternative to "being imprisoned in the house" as being a "clinching [of women] to desks or machines" that would provide "another degree of capitalist control and regimentation" (50).

However, neither Dalla Costa nor Selma James, on whose political analysis from the 1950's Dalla Costa draws, concretely imagines what kinds of social organization would follow from a refusal of domesticity *and* work,[5] nor do they assess or reflect on Marx's notion that work produces the consciousness of emancipation in the practices of reshaping primary materials and of controlling the temporalities of objects:

The transformation of the material by living labour, by the realization of living labour in the material—a transformation which, as purpose, determines labour and is its purposeful activation (a transformation which does not only posit the form as external to the inanimate object, as a mere vanishing image of its material consistency)—thus preserves the material in a definite form, and subjugates the transformation of the material to the purpose of labour. Labour is the living, form-giving fire; it is the transitoriness of things, their temporality, as their formation by living time. (*Grundrisse*: 360–361)

Second-Wave feminist theory provides some additional tools, not available to Dalla Costa or James, for reconceptualizing "women's work" as neither dominated by the factory nor by the domestic model but rather as formulated in reference to subjective processes that still might escape, at least in part, from total immersion in objectified cultures of quantifiable profit: the production of subjectivities, language acquisition, corporeal realignments, the management of ideas, and, of course, the socialization of the imagination. Though *Gender Work* can only suggest where the redefining of "women's work" along the lines of poststructuralist feminist concepts might lead, it insists that even poststructuralist feminist theory was always proceeding toward such a redefining and needs, now more than ever, to acknowledge this tendency and make it explicit.

"Women's Work"

Philosophical strains of feminism are not the only places where "women's work" is producing new symbolic structures that enhance and multiply possibilities for profit within neoliberal economies, though these are the main foci of *Gender Work*. The mainstream media, too, sometimes recognizes that workers' issues and women's issues not only overlap but more than often coincide and that "gender" is often a placeholder for "class." There has been marked interest in how the changing structure of work infiltrates the organization of social relations in reference to gender and how gender can prepare the terrain for creating new profit resources in labor. Two articles can serve as examples: "Why Women Still Can't Have It All" by Princeton University professor of politics and international affairs, Anne-Marie Slaughter, in the July/August 2012 issue of *The Atlantic*, and "Two Classes, Divided by 'I Do'" by Jason DeParle in the 14 July 2012 edition of *The New York Times*. The first article reenvisions women's professional labor as a model for labor flexibility in general; the second worries about the dissolution of the nuclear family because of its negative impact on children while still touting the inevitability of this alternative family structure that allows the depreciation of wages, starting with women's wages. Together, the two articles reveal how "women's work" is site registering an ideology of emergent types of class struggle across the spectrum of class positions.

Slaughter starts by attributing to "feminist beliefs" (86) her success-ful career as the first woman director of policy planning at the US State Department under the directorship of Hillary Clinton, for which she got a leave-of-absence from her job as a law professor and dean of Princeton's Woodrow Wilson School of Public and International Affairs. Before her stint in Washington, Slaughter participated on a lecture circuit, encouraging young women that they could realize the feminist dream of entering the pro-fessional workforce while still having a quality family life. When Slaughter leaves Washington for the sake of her family who needs her attentions and care in ways her husband alone could not give, she notes that the claims on time demanded by government service or other similarly power-driven employment made it impossible to be a leader and have a family at once. The solution to the problem originally raised by a pioneering generation of feminists, according to Slaughter, is for women to hold positions and wield power, where they can change how work is configured to be more family friendly: more allowances for work to be done remotely, more "space for play and imagination" (101), less work restricted to long hours in the office, more policies that let parents take breaks in their careers for extended periods, with pay and without consequences to their career track.[6]

Though Slaughter does admit that "I am writing from my demographic—highly educated, well-off women who are privileged enough to have choices in the first place" (89), she does not outwardly realize that she is describing, in a sense, exactly the way "women's work" has been revised in accordance with neoliberal ambitions. Not only does she disregard, as Naomi Wolf remarks in "Why Women Still Can't Ask the Right Questions," "the fact that afflu-ent working women and their partners overwhelmingly offload the work-family imbalance onto lower income women—overwhelmingly women of color"—, acclaiming a type of work organization that forces migrancy for the sake of cheapening wages. Also, as she apologetically surrenders her job in the State Department and concedes apologetically, to return to her ten-ured position at Princeton, troubled that she might be seen as forsaking her commitment to feminism, she overlooks that frequent lags in working-time are often experienced by working women and men under conditions of flexi-bilization (or unemployment), most times without choice: paid time, or nec-essary labor time, has been substantially reduced rather than surplus time (time of reproduction) increased and compensated. Additionally, Slaughter has no perspective on how creative service work *has* become an increasingly prevalent type of work where women workers in particular are undervalued, and where much of the labor that goes into the production of profits is done for free, often without even the protections that come with the wage. Lastly, Slaughter does not figure how much work has moved away from offices (or factories) and into homes, burdening women disproportionally, lacing them with the overhead costs of production, indebting them to financiers, and extending the time of work into both leisure and family time. Such a trend does not bode well for quality family time for many.

Slaughter's article exhibits how new social relations of work are communicated through and as gender. This effect is achieved predominantly by a displacement of class onto gender, a displacement that serves to give a positive moral gloss to capital's side in its struggle against labor. In addressing what it calls "striking changes in family structure," the *New York Times* article performs a similar displacement at the level of the middle and working classes. In contrast to the *Atlantic* article that glosses the structures of labor oppression as a morally positive aspect that liberates the work of elite women, the *New York Times* article blames changes in gendered lifestyles for women's wage depression. "College-educated Americans," DeParle specifies,

> Are increasingly likely to marry one another, compounding their growing advantages in pay. Less-educated women ..., who left college without finishing [a] degree, are growing less likely to marry at all, raising children on pinched paychecks that come in ones, not twos... Changes in marriage patterns—as opposed to changes in individual earnings—may account for as much as 40 percent of the growth in certain measures of inequality.

"The middle is shifting to the bottom," DeParle further explains, and the reason is "not the impact of globalization on their wages but a 6-foot-8-inch man named Kevin." In other words, women themselves are responsible for the impoverishment of the middle class by choosing a particular gendered demographic life-pattern, a life without men.

For *The New York Times*, the problem with the way women have entered the workforce at the expense of married life has been the effects on children. Whereas conventionally married parents have the time (as well as the money) to send their kids to Boy Scouts as well as summer camp, karate lessons, Disney, and singalong, for single mothers—who are "more likely to have children with more than one man"—"time away [from work] is money lost." That is, mother's time is shifted away from reproduction, now directly exploitable in the workforce, and as a result, children are not being prepared as the next generation of "good labourers," causing a general economic downturn. Whereas children of conventionally married parents can overcome obstacles, succeed, and move up, according to the Brookings

Institution, "there are suggestions that the absence of a father in the house makes it harder for children to climb the economic ladder." The effects of single mothering, as presented in DeParle's anecdotal evidence with the appropriate level of pathos, are economic but also physical, spiritual, and psychological, ranging from hunger to problems in school, including autism. Though statistics are given that demonstrate the relative hardship of children growing up in homes with single mothers rather than married ones, no comparative data is presented for children growing up in households with single fathers (or any other arrangements). The article refuses to consider that absent fathers may influence their offsprings' economic future and instead insists that only mothers are to blame (in the example given, the mother is to blame for a pregnancy during college where the father is African-American, though racial designations are not otherwise assigned, marking the act even further—the article seems to suggest—with a sense of failure, depravity, and wrong-doing, even maybe deserving of such dire economic punishment).

According to "Two Classes," the growing economic polarization between children of families with single mothers and children of families with married mothers (a disparity which extends even to adulthood, according to the studies) can be said to result from many different historical factors, though marriage for women is touted as the most significant parameter. Less significant are: "the growing premium a college education commands, technological change that favors mind over muscle, the growth of the financial sector, the loss of manufacturing jobs to automation and foreign competitors, and the decline of labor unions." The influence such factors play on the economic standing of women and their jobs is not explained because the article funnels all such causes into the higher potential of women's marriage to elevate, and of women's nonmarriage to denigrate, regardless of the broader structural frame. Women's decision not to marry is the primary catalyst toward economic dissolution, the cause for which these other factors are but effects.

Additionally, as women and their work stand in for the failed economy (because of their moral failing), they also are positioned as exhibiting the failure of public supports for work: "After Ms. Schairer [the unmarried example] had an operation for cervical cancer last summer, the surgeon told her to take six weeks off. She went back to work five weeks early... 'I can't have six weeks with no pay.'" "Women's work" indicates a lapse in the public obligation of supporting workers through, for example, health care, sick leave, and childcare but also a lapse in the politicization of work that collective bargaining might ensure. Instead, as a model of the impoverishment of workers through work, "women's work" is only to be thought as the antithesis to marriage, a transfer of time away from the "free labor" of reproduction, yet it still is imaginable only in a privatized, domestic arrangement where protective public rights are not even thinkable let alone negotiable.

Gender Work

Gender Work examines indications that gender has similarly assumed the functions of class and productivity in critical theory and literature. The current organizations of production relies on gender as a heretofore undercapitalized zone of primary accumulation and profit because of *women's work*'s relation to time, language, socialization, education, care, affect, private domesticity, and the production of subjects. Further, *Gender Work* also teases out openings for different types of feminist interventions, arguments, and analytical constructions that the "feminization of work" makes visible.

Chapter 1 reviews the scholarship that tried to reconcile Marxism with Feminism during the emergence of Feminism's Second Wave. At first, feminist research assumed women's work as outside production in a sphere of reproduction, adopting the model of ideology critique to explain that the oppression of women is "relatively autonomous" and, therefore, has an independent history from the oppression of labor. Other feminists countered that women need to be understood in relation to production, but including them would mean that the category of class would be abandoned. This chapter looks at how Marx, in contrast, posits the gradual feminization of labor and labor-time as necessary for capitalism's historical project. It argues that the current economy demands, with Marx, that feminism develop a gendered theory of class that can claim back women's control of their working time.

Chapter 2 looks at Julia Kristeva's detective novel *Possessions* in light of her philosophy of the Semiotic, or pre-linguistic bodily thought, and the Symbolic, or the social conventions of language. Kristeva's theory of the Symbolic depends on an original, infantile separation with the mother and her language. *Possessions* illustrates this loss in a murder plot where the mother's language is lost: the hired language teacher beheads her, taking her place. By adopting a popular form for her philosophical concepts, Kristeva shows that the necessary resolution of the conflict between the Semiotic and the Symbolic results from a commodifying of the maternal function of language socialization as paid service. This article indicates how feminist philosophy's work on language and the subject intersects with a narrative of neoliberal labor reorganization.

Chapter 3 suggests that the anthropologist Aihwa Ong represents the next step of the critical conversation that culminated, for the most part, in the generation of Judith Butler and Donna Haraway. Where Butler and Haraway use language as the primary category where identity is constructed, Ong presumes work as the primary social lever that places value onto bodies as it is manipulated, like a language, through a series of historical recon-figurations, relations between institutions, and governing forms in mobile globalization processes. As the main concepts of feminist theory move from their roots in the Humanities toward a new dominant basis in the social sciences, "women's work" serves as a quasi-linguistic "flow" between first and third worlds, corporate governance and state sovereignty, national citizenship and postnational, "deterritorialized" rights regimes. This chapter analyzes what is gained and what is lost in this transition in scholarly focus. In particular, I discuss how this "sociological turn" has meant a reconsideration of concepts important to feminist theory like biopolitics, civil society, consciousness, agency, subjectivity, signification, norming, and the politics of desire.

Though socialization process and language acquisition have historically been feminized, their tendency now to be in the foreground of the creation of new labor markets is leading large portions of the economy to become increasingly feminized as well. This tendency can be read throughout narratives of school which focus on the economization of subject production as a gendered construction, influencing a reorganization in the division of labor. Most recently, the separation of the sexes in public school classrooms has been lauded as an innovative educational initiative that increases "choice," while the education of girls in needy countries has, in parallel, been praised as "spreading democracy" and connected with the building up of women's work regimes in Third World nations. In fact, the rise in interest in publically mandated sex-segregation in schools is symptomatic of a broader economic and cultural focus on the production of subjects. This chapter argues that the political rhetoric surrounding sex-segregated schools is, in part, borrowing from literary conventions. In contrast to the social scientific study of essential gender differences in learning, the "girls' school" genre presents the school itself as an aesthetic, sexual, or epistemological break in the social order that responds to a change in the division of labor. In chapter 4, I look at the tradition of literary texts on girls' schooling, from Charlotte Bronte's *Villette* to Modernist fictions like Lillian Hellman's *The Children's Hour*, Dorothy Sayers's *Gaudy Night*, Dorothy Richardson's *Pointed Roofs*, Gertrude Stein's *Fernhurst*, Colette's *Claudine in School*, and Michel Foucault's *Herculine Barbin*. Distinctively, the current literary treatment of girls' schooling—in books like the much celebrated/much reviled Greg Mortenson's *Stones Into Schools* and *Three Cups of*

Tea—takes this Modernist break into a new context. The "girls' school" genre in the imperialist setting situates girls' education as initiating new forms of temporality that break through "cultural stagnancy"—or "native traditionalism"—with promises of democracy as "the new." Unlike in the earlier Modernist texts, where the break challenged conventional temporalities through a deinstitutionalization and detemporalization of subjectivities, I show that in the imperialist texts the break foregrounds a new temporality based on privatizing women's work.

Gender Work is contributing to ongoing scholarly debates about the centrality of women's work under neoliberal regimes of capital. Recently, Michael Hardt and Antonio Negri's theories of *Empire, Multitude*, and *Commonwealth* have envisioned women at the center of neoliberal globalization. They see that this current nexus of primitive accumulation through corporate growth and consolidation expands production in ways that capitalize on the types of work women have traditionally done in private and the meanings attributed to that work, and they also understand that women's work offers a particularly rich symbolic setting for thinking through biopolitical life-in-common. Hardt and Negri argue that globalization is transforming work into new formations of exploitation—like contingent, service, care, cognitive, or affective labor—that are particularly concerned with the production of subjectivities—educative and socialization processes, the management of life—and not predominantly organized around the production of commodity-objects. Following Marx in the *Grundrisse*, Hardt and Negri characterize neoliberalism as an economy where most production is realized in recognizable forms of reproduction like language, creativity, and social interaction, and so the difference between production and reproduction has disappeared. Chapter 5 considers what it means for feminism that femininity has become the basis for a new form of universal subjectivity, and what is at stake for Feminist Theory in adopting some of Hardt and Negri's insights about this "feminization" of the economy in terms of formulating innovative frameworks for critique and action.

Gender Work seeks to ground a theoretically informed politics about changes in the gendered structure of labor. In this, it looks to critical theory and literature to analyze representations of how the symbolic power of gender is put in the service of neoliberal practices. It retraces traditions of Marxism within critical theory in order to look for a greater focus on the necessity of gendered productivity in Marx's work and after, and then integrates this reading of gender with more current poststructuralist analysis in order to place the construction of gender as always and necessarily in relation to work, even in its deep fascination with the linguistification of social life. It therefore discusses how lifeworlds, socialization processes, and educative development have been concretized as part of a discourse about accumulating the surplus of unpaid women's labor. Lastly, it suggests extracting from such representations of gendered economy a possibility of imagining a transformative politics of gendered work.

CHAPTER 1

The Gender of Working Time:
Revisiting Feminist/Marxist Debates

In the mid-1970s till the mid-1980s, feminist scholars in both the humanities and the social sciences engaged in a vibrant debate about the relationship between Marxist theory and feminism. Following on Juliet Mitchell's call in the late 1960s for a socialist criticism that took seriously "the subordination of women and the need for their liberation" (1966: 12),[1] feminists tried to grapple with concepts like ideology, exchange, labor, and class struggle, and ask if and when they could be applied to oppressions in women's social conditions, collected under the umbrella-term of patriarchy, or if women's forms of subordination were so culturally specific that they needed their own, independent rubric. In about 1985, such inquiry lost its fervor. It was replaced by a much more linguistic and locally focused orientation structured around difference and experience: in other words, in the humanities, thinking about the irreconcilability between the two discourses was buried under a poststructuralist surge: feminism developed a really lively debate around the Symbolic and how meaning was produced in reference to gender without easily being able to connect this discussion to economic thinking or thinking about changes in the nature of work. Meanwhile, in the social sciences, class discourse in feminism was overtaken by a particularizing empiricism, much of the time both history- and theory-avoidant.

At the same time, more women than ever were entering the global workforce while economic polarization was on the increase both nationally and internationally, and women's impoverishment was on the upswing.[2] In other words, the more women worked, the poorer laboring people got globally, and the larger the percentage of wealth was accumulated by the wealthy. The end of a heated discussion about feminist and Marxist connections therefore coincided with a rise in an expanded corporate profiting from women's work in the new neoliberal economy.

While I acknowledge the validity of contentions over Marxist historicism and the difficulty of its applicability to our postindustrialist productive worlds, I believe that Marx offers a basic premise that can be expanded to explain social relations and power structures in the present: that is, that labor produces profit,[3] and that women's labor produces more profit. This premise makes Marxism indispensable for explaining distributions of gender in the current juncture, and therefore for understanding power. For Marx, in capitalist production, unpaid labor time creates profit. Even as women's work has symbolically captured free time, Marxist analyses have not yet identified capital's grasp at unpaid labor time with the accumulation of women's labor time. As the first volume of *Capital* prosaically notes:

> Hence it is self-evident that the labourer is nothing else, his whole life through, than labour-power, that therefore all his disposable time is by nature and law labour time, to be devoted to the self-expansion of capital. Time for education, for intellectual development, for the fulfilling of social functions and for social intercourse, for the free-play of his bodily and mental activity, even for the rest time of Sunday (and that in a country of Sabbatarians!)—moonshine! But in its blind unrestrainable passion, its were-wolf hunger for surplus-labour, capital oversteps not only the moral, but even the merely physical maximum bounds of the working-day. It usurps the time for growth, development, and healthy maintenance of the body. (252)

Many critics have underscored Marx's emphasis on capital's need for the freeing-up of time, from Fredric Jameson—who calls capitalism "a process of perpetual breakdown" (2010: 1) and *Capital, Volume I* "a book about unemployment" (2010: 5)[4]—to Herbert Marcuse—who lists as a condition of freedom the "reduction of working time to a minimum" (44)—to Marx himself who, in "The Fragment on Machines" in the *Grundrisse,* relates profit to the "*creation of a large quantity of disposable time*" (Marx's emphasis; 708). "The whole development of wealth," Marx specifies, "rests on the creation of disposable time" (*Grundrisse,* 398).[5] Whereas industrial capitalism, in its processes of primitive accumulation, destroyed, claimed, and centralized independent spaces of production—for example, agricultural, domestic, etc.—to set labor in motion, postindustrial capitalism seeks to capture independent time, until now identified through autonomous domestic employments, leisure, and consumption whose temporalities are distinctly gendered.

Many feminist critics have justly attributed to Marxism an assumption of masculinity behind the proletariat subject. Heidi Hartmann succinctly reproves, "the categories of Marxism are sex-blind" (1981: 20). Others have indicated that such abstraction is not only neutral or sex-avoidant but distinctly excludes consideration of the feminine in the characterization of labor. As Leopoldina Fortunati, for example, remarks, "The woman, at the formal level, came to be excluded from any direct relation with capital" (28). Additionally, feminists have objected to the tendency, in Marx as well as in Marxism, to marginalize questions of reproduction. Linda Nicholson, for instance, contends that "Marx has eliminated from his theoretical focus all activities basic to human survival which fall outside of the capitalist 'economy'" (133). Many feminist readings of Marx protest that since Marx did not assume women as working in a separate or private sphere, he was not assuming their existence at all, as though a recognition of women could only occur in the essentialized context of nuclearization, caregiving, reproduction, or domestic seclusion. Roisin McDonough and Rachel Harrison allege, "a wife cannot be regarded as 'free labour', because she is bonded to her husband for the purpose of procreation and the reproduction of the bearers of labour power" (31). Christine Delphy agrees that "the oppression of women is held to be a secondary consequence of (and derived from) the class struggle, which is currently defined exclusively as the oppression of the proleteriat by Capital" (1984: 58). Rita Felski concurs: "Most writers agree that the traditional Marxist view of class as a polarized struggle between bourgeoisie and proletariat is of little use in the contemporary Western context" (34), particularly for feminism and popular culture. Heidi Hartmann and Ann Markusen attribute this split between commodity production and the production of labor power (reproduction) in Marxist analysis to the lack of attention to a specifically "woman-defined" context within Marxist analysis of reproduction: "A truly holistic view of the nature of capitalism must explain both the production of commodities *and* the production of labor-power. The silence of mainstream Marxist theory on women's work and the absence of a fully worked-out Marxist theory of the value and sources of labor-power both stem from the failure of Marx and his predecessors to explore this other half of the material process" (1980: 89).[6] Contingently, and perhaps most injurious to his theory's applications within the current global context, Marx, particularly in *Capital,* is predominantly interested in the production of objects, a focus which leaves to the wayside the growing dominance, in certain regions, of commodity markets based in services, affects, and the production of subjects.[7]

Not only do Marx's descriptions of the processes of production seem, to many critics, to cast women as barely existing phantoms within capitalist productive relations, but also, women seem particularly diminished because of Marx's emphasis on an overriding historical narrative hinging on class. Andrew Parker, for example, objects to the marginalization of sexuality habitual in Marx and Marxist analysis that feminism can address: "not only...has Marx's typical proletarian long since been identified as male (his industrial labors forming the norm against which domestic work appears as *non*labor), but even the concept of class...can itself be viewed as masculinist in its implicit assumption of a familial division of labor" (22). Rejecting a possible connection between Marxism and feminism in favor of a "materialist feminism" more concerned with the discursive construction of gender, Rosemary Hennessy concurs: "With its class bias, its emphasis on economic determinism, and its focus on a history exclusively formulated in terms of capitalist production, classic Marxism in the seventies had barely begun to analyze patriarchal systems of power" (1993: xii). Nearly 20 years later, the same critique holds up, as Kathi Weeks has pointed out: "The problem was that to the extent that class was conceived—as it typically was—as a gender and race-blind category, its ability to register the contours of even narrowly economic hierarchies was limited as well" (17). Though Nancy Hartsock does draw an epistemological or meta-theoretical connection between Marxism and the feminist critique of Enlightenment (1998: 107)[8]—the focus on engagement, the "embedded understanding of subjectivity" (1998: 77), the "importance of processes" (1998: 76), the skeptical account of the "relation of knowledge and power" (1998: 77)—, she still dismisses Marx's critique of capitalism because: "class [is] understood centrally...as the only division that counts"; and, women "are profoundly absent from his account of the extraction of surplus-value" (1998: 75).

On the contrary, I believe that Marx not only includes women in his story of surplus-value, but makes that inclusion into the crux of the process. Rosa Luxemburg, for example, professes that, in Marx, "variable capital is directly attributed to the natural physical increase of a working class already dominated by capital" (341). In other words, in one area of capital growth—variable capital—women's work is a recognizable factor in the making and increasing of surplus value as well as its capitalization. Luxemburg understands that natural propagation cannot account for women's full role within the process of extending and realizing the surplus. Rather, Luxemburg remarks, women's working role in production is essential for realizing the excess product in order for capital to expand and accumulate.[9] Following Marx, I give here an account of women's work as accumulating the surplus time of production not totally circumscribed in traditional reproductive functions. With Gayatri Spivak, I argue that "In the current financialization of the globe all critiques of hegemonic humanism"—including feminism—"must digest the rational kernel of Marx's writings in its own style of work, rather than attempt to settle scores with Marxism" (98).[10]

Marx's abstraction of the individual into a marketable commodity called "labor power" does masculinize the proleteriat subject, stamping the working body as an emptied-out form defined through equivalence, comparability (exchange), and abstraction and contoured around metaphors of mastery, self-possession, power, and rights. The laborer is (ironically, in this particular passage) "untrammeled owner of his capacity for labour, *i.e.,* of his person" and "equal in the eyes of the law" (*Capital I,* 165), while labor power "exists only as a capacity, or power of the living individual" (*Capital I,* 167) and, in particular, as a power to transform nature. As well, the proleteriat's loss of property in "The Communist Manifesto" is lamented as the loss of wife and children (482), that is, as an inability to assert oneself as the center of the bourgeois nuclear family. Additionally, in Marx's view of history, the class relation transcends the family relation as capital advances. Yet, at the same time, Marx makes it abundantly, even prophetically clear in the first volume of *Capital* that the gradual feminization of the proletariat is necessary for the expansion of capital. Over and over again, Marx gives examples to show that capital's drive for profits requires the expropriation of women as time.[11] "Legislation was, therefore," Marx understands, "...to declare any house in which work was done to be a factory" (282), and the "division of labour is thenceforth based, whenever possible, on the employment of women" (434). This theme repeats in "The Communist Manifesto": "the more modern industry becomes developed, the more is the labour of men superseded by that of women" (479). Marx's account of labor power emphasizes the integral relationship between labor and captured time, a relationship that requires the appropriation of women's work as capital advances.

In fact, femininity is intimately involved with the symbolic production of profitable labor time under capitalism. Beyond the paradigm that women store working time by working in a separate sphere of reproductive labor, Marx's treatment of women's work uses the separate domestic sphere of reproductive labor as *only a sample case* of the ways women's work stores unpaid time, replaced by other historical forms in different historical configurations, like reproduction, credit, hoarding, and circulation. That is, women's work stores surplus time because of its ties to reproduction, and even though the domestic sphere is its current mode of time storage, different historical moments will see different modes of time storage; no matter what the mode of women's time storage, time stored now in reproduction creates surplus labor time when it is realized later in circulation and production and is therefore exploitable for profit.

Marx's insight that rising profits for capitalists coincide with the increasing feminization of the workforce is prescient, even determining for a shrinking, post-Recession, neoliberal economy. The way profit is created through the split between "paid" and "unpaid" labor—or, in Marx's terms, "necessary" and "surplus" labor time—is still constructed through gender, even as what counts as "unpaid" takes on different forms; for Marx, "unpaid labor" was labor that exceeded what the wage paid for in the productive process, that is, what was necessary for the worker's subsistence outside the factory, whereas the current economic forces are generating novel mechanisms for exceeding the time of the wage (taking work for free), redefining jobs as surplus to the wage, its organization, its regulatory traditions, its benefits, and protections in order to appropriate such surplus more energetically. For example, according to a 2010 brief from the Center for American Progress that analyzes US Department of Labor statistics, the 2008 financial crisis reduced the number of dual-earner households because more men became unemployed, and the proportion of married women in the workforce thus reached a high. This period, with male unemployment in married couples growing to 3.7 percent and men altogether "lost 70 percent of the jobs" (Boushey, 3), was unprecedented, contrasting sharply with the period of 1979–1997 with its marked lesser degree of polarization. This gendered pattern of job loss was particularly true for couples who were close to retirement, causing a postponement in the age of retirement that was augmented more by cuts in employer pension contributions, and when the time of employment was reduced through the creation of part-timing or temporary positions, and, as Louis Uchitelle reports in *The Nation*, "helps to explain the rise in mortgage defaults and home foreclosures." As US gross domestic product (GDP) evinced sustained growth while the unemployment rates remained sharp, prolonging a polarized recovery, some economists like Mark Provost demonstrated that keeping workers' wages low also keeps inflation low, increasing the gains on assets as well as securities and other speculative investments: "High unemployment constrains labor costs and, thus, also functions as an anchor on inflation and inflation expectations—protecting bondholders' real return and principal." More than just encouraging a policy of "total unemployment" in advanced countries, such an outcome also encourages semi-employment and part-time employment. Such a labor-adverse political climate not only weakens labor by weakening labor unions and labor-friendly legislation, by cutting supports for reproducing labor, like education, pensions, and healthcare; it also produces unemployment by employing women in greater numbers.

In other parts of the world, as well, expanding poverty frequently partners up with expansive capitalizing on women's working time. As Martha
Gimenez summarizes the "Facts on Women" of the National Council of
Women's Organization, "the vast majority of the world's working population is female; women are the poorest of the world's poor. Seventy percent
of the 1.3 billion people who live in absolute poverty are women. Women
work 2/3 of the world's working hours, produce half of the world's food and
yet earn only 10 percent of the world's income and own less than 1 percent
of the world's property" (2010: 98). Maria Mies has shown how the flexibilization and informalization of labor—in which "women are the immediate
targets" (15)—have also become methods for securing women's labor time
in profit regimes for which others benefit. Mies states that the unpaid work
of women in the domestic sphere under industrial capitalism was replicated
in "non-wage work in the colonies" (33), former colonies, and other sites
of capitalist penetration, particularly in "the work of small peasants and
women in Third World countries" (33).

An absorption of reproduction into production in neoliberalism jacks
up possibilities for the exploitation of unpaid reproductive labor, both
inside and outside production. For example, in Ananya Roy's descriptions
of microfinance schemes in the Third World, "Women are seen as particularly important conduits of microfinance loans" (3), first in Bangladesh
and then across the developing world, as, for example, "a Mexican microfinance institution...makes a healthy profit at $80 million a year by serv-
ing about 1 million women at 90 percent interest rates" (27).[12] As Heloise
Weber elaborates, "In some cases it is a condition that Non Governmental
Organisations (NGOs) or Microfinance Institutions (MFIs) do *not* lend
to the poor below a given commercial rate," and then in a footnote: "In
general, interest rates may range from anything between 25–40 percent or
higher" (540), according to a World Bank report. Women borrowers, Roy
goes on, are considered good investments because the credit agency is able
to mobilize the ethical codes of rural life and use intimate rules and local
and domestic organization, including informal surveillance more than often
gendered, to manage and ensure timely returns.[13] Microfinance also seizes
women's time by increasingly shifting responsibilities onto women as well as
increasingly often lending to more middle-income women, even "successful
entrepreneurs...with existing job skills and training" (Keating et al., 2010:
164) so that the costs of preparing and educating financed labor is transferred back onto the laboring women, even as such laborers are required to
provide their own equipment, often collateralized.

The symbolic placement of women's reproductive labor time "outside of production"—and therefore outside of production's regulative

rules—even when it is succinctly *inside* productive processes—has been particularly relevant in Third World contexts, where much of the work of reproducing labor has fallen onto the shoulders of women, whether as immigrants or as cheap corporate and service labor. As Silvia Federici has pointed out, "We can recognize, first, that the expansion of capitalist relations is premised today as well (no less than at the times of the English Enclosures, the *conquista* of the Americas, and the Atlantic slave-trade) on the separation of the producers from the means of their reproduction" (53). Geographer Melissa Wright chronicles how women's labor in *maquiladoras* on the Mexican border has turned into a quick source of profit for multinationals, a production of commodifiable value, because of its quick turnover and unreliability, its temporal "coming and going" (78), where employers can say they expect women of being "loyal" to their family rather than to the company and so only to be employable on a temporary basis. This gives the employers flexibility as well as an excuse for not training the women and then for paying them less as "unskilled workers." In all these scenarios, the new economy is being reorganized across classes and nations for capital to make claims on women's unclaimed labor time.

Women's Labor Time and the Time of Reproduction

The reason that women's labor produces more profit, or that women themselves are positioned within capitalist relations as containers and releasers of saved and utilizable surplus time, is not self-evident. Why would women get paid 79 cents on the dollar for the same work as men in advanced industrial counties, why does such a situation persist, why is the situation maintained even when women are reaching higher levels of education and leadership, and why do women earn less cross-culturally? David Harvey offers a reading of Marx that suggests a possible interpretation. For Harvey, the value of a commodity is measured in relation to "socially necessary labor-time," or "as the embodiment of abstract human labour"—time as congealed in the object. "Socially necessary labor-time" depends on the average time it takes to produce that object within a given level of technology and knowledge development at a particular historical moment and within a particular spatial and cultural matrix: value is "phantom-like," that is, "subjected to perpetual revolutions" (2010: 24), "not static and closed but fluid and open and therefore in perpetual transformation" (2010: 24). "Socially necessary labor-time" is not, as Harvey reads it, completely technologically determined, or calculable as a series of uniform and countable units, but rather the work-time that can be attributed to producing the worker and his knowledge, the time of socializing and educational processes varying with historical demands, provisions, and needs.

This does not adequately explain why women represent accumulated time (that is, why women necessarily do the necessary work of storing time, transferring the value of past labor time into the commodity—labor power—to be exchanged, and thereby creating the conditions for surplus labor time)—why, that is, their time is the time of reproduction. Yet, it certainly insinuates that the work of women during industrial capitalism circulated as "free time," or time that contributed without cost to the commodity's value for capital, and that this sense of women's time as producing an expanding value is adopted as well within neoliberalism. The value that women's "free time" adds to production is, like the level of technology, subjected to historical fluctuation. "If the owner of labour-power works to-day," observes Marx, "to-morrow he must again be able to repeat the same process in the same conditions as regards health and strength. His means of subsistence must therefore be sufficient to maintain him in his normal state as a labouring individual. His natural wants, such as food, clothing, fuel, and housing, vary according to the climatic and other physical conditions of his country. On the other hand, the number and extent of his so-called necessary wants, as also the modes of satisfying them, are themselves the product of historical development" (*Capital, Vol. I,* 168). Though Marx does not explain the process through which the food gets to the table or the housing gets tended—assuming that once the food appears as a commodity, it is already set to be digested into energy, for example, without preparation—, his descriptions of the reproduction of labor power presuppose women's reproductive work as the foundational pipeline through which historical time makes labor power into a commodity with a surplus to be commodified and then realized in production.[14] Because history is itself indeterminate in what it determines to be "socially necessary" at a particular moment, the time that is materialized through women's work makes the value of the commodity open to speculation, or invisible but symbolically and materially expandable as surplus, even after the division of industrial labor regimes no longer fully segregates productive and reproductive time by gender.

Harvey is interested in rehabilitating Marx as helping to explain current political problems against critics who might dismiss Marx's work as resolutely out-dated or as proven irrelevant by the fall of the Soviet Union and the end of the Cold War, or by the historical transition away from Fordism. He focuses therefore on the aspects of Marx's critique that view history as constantly transformative in its interactions with things, their temporalities, and their social relations, where "value is sensitive to revolutions in technology" (21), for example, as well as to other revolutions in need, average skill, scientific knowledge, and the perpetual interactions of use value and exchange value within the commodity. In fact, Harvey is expanding on a trajectory of Marxist thinking which, since Althusser, has interpreted Marx's historicality in an alternative sense to the traditional view of Marx as teleological or determinist. According to this interpretation, Marx's work can be divided into "early" and "late,"[15] with the "early" works concerned with alienation and its loss of the "truly human" progressively over time, and the "late" works—starting with *Capital*—tracing a more synchronous picture of industrial capitalism, with different historical moments still operative simultaneously within the productive maps of the present, with overlapping sequences of production and reproduction and with movement between them both circuitous and dislocating as some moments of one circuit interact or protrude at different moments of another.

Within Marx's global system of complex industrial circulation, objectified past labor time is transferred by living labor into the commodity during production (like a ghost story). The commodity then holds onto the value of this stored past labor time until it is brought to market and exchanged. At this point, the extra value added into the commodity by living labor (surplus labor time) is realized along with the stored value, first as money and then either as individual consumption (where value is used up) or productive consumption, where value is re-invested. In such a system, the realization of value is not instantaneous because cycles of production do not necessarily line up, with one ending in time for the next one to begin without hiatus: sometimes purchases are needed to accommodate a new round, or money cannot be immediately concretized into an equivalent object, or an object to be exchanged has to accumulate equal value for the exchange. If production has to cease temporarily to await inputs, both money and capital are removed from circulation, or "hoarded" in Marx's terms, waiting to be turned back into productive capital. During the waiting time, when capital does not yet have contact with the productive labor that sets it into motion, capital has no way to realize its value and is devalued. This constitutes the cycle of reproduction, for example, the business cycle that sends the system into crisis.

Capitalism, in this sense, must have skipped the first productive cycle, because it always needs reproduction to start it moving—it always needs to be realizing the value of past labor stored in the object. It starts up only through the delay. Past or stored labor time is necessary for surplus value to be accumulated and then realized. The storage of the surplus for a later time accounts, in part, for the growth of capital in the next (or the first) productive cycle. It also ties women's work paradigmatically to reproduction, as the work of socialization does not realize its value until it enters into the productive cycle—that is, women's work in socialization and education is a prototype of "hoarding." In *Capital, Volume I,* women are the concrete instances of capitalism's temporal contradictions: that the future cycle of production needs to realize objective past time in order to turn a profit, and that therefore objectified past time is both the necessary condition and the necessary response of the productive cycle.

Following Althusser, Etienne Balibar points out the role that reproduction plays in stabilizing the production of objects (the stored value of past labor time) and the subjects that make them: "reproduction appears to be the general form of permanence of the general conditions of production, which in the last analysis englobe the whole social structure" (259). However, this same model of reproduction, he goes on, gives an account of historical transition, or changes in the structure. Balibar describes Marxist temporality as different sequences of production and reproduction from different, independent, and often contradicting historical origins that are lined up as a plurality on the same plane and happen simultaneously even if they appear temporally differentiated: "the production of social relations is not subject to the determinations of the preceding and the succeeding, of the 'first' and the 'second.' Marx writes that 'every process of social production is at the same time a process of reproduction . . . : in this sense the 'first' process of production . . . is *always-already* a process of reproduction" (271). Subjects, Balibar reasons, can only produce objects that already presuppose them as subjects (as their prehistory), and yet these subjects can only exist once these objects already exist: "periods of transition are therefore characterized by the *coexistence* of several modes of production, as well as by . . . forms of non-correspondence" (Balibar's emphasis; 307). "Non-correspondence" implies that the cause for transition is a temporal dislocation, where certain productive stages contradict earlier or later ones but coexist with them on a plane of simultaneity. As Marx himself details in the *Grundrisse,* "The first glance shows what a nonsensical circle it would be if on the one hand the *workers* whom capital has to put to work in order to posit itself as capital had first to be *created,* to be brought to life through its *stockpiling* if they waited for its command, *Let There Be Workers!;* while at the same time it were itself incapable of *stockpiling* without alien labour" (506). In other words, with capital's utterance of its command phrase, women pop out babies that line up at the factory door. Women are "first"—therefore autonomous, even metaphysical Creators—, bringing workers into being as if by fiat (as stockpiled time). Women's time is the primary, objective form of labor that has already been alienated, stored up, and objectified; women's time is stored time that expands surplus value in the commodity.

This time storage that women's work represents in reproduction is repeated as capitalism's own origin story, or "primitive accumulation." The reproduction of the conditions of production, for example, can only occur within a money economy, that is, once the worker and the means of production have been separated, and the worker needs the capitalist to supply the means of production in order to put his labor power into motion. Capitalist production thus needs to imagine itself as following on a period of primitive accumulation, where the worker is forcibly driven away from his (natural) means to land and livelihood. But such an event would only be possible if a money economy already existed, that is, if there were already an accumulation of objectified labor held by the capitalist. What Althusser's and then Balibar's analyses make evident is that capital can never be in its first round of circulation and is always, in this sense, reproduction.

In the industrial moments that Marx foregrounds, this means that the separate sphere of women's reproductive labor is a backward projection of a contemporary productive need. Perhaps Marx gives a partial gloss on this in his analyses of the relationship between women's labor-time and the work of reproduction. On the one hand, women are isolated from production because of their roles in reproducing labor power. Women represent a type of economic profit-making that has been made autonomous from production. The laborer works, and then consumes. When he consumes, labor-power is reproduced for the next laboring day. This individual consumption is completely separated from productive consumption, or the reproduction of capital, because during its process, "he [the laborer] belongs to himself, and performs the necessary vital functions outside the process of production" (*Capital, Vol. 1,* 536)—it is outside the capitalist's concern, and so the capitalist leaves the laborer alone to attend to his own vital functions (to "hoard" them), an activity of "care" from which only the capitalist profits as soon as the labor power is reconverted back into the productive process. In this sense, women add supplemental labor-time to the commodity by reproducing labor power for free, and the value is only realized once it enters into contact with the productive forces. The capitalist, however, also profits because the worker is buying his subsistence consumables from him, so that, in fact, the consumption has to happen before the worker can sell his labor power on the market. Just like the original, primal attachment to community before the peasant is driven from the land, "women's work" enters into production as an originary story of alienation, as a fiction of expandable, surplus time, of historical objectified time, of time outside of production that the productive forces can add onto value.

On the other hand, the capitalist also wants to grab as much free and profitable time as possible for production, reducing the time of labor power's reproduction: "All the capitalist cares for, is to reduce the labourer's individual consumption as far as possible to what is strictly necessary" (*Capital, Vol. I,* 537). The capitalist argues against education, because it forces the working life to start at a later age, just as he demands that workers eat at their working station, so that less time is subtracted from the working day, and live nearby, so that less time is wasted in journeying to work. Marx differentiates what the capitalist wants for his own workforce, or no free time for reproduction, and what he wants for the workforce of other capitalists, that is, an abundance of time for purchasing his products. The capitalist's primitive accumulation of women's time leads to the absorption of the laborer's family into production as free labor power, and the consequent dissipation of the laborer's individual consumption along with its separate tasks of reproducing labor power for free: "Compulsory work for the capitalist usurped the place, not only of children's play, but also of free labour at home within moderate limits for the support of the family" (*Capital, Vol. I,* 372). Like individual consumption, unpaid and autonomous women's work is necessary to offset the capitalist's costs of reproducing labor-power for the next day and the next generation of production (as the capitalist steals increasingly more of the laborer's own reproductive time), but its needed autonomy presents a block or a limit to capital's growth. If the capitalist continues to steal reproductive time, he will lose the stored time of past labor that will create surplus value in the next productive generation. As Marx writes in the *Grundrisse,* "*Surplus time*...can also be created...by means of forcible prolongation of the working day beyond its natural limits; by the addition of women and children to the laboring population" (Marx's emphasis; 398–399). Capital must make free time. Reproduction is, then, always a resistance to capital that capital itself needs to produce.

Marx foresaw the dissolution of the private family whose signs now pervade the social landscape,[16] as well as the historical limits of a type of reproductive "separate sphere" whose value had yet to be realized. He also anticipated the diminishment of sex role differences through the abstraction of the individual worker first with exchange and later with the advent of machinery. Marx understood that capitalism would make autonomous family labor obsolete and annex that time into the time of production, and that other forms of reproduction would take its place. Marx predicted the symbolic status of women as autonomous and expandable stored-up reproductive and unpaid productive surplus labor time as future profit that neoliberal capitalism ultimately realizes and exploits. In attributing to women's work the stored up past labor time that, as surplus, ensures future profits, Marx may have conceptualized why women continue to be ideologically linked to the domestic, its labors, and its values even long after there is no longer a historical necessity for them in that role and long after that linking has become no longer useful to capital. Marx is concerned at every level about how capital sucks profits out of unpaid time. He also understands how such value needs to be "hoarded" as it circulates outside of production, to be realized and reproduced in intervening temporal sequences. Women's work is the historically necessary "origin story" for the circuits of reproduction and accumulation that feed the productive process, the humanization of the narrative through which such processes are rationalized.

In the second volume of *Capital*, Marx constructs an elaborate calculus for circulating money and commodities to show how past time gets stored up as value—in unused machinery, amassed ancillary materials, and/or money hoarded outside of the productive process—, circulates, and eventually gets realized in consumption expenditures that turn over in the next, autonomous productive cycle. "In order for the process to keep flowing—quite apart from whether this stock can be renewed daily or only at definite intervals—there must always be a greater store of raw material, etc. at the place of production than is used up daily or weekly, for example" (*Capital II*, 219). The processes of production are always methods of storing-up unpaid labor time, or surplus value, in various intersecting pathways. Marx sees this unpaid time as formulated in gendered terms. The unpaid surplus time is then embedded in the object whose value circulates, awaiting its eventual realization. The symbolic status of women as autonomous to production, adding unpaid labor time that becomes the surplus value of the future commodity, as expanding unpaid labor time within present production, reflects the symbolic status of reproduction—of storing time—within the valorization of profits in circulation (exchange). Though feminist theory has faulted Marx for paying too little attention to autonomous cultures of reproduction linked to patriarchy, neoliberalism has overseen the process of the contemporary dissolution of the family and the symbolic absorption of its value into expanding profit-production

Separation of Women's Time from Productive Time

Unlike my reading above, much of feminism's reading of the "separate spheres" envisioned women's work was in a sphere of reproduction that could be split away from production, or autonomous, or framed through a sense of culture or ideology fully or partially divorced from economic forces. Feminist theory's de-emphasis of working time's role in constructions of difference within production meant that there would be a gap or incongruity between descriptions of labor time and descriptions of women's time. Though often attributed to Marx, such a gap cannot—as I show above (and below)—be attributed to Marx. Rather, such a gap was part of an interpretation of Marx that sought out a diversification of political subjects, a search for new actors on the part of the left, that is, what Christopher Nealon talks about as a generalized "political agnosticism about who might replace the working classes" (25), or the need in the face of a rightward political shift to find "an ongoing relevance of Marxism" (26) that "makes sense of a defeat" (26) as the industrial working classes could no longer be identified in themselves as autonomous or revolutionary agents. Such a shift witnessed, as well, a diminution in the category of "work" either in identity formation or in historical causality, as though once the industrial working class were fragmented, distracted, or defeated, "work" itself, in any other form, would stop being legible, credible, recognizable, collectivizable, or amassable across categories of identity. Yet, as Kathi Weeks has demonstrated, "Work is one politically promising way of approaching class—because it is so expansive, because it is such a significant part of everyday life, because it is something we do rather than a category to which we are assigned, and because for all these reasons it can be raised as a political issue" (20).

The diminished relevance of the central category of "work" is a significant loss. Most notably, "work" for Marx, is the potential of human action: the possibility that human activity can transform the world and, by transforming the world, can transform, as well, the human self. As he says, for example, in the *Grundrisse,* work is not only important because it requires a relation with others or social relevance, but also because it "is a *positive, creative activity*" (Marx's emphasis; 614). As Kathi Weeks remarks, "The focus on laboring practices, on the labor process and the relations of labor, can register the workers' power to act" (19). That is, Marx positioned "work" not only as the singular moment of consciousness—a configuration that does seem limiting—, but also as a dialectical hinge, the process where natural and social existence, social relations and ideas, come to appear as human-made and human-re-makable products. This is not to say, with Teresa Ebert, that gender and sexuality can only be situated "in the world of historical processes of labor and capital" (34), or that class "is the only site of historical agency" (37). Such statements tend to hierarchize suffering and oppression as well as hierarchize certain people and positions as the sites of historical, even revolutionary change. Rather, what I am saying is that the current historical moment cannot afford to give up on understanding work as part of the way the world we live in is constructed and known, including the identities we inhabit. Additionally, Ebert's analysis draws a strict separation between ideology and materiality. My question of why women in particular have become sources of unpaid labor time in a shrinking economy cannot be addressed without theorizing the symbolic. Though Weeks criticizes Marx and others for adopting a work ethic where waged labor is the main source of identity, Marx's descriptions of waged work as the freeing of time makes work into a "creative practice" (22) or an imaginative capacity implicating the immanent possibility of freedom.

The separation between production and women's time within feminism made it increasingly difficult to talk about gender as a class category, even relationally, or to talk about class at all as a feminist topic. Instead, time in feminism became increasingly experiential and phenomenological and, as such, aestheticized. For example, Rosemary Hennessy's recent ethnographic study on affect and labor organizing in the *maquiladoras* on the Mexican border argues for a more developed critical feminist engagement with "the passionate politics of political engagement" (2009: 311) or "affective relations" (2009: 311). Though Hennessy recognizes that such relations are forged within regimes of surplus labor extraction, her descriptions focus on personal choices, social bonds, and erotic desires that influence the ways associations are formed and responded to outside of direct economic activity but deny the theoretical or ideological aspects. Similarly, feminist theorist Elizabeth Grosz elaborates that what feminism needs is "an account of the place of futurity" inducting "a future different but not detached from the past and present" (2004: 91)—that is, a phenomenological account of time that privileges "a wide range of possible variation or development of current existence" (2004: 91), where the past is called into the present by the future as difference (Grosz seems to be constantly arguing against a haunting claim that the past and the future are the same as the present, or repetitions of it, or undifferentiable from it, though the person who would make such a claim remains unnamed). This assertion depends on a prior reduction of labor—read through Marx!—as "individual variation" closely linked to life, or the "innate particularities and learned skills of the laboring body" (2004: 37). As pure corporeality, labor disappears as exploitable labor power or historical necessity, and now, according to Grosz, is called into the present in its semblance to evolutionary time (or the time of natural variability and selection) rather than to work, that is, as an endless process of transformation that resists closed-systems, past restraints, and historical inevitabilities. Labor, for Grosz, is a matter of bodily style, of appearance, of choice. In pluralizing hierarchies, this reading of Marx cuts a rift between labor—as a historical, oppositional, singular class category, defined through its social position and identified through its alienation—and time, presented as a set of free body movements opening to the world. In a way that erases Marx's idea that the value of past labor (congealed time) is preserved and transferred to the present through machinery or consumption, for Grosz, the virtuality of the past can be reactivated in the present, but only through a leap, or disengagement—what Grosz calls "radical politics" that has no consciousness but only capacity, tendency, choice, and movement. Because the past depends on what the future makes of it, Grosz rejects the possibility of preserving any thing or idea; she also, in rejecting work as a category of experience, rejects the possibility of being stuck in time or of being subjected under yokes of objectified time, or experiential time that belongs to others or is controlled by them, in a field of power. Instead, time is cheered on in its process of becoming and forgetting, forever freeing itself from its past easily, realizing its "capacity to initiate something new and unpredictable" (2004: 163), blindly celebrating the constant coming of a future that escapes from its past, wherever it may lead.

Grosz' idea of time insists that Marx's descriptions of labor as a class needs to be rejected because they cannot account for diversity, change, movement, and, most emphatically, "becoming" of culture, position, temporality, or identity, and that such a class is so rooted down in its material structure, its need to work, that it cannot differentiate itself from what it always was, from repetitions of congealed time (Marx claims that capital abstracts labor from the diversity of its cultures, so that the schism with the past that Grosz celebrates is one that Marx presents as the condition for exploitation. For Marx, capital breaks diversity by breaking origins. Marx's laborer encounters the restraints of past labor only inside machinery and commodities). Instead of work, Grosz turns toward a model of diversity and continuous variation in evolutionary theory; this sense of corporeal or experiential time underlies what Grosz calls "work" and its temporalities, having nothing to do with the making of actual things (what Marx calls labor) but rather with the development of forms without content, of corporeal expression. Though Grosz does insist that she is not equating nature to culture, the transformative force of time moves the present into the future by calling in the past, but without human intervention, and change happens without controls, plans, or strategies, in something like primitive, evolutionary time or the time of living beings, often compared to cellular flux (though clearly Marx does borrow from Darwin and is interested in labor as the production of forms, to equate labor schematically to evolutionary time, change, and transformation is to ignore the laboring and its effects on time as well as to ignore that there is a wizard behind the curtain—i.e., that capital has designs). Such referencing of the biological evokes a substratum to culture ("desire"), or a universal force of circulating, self-generating, undefinable, phenomenological energy or vitalism that underlies equally geographical as well as political behavior, matter as much as perception, outside of human subjectivity. The disconnecting of working time from women's time creates a rupture between the feminist pursuit of women's agency and the historical categories of Marxism, including those linked to the necessary social and historical relations of liberation.

The rest of this chapter starts out by looking at feminist theory that tried to find intersections between feminism and Marxism in the 1970s and 1980s, and asks how this debate finally led to the conceptual separation between labor time and women's time that we witness in Grosz' theory, but not only in hers. Much of this early Second-Wave scholarship questioned whether the critique of capitalism would suffice to explain the specific oppressions of women, or whether an alternative critique of patriarchy was necessary that was more historically transcendent. The idea of the autonomy of women's oppression eventually merged into the critique of gender difference that framed much poststructuralist feminism. The autonomy of women's oppression became a rallying point for addressing the limitations of Marx's historical privileging of class struggle and the need for a more fluid and multiple definition of the work of difference. As the prewritten backdrop of history, class struggle seemed to determine history's outcomes as well as its players. Class struggle as a paradigm for understanding history gave way to an analysis of the division of labor, which multiplied social stress-points; feminist critiques of difference then evolved toward a vision of language and identity, emphasizing social division and multiplicity over the dualisms of class theory. This proliferation of difference replaced labor as a lever from which social and historical change could be projected.

Yet, as the rest of the chapter goes on to suggest, what got left behind in the feminist framing of autonomy was Marx's sense of gender difference as stored up historically necessary surplus labor time. By reinserting circulation and reproduction as motors of history, the complex idea of time that is constitutive in Marx's story of gender difference is not necessarily historically determinative or class reductive, nor is it negligent of the historically contingent, diverse, and disjointed ways gender difference is produced and reproduced first as value and then as contradiction and crisis. Marx's descriptions show gender difference to be tied up with the fluidity of past time in the present time of production. As their working time repeats and preserves the past, it is inconsistent with the present, opening it to historical separation, irresolution, and transition

Patriarchy, the Autonomy of Culture, and the Critique of Ideology

The relationship of women's work to the category of productive labor can be said to be a question that governed the development of feminist theory from the late 1960s on. In fact, poststructuralism, with its focus on language and the subject, can be said to have developed out of a feminist insistence on marginalizing class in its analysis and posing alternative origin and development stories to explain culture, identity, and consciousness. The trajectory of feminist thought went from asserting, on the one hand, that women's oppression could not be explained as class exploitation and wage exploitation and trying to understand its own specific dynamics, to, on the other, rejecting the category of class in favor of the categories of culture, language signification, and variability. In the former case, women's oppression appeared excessive to capitalism, and therefore existed as pure ideology. The premise of a separate space and status for women's oppression, outside of the social relations of production in a sphere of reproduction, was adopted by feminists from Marx's indication, in "The German Ideology," that all ideology—as the reproduction of social relations—seemed independent from the material base ("upside-down as in a *camera obscura*" (154)): "Thus all collisions in history have their origin, according to our view, in the contradiction between the productive forces and the form of intercourse" (196), including the family, the law, and civil society. Marx identifies the family here as the first instance of a social stage or superstructure, as divorced from practical activity, set apart from productive forces, both reinforcing their material interests and autonomous, unbound by production, even outside the time of production. Feminism interpreted this cut between, on the one hand, production and, on the other, the ideas that reproduce it and distort its realities as the split between men's paid work in industrial social relations and women's unpaid exchange, often as symbols, in excess of capital.

In the 1970s, when feminism was bursting onto the theoretical scene, many critics were interested in understanding the psychic relationship that informed patriarchy, but still had to contend with a strong leftist tradition that explained social forms through means of production and was still more or less invested in Marxism. Feminist critics, however, were becoming increasingly impatient with the determining primacy that means of production explanations seemed to hold on formative theories of the subject. Theories of ideology envisioned the family, for example, as Annette Kuhn remarks, as "simply a vehicle for the transmission of representations of those relations [of production]" (63), that is, as a transparent or functional lever for the transmission of ideas already established elsewhere (e.g., in production) in the interests of the ruling class. There was a growing tendency to separate out the critique of patriarchy—defining culture as what was outside of production—in order to free considerations of the subject from its role as a reflection of a history managed solely through economic processes.

Many here came to appreciate Engels more than Marx, since Engels—in *Origin of the Family, Private Property, and the State*—took seriously his assertion that the division between men and women in the household was the first class division, and granted analytic primacy to the patriarchal household as a precapitalist social arrangement that overturned an even more primitive Mother Right[17] and that capitalism would, in its own right, overturn. For Engels, the oppression of women was based in a residual family form, where the father controlled the tools of production and wanted to transmit them to his legitimate offspring, meaning that household production lost its formative collective character. Because family nuclearization was becoming inessential to a working class without property to transfer, it would, according to Engels, eventually devolve, as "no basis for any kind of male supremacy is left in the proleteriate household" (38), except as a brutality left over from the old practices of monogamy. The offshoot of Engels focus on intrafamilial inheritance rather than production was that women's oppression was made to have a narrative of causality divorced from considerations of labor or labor time under industrial capitalism.

Gayle Rubin's 1976 essay "The Traffic in Women" exposes the muscular analytic efforts feminists exerted to think a platform for subjectivity that had its own trajectories and causalities, outside of capitalism and its modes of production, but could still shed some light on social inequalities and oppressions. This canonical piece inaugurated a set of inquiries into what Rubin first labeled as the "sex/gender system"—the mutual indeterminacy between the material world of bodies and the cultural world of symbols that would open up into poststructuralist interest in the arbitrariness of signification, the signifier-signified split, that is, in difference. Rubin was following in the footsteps of Juliet Mitchell who, for example, proposed that "The working class has the power to take back to itself (for mankind) the products of the labour which are now taken from it; but no simple extension of this position can be taken to apply to patriarchal ideology" (1974: 412), arguing, similarly to Engels, that the patriarchal psyche no longer matches the realities of the base material structures of modern society and therefore belongs to an archaic residue within ideology.

Rubin starts out thinking about the "genesis of women's oppression" (157) which, she says, cannot be rooted within the classical categories of Marxist historicism because women's oppression existed before capitalism began. She grants that Marx is able to elucidate more aspects of women's oppression than other theories—for example, the relationship between production and reproduction, the role of women in producing surplus value by contributing unpaid labor. Yet, "to explain women's usefulness to capitalism," she continues, "is one thing. To argue that this usefulness explains the genesis of the oppression of women is quite another" (163). Sifting through the ethnographic record, Rubin observes instances of patriarchal power that exceed women's induction into industrial capitalism. Therefore, she concludes, one needs to find a "historical and moral element" (164) that is the key to explaining the cultural heritage of sexism. Rubin never defines the "oppression of women," nor catalogues what types of behavior, institutions, or social routines might fall under that term, but instead keeps it vague, merging all its instances into one arching problem to be resolved by one arching solution outside the economic. For Rubin, since the oppression of women is so all-pervasive in time and space, there must be a singular cause of patriarchy, and since the oppression of women cannot be totally subsumed within the political-economic critique of capitalism, the singular cause of patriarchy had to reside not there at all but totally elsewhere, within an autonomous cultural structure.

As is well known, Rubin locates the cause of the oppression of women in the incest taboo and, in particular, following Freud, Lacan, and Lévi-Strauss, in the exchange of woman that the incest taboo incites. In this, women are "like words" (201), values or symbols exchanged between men of different population groups for the purpose of communicating an alliance, carrying meaning. Rubin uses the instance of the "primitive tribe" to illustrate the formative moment of the exchange of women as also the moment of the birth of the human and its culture, using anthropological retrieval as the point of identification of the universal, even while citing contemporary exemplars. The shift to culture here, however, does not absolutely escape economic determinants (only relatively), but rather separates out a critique of production as value creation in order to devise an alternative place of "gift exchange," or exchange-before-money, defined as language, symbolic circulation, and culture—or ideology. Communicative value here arises from the expansive symbolic meaning stored up in women as they are moved between groups, as desire passes through them. Rubin willfully abandons the time of paid production in order to set into play, exclusively, the timelessness of unpaid exchange. Contrary to Marx, who understands circulation as the realization of the surplus value that eventually passes back into production as commodity (and thus is sutured to it), Rubin ascribes exchange to an archaic and the tribal past, estranging the perfectly contemporary event of exchange and circulation from contemporary production, calling it "gift-giving" to present it as the universal in its "primitiveness," beyond labor's present and not historically bound by it. As she says, the work on "gift-giving" and incest by Freud and Lévi-Strauss "enables us to isolate sex and gender from 'mode of production,' and to counter a certain tendency to explain sex oppression as a reflex of economic forces" (203).

This disassociation of women as timeless culture symbols from the time of labor (history) is not isolated. Like Rubin, French feminist philosopher

Luce Irigaray privileges circulation and exchange—symbolic exchange—over production and in contrast to it. In the essay "Women on the Market" published in French the year after Rubin published hers, Irigaray's project in reading Marx is to prove that Freud is Marx (as well as Hegel, Descartes, Levinas, and Plato, among others), that is, denying a place for women subjects within symbolic representation while still framing the logic of representation around women's not-to-be-seen-ness: the reflectiveness of the signifier must pass through the repression of femininity. Marx is prone to the same tendencies of mimesis displayed in the entire Western philosophical tradition that uses the feminine as the negative to shore up men's self-representation, his value to himself.

Irigaray's critique collapses historical time within representations of women in philosophy, where women come to represent the flattening of time: all philosophy is but a reflection, a repetition of women's lack of reflection. Marx's formula "C-M-C"—commodity-money-commodity (explaining how commodities attain value apart from their use-value when they enter the market, by passing through a "universal equivalence" of exchange value with the advent of market trades)—gives Irigaray a point (translated into Lévi-Strauss) to identify the man mirroring himself through the negative of the feminine, parallel to castration (where women, for Freud (reads Irigaray), are the "nothing to be seen" between men that gives men the assurance that that what they have is real and cannot be lost because it is reflectable): "In order for a product—a woman?—to have value," she notes, "two men, at least, have to invest (in) her. *The general equivalent of a commodity no longer functions as a commodity itself*" (Irigaray's emphasis; 181). Exchange is a desire for representation between two men expressed through a woman traded between them, just as in trade desire is expressed through a relation between two commodities represented through money. Needing to defend themselves against the negative and the invisible (feminine), men circulate symbols that reflect their own value in things, in an equivalence, a self-image: "The body of a commodity thus becomes, for another such commodity, a mirror of its value" (179). Money is capitalist society's mirror stage. For Irigaray, this circulation, or exchange value (the Symbolic), is defined against the use values, relations, and meanings made in production and, in fact, disqualifies them (unlike in Marx where use value comes back changed through production and exchange). "The circulation of women among men is what establishes the operations of society, at least of patriarchal society" (184). Like Rubin, Irigaray is placing women as the dividing line between production, on the one side, and, on the other, timeless culture, reproduction, symbolic exchange, and patriarchy, where women's oppression occurs. What defines the oppression of women is not hooked up to money, wages, and commodities, as money, wages, and commodities are relegated to only explaining the later historical formation of class. Like Rubin, Irigaray links circulation and exchange to culture (ideology) and, in doing so, makes circulation into a category that is incompatible with considerations of production: that is, into a separate sphere of reproduction. This becomes a feminist standard.

Division of Labor

The theoretical split between patriarchy and capitalism within feminism was partly grounded in an interpretation of Marx that projected production and reproduction (or, circulation) into relatively disparate, noncommunicating, and incompatible conceptual spheres, even different historical stages (the division between material/manual labor and ideal/intellectual labor, or ideology).[18] This perceived rift between women (symbols and ideology) and productive forces (or, class) limited feminist inquiry.[19] By placing the circulation of gender, symbols, and culture in a precapitalism, before production was oriented around paid labor, feminist theory was not recognizing that women's unpaid labor time was already a constitutive ingredient in paid labor's profits and that the distinction between paid and unpaid labor is already filtered through the construction of symbolic exchange. In order to resituate women as agents of production and not just objects of culture, some trends in feminism therefore insisted that women's work had to be considered inside of the productive process. These trends did not consider women workers as abstracted into a universal equivalence defined singularly as the seller of labor-power, devoid of bodies and differences, but rather they found that describing the division of labor within production would indicate how class itself was culturally divided rather than singularly motivated, and that cultural differences were not economically insignificant, inelastic, or superfluous. Considering reproductive work on the same historical plane as capitalist production allowed such theorists to understand paid and unpaid labor time as a structural or formal difference that managed and distributed inequalities for greater profitability.

Perspectives such as Juliet Mitchell's and Gayle Rubin's were adapting to feminist analysis the methods of ideological critique, such as Louis Althusser's, where mental (superstructural) and manual (infrastructural) forces operated effectively in "relatively autonomous" but reciprocally interactive levels of a singular edifice erected on a singular base (production), in the last instance. For Althusser, this descriptive view allowed Marxism to illuminate the ways that the elements of the superstructure interacted with the base "*on the basis of reproduction*" (Althusser's emphasis; 1971: 131), within an overall effective structure. Given this separation, one area, for example, that seemed particularly difficult to broach with women's oppression positioned outside of production, was why women's productive wages were lower than men's. Some feminists noticed that the conceptual vocabulary for describing women's relation to production, and the problems involved in that relation, were becoming harder to access or analyze. "Nothing about capital itself," writes Heidi Hartmann, "determines who (that is, which individuals with which ascriptive characteristics) shall occupy the higher, and who the lower rungs of the wage labor force" (1981: 24). The feminist conceptual apparatus was failing, as Veronica Beechey remarked, "to integrate a feminist analysis of the sexual division of labour with a Marxist analysis of the labor process" (158), or rather methodologies did not develop for thinking about how production and reproduction mediated one another, nor how the symbolic and the cultural circulated inside of historical productive processes, nor how women's unpaid labor time and symbolic exchange created opportunities for profit exploitation within production.

In response to this stalemate, feminist theorists questioned the dichotomous view of class that Marxist historicism offered. While the critique of patriarchy as ideology interpreted women's reproductive work as independent of the productive base (what came to be known as "dual systems theory"), other feminists developed analytical categories that could account for women's separate status inside the productive apparatus. Instead of a history that progressed through the dualism of class struggle, where women's work would be described on the outside of production—in the "ancient" or "primitive" world, for example, or in the home—, feminists like Iris Marion Young proposed a model where the family would no longer be considered as a separate sphere from capital or as a primary place of socialization or consumption. Instead, patriarchy would be examined as internal to productive processes. This would mean a breaking-apart of class as a singular conflicting force, and substituting more various, concrete, specific accounts of the "*activity* of labor itself" (Young's emphasis; 51) and the specific, multitudinous forms of cooperation, consciousness, and institutions that such activity demanded. In lieu of a type of difference conceived as a historical and unbridgeable cleft, a battle between two nonmediating but self-identical forms: culture (intellectual labor) and production (manual labor), Young advocated that a gender division of labor must describe "the major structural divisions among the members of a society according to their position in laboring activity" (51). Rosemary Hennessy agreed that "marxism cannot adequately address women's exploitation and oppression unless the Marxist problematic itself is transformed so as to be able to account for the sexual division of labor" (1993: xi–xii). The separation between production and reproduction would then be an internal limit rather than a definitional enclosure or identity, an unbridgeable exclusion.

A division of labor thesis would not assume that all women fall under a unified oppression but would be able to notice how diverse, variable tasks, values, and functions were assigned value usually, within a particular society, through gender. Patriarchy would no longer be considered as prior to industrial development, as archaic, of a singular cause (primitive), or as only contextualized in the anthropological record. Answering to the allegation that Marxist categories like class were "gender-blind," division of labor gave a view of gender as structured through chains of signifying difference, cross-culturally variant, a distribution of internally changing but interrelated action- and value-variables, a network in motion, like language as poststructuralist or deconstructive theories would go on to conceive it. The division of labor thesis was responding to the separation of ideology or symbolic exchange (reproduction) from production via the separation of women. In response to such premises of ideology critique, the division of labor thesis merged cultural circulation (reproduction, or language) into production, made them seem interchangeable, or revealed them as overlapping instances of a process (as they are in Marx).

As "women's work" was absorbed into production, sites of production would multiply. For French feminist sociologist Christine Delphy, for example, in her groundbreaking work *Close to Home,* the types of exchange systems in which women circulate are not to be differentiated from productive exchange circuits (markets) but rather explain their internal hierarchies. Delphy states her ethnographic interest to be to "study the inheritance of property" (1970, 15). This put her in line with Engels and his definition of patriarchy as an effect of inheritance. She hoped that the focus on inheritance would lead her to answer "the criticisms of the women's liberation movement which come from the left" (1970: 15)—she hoped to show that an analysis of patrimony and the transmission of property would help her understand why gender was important for understanding how markets worked. Within the systems of agricultural production Delphy observed, as property is passed down usually to one family member with the interests of keeping it intact, the other family members will often continue to labor for the family farm, in unremunerated roles, doing devalued tasks. "In my research," she notes, "I discovered first what a huge quantity of goods change hands without passing through the market. These goods change hands through the family—as gifts or inheritance" (1984: 15). Transmission of property or "gift-giving" is not prior to markets but coincident with markets. Delphy learns that the division of labor between paid and unpaid pre-exists the gendered division of labor in industrial markets but gets absorbed into industrialism as gendered value. Gender gives a name to different aspects, elements, and moments already existing in the productive/circulation process in order to create differential value between them.

Delphy uses Engels to skip over the centrality of industrialization in Marx's descriptions of modernization, where the Symbolic of money circulates often outside of production but also within it. Because transmission precedes production, the hierarchy between paid and unpaid labor came first, and then gender was produced by gathering together disparate traits of the "unpaid" into a particular vision of the sexed body. Farm life, for Delphy, does not represent a rustic or quaint example of a precapitalist mode, removed from production, a "symbolic exchange" that precedes capitalism's emergence, nor an originary scenario dug up from the anthropological or evolutionary record, tracing the shape of the human, the cultural, or the universal. Rather, embedding domestic culture into the construction of value in markets, farm life gives a capsule-view of a labor market *within* a family and the construction of gender as a response to the construction of value. "This is indeed one of the times when the domestic mode of production *meets* the capitalist mode and where they *interpenetrate* each other" (Delphy's emphasis; 1984: 19). Domestic production—because it initiates the division of labor between paid and unpaid work, because it exhibits the transfer of the uncountable time of use value into the quantification of exchange—*is* the structure of all production.

Delphy develops her thesis about the patriarchal family as a disagreement with Engels. For Delphy, the patriarchal family organization in the farming context brings out the historical division that Engels projects into the past to be a product of the present: women's domestic production coexists inside industrial forms as devalued because of an arbitrary attribution that initially referred to something else: to the work of those who did not directly inherit. The agricultural setting makes clear, however, that unpaid work (symbolic exchange) and paid work interact in shared-time, bestowing meaning by differentiating their arbitrarily designated tasks: patriarchy and capitalism intertwine. Exchanged commodities gain value through the contributions of unpaid labor.[20] Instead of seeing women-directed, extended family households as a historical and "primitive" relic, made irrelevant by male ownership and transmission of productive tools in the evolution of capitalist productive processes, Delphy describes domestic agricultural production as a set of productive tasks organized to keep a certain set of workers—through the transmission of inheritance—working without pay while others expropriate their labor and profit, only later carrying an arbitrarily gendered designation. The class structure is internal to the symbolic of kinship relations, producing profit. This explains why—as Engels himself predicted though did not fully realize why—kinship persists even after its utility has all but dissolved.

Delphy's intention is to challenge feminist (or "protofeminist") perspectives that place domestic life in its own alienated category with women at its center, not only removed from production but also irrelevant to the money form, inconsequential to class or to the commodity. In a barbed attack against one such critic, Delphy vituperates against popular "women's liberationist" views professing that the oppression of women comes down to subjective values that can easily be revalued, so that what makes domestic work miserable is the social attribution of misery and inferiority to such tasks rather than the system of domination that requires such tasks to be (gendered) inferior. Delphy believes that such idealism masks "the relationship between *division* and *hierarchy*" (2000: 63; Delphy's emphasis) embedded in the organization of the means of production. Intending to show that the Symbolic of gender is not relatively autonomous from the class structure but fundamentally integral to it, Delphy sets out to show that the Symbolic of gender comes first as the expression of hierarchy between paid and unpaid labor in its particular historical form: "men" and "women" are the bodies that get captured in different positions of the hierarchy leading into industrial capitalism; before then the hierarchy designated only the primogenitor in the position of paid labor, where wives', younger siblings', and children's productivities were gathered into the subordinated position of the unpaid. She thus refutes feminist analysis based on the idea that sex is the ground of gender.

Though focused on production in the agricultural setting in *Close to Home*, Delphy maintains that the relations of the farming family parallel all modern forms of kinship and family nuclearization where the labor of the housewife is expropriated. The atemporalized naturalization of the division of labor found in theories such as Engels'—by making gender prior to history—has led, she says, some mainstream feminist analysis, like Leclerc's, to assume value, essential content, moral meaning, work product, intrinsic utility, status, and hierarchy within unchanging, timeless gender categories, that is, to affirm and legitimate ideological gendered traits as needing to be respected in order to give women the self-esteem they need and deserve. Women are supposed to do housework out of a love that forms from their "feminine nature," and society needs to value such commitment rather than make women suffer from embarrassment or derision. In contrast, Delphy believes that such perspectives start with the ideological supposition that women's work is inferior, and then make that into a cause of why women are dispossessed of the product of their work, or are "doing a task *unpaid for someone else*" (Delphy's emphasis; 1987: 100), as "housework." Delphy goes on to show statistically and descriptively that, though unpaid, domestic production is only different as an ideal, arbitrary reflection from other types of commodity production: that use value cannot really be distinguished in content from exchange value,[21] that services provided by wives are not distinct in content from services provided by markets, and that producing for personal consumption is really "on a continuum" (1984: 64) with production for a wage. "In our society," she explains, "... it is not a case of certain tasks being forbidden to women, but of our being allowed to do them only in certain conditions. It is not that women may not act diplomatically, but that we may not be diplomats; it is not that women may not drive a tractor, but that we may not get on to one as the boss, nor even as a *paid* worker, etc." (Delphy's emphasis, 1987: 103). Gender arises to preserve unpaid labor, or reproduction, for value-maximization within markets.

Delphy does not escape from the problem in Marxism which envisions the singular conflict between capital and labor as the singular motivating force of History, even as she allows a diversity of types of unpaid, reproductive labor at different stages of History. She also is unable to resolve the critique of Marxism as economically deterministic—the Symbolic can only function in the service of capital and exchange and cannot, as later feminist perspectives like Kristeva's and Butler's allowed, unleash creativity, changing institutions and subjectivities by making them unstable. However, the important question that Delphy does ask is about the relationship between the Symbolic—the social production of gender in circulation—and class conflict, that is, how the Symbolic of gender is needed by capitalism to produce and preserve a sphere of unpaid labor as pure surplus.

Delphy's analysis is symptomatic of how a change in linguistic concept affects a construction of class. Language operates as an arbitrary veil that pieces together, into a singular category of gendered reproduction, a multiplicity of *activities* of unpaid labor. Once the division of labor thesis opened up the category of work to diversification through lingustification, class would become one instance of a wide array of symbolic divisions, each contingent and replaceable by other links in a chain of difference. Feminist theorists like Ernesto Laclau and Chantal Mouffe would then be able to generate a concept of civil society—"the political"—modeled on the structure of work in the division of labor thesis though without work at its center. Laclau and Mouffe attest that even at the time of Marx's writing, class and class antagonism were not the principle divisions demarcating historical action: they reject "the vanity of the aspiration that the 'class struggle' should constitute itself, *in an automatic and a priori manner,* in the foundation of this principle [of social division]" (Laclau and Mouffe's emphasis, 151). The category of class was insufficient because it depended on the assumption that class struggle was monolithic, constituted through an opposition that was dualistic and determining throughout history, whose players were pre-defined and invariant, and whose outcomes could be predicted. Instead, the political field was composed by multiple unstable identities constantly being redefined by passing through a series of unstable, structural, linguistic oppositions, including both class and gender but not rooted in either. "The decline of a form of politics for which the division of the social into two antagonist camps," they read in the historical record before and after Marx "is *an original and immutable datum, prior to all hegemonic construction,* and the transition toward a new situation, characterized by the essential insta-bility of political spaces, in which the very identity of forces in struggle is submitted to constant shifts, and calls for an incessant process of redefi-nition" (Laclau and Mouffe's emphasis, 151). The democratic revolution's affirmation of equality made subordinated identities into articulations of difference (e.g., social movements) that kept changing in content, depend-ing on changing mechanisms of subordination. Antagonisms were, then, practices of such articulation. Laclau and Mouffe released the hold of the universalizing category of class on activities and identities that were con-flated into this category. They exposed the field of social relations—or "the political"—as broader and more expansive than their strict designation of class would imply, splitting class identities away from the many other social identities, including gender, that they subsumed. Identities become more localized and singularized.

Though the division of labor thesis did not pose women's work outside of production, neither would women's relation to production (to labor) be its defining moment. Whereas in ideology critique, a fundamental schism between production and reproduction was built on a fundamental sense that capitalism had limits—for example, that the anthropological record would teach us that patriarchal culture had a life exterior, prior, and excessive to capitalist relations—, the division of labor thesis, like the language theo-ries linked to poststructuralism and deconstruction, envisioned difference as symptomatic of capitalism, that is, as an arbitrary errancy, aberration, rupture, absence, limit, or crisis produced inside of it and integral to it, with no outside. Though clearly the division of labor thesis opened up femi-nist analysis to a broader array of topics, identities, and perspectives, it also re-interpreted the category of class: class would become an emptied-out and indistinct form, without autonomous historical force or agency, and, con-ceptually unimaginable.

Division of labor divided the way language worked as a binary class ideology—referential, reflective, mimetic, or reproductive language—from the way language worked within the divisions of work, as a slippery, nonreferential, arbitrary process in a chain of processes: the production of signifying variety. For example, in Chandra Mohanty's canonical piece, "Under Western Eyes," the ideal image or hegemonic representation of "Woman—a cultural and ideological composite Other constructed through diverse representational discourse (scientific, literary, juridical, linguistic, cinematic, etc" (50) is contrasted with "women—real, material subjects of their collective histories" (50). Mohanty dismisses the symbolic of sexual difference which, she notes, puts women into a coherent and universal classification, frozen into binaries such as the powerful vs. the powerless. Though, Mohanty points out, within such symbolics, "Woman" is monolithic, linked to humanism, its authorities, its norming, and its production of "third-world women" as powerless victims of patriarchy, "women" has an uneasy ability to reference. Like ideology, "Woman" as purely symbolic form that exists overarchingly, cross-culturally, prior to its entry into particular social systems, exchange networks, or kinship structures, whereas, in contrast, "women" is meant, Mohanty insists, as various, locally differentiable, nonabstractable contextually and historically singular. Instead of the ideology of difference, Mohanty understands women in what she calls historical materialist terms, that is, as nongeneralizable: as so context-bound, situated, and immediate as to preclude the possibility of theory, abstraction, and concept altogether. Appearing within global circuits of work, "particularity" stands against the ideology of the grand signifier "Woman" by touching on material practices, the multiplicity of forms and instances but, as such, has no viable concept to grasp it. Instead, she advocates a heterogeneity of particularities "constructed in a variety of political contexts that often exist simultaneously and overlaid on top of one another" (61), like the division of labor.[22] This radical particularity becomes visible for Mohanty through an analysis of lacemakers in India, where women's positionalities within the organization of production are not generalized "in the direction of 'women' in India, or 'women in the third world'" but rather generated from "within the situation and context" (61)—in other words, the division of labor allows a multitudinous variety to break apart general, reproductive ideological categories by refusing the reduction of identity to the predetermined binary split between the exploiting and the exploited. This critique of the binary of class underlay a revision of labor theory away from language as reflection or reproduction of reality (set within a binary of class division between ideological labor and manual labor) and toward language as a nonreferential signifying chain (a multiplicity of laboring tasks).

This disappearance of class and of theory was developing at a time when manufacturing and industrial laboring were seen to be disappearing, dispersing, and decentralizing in first-world production (it could even be predicted, however preposterously, that first-world production might eventually cease entirely), even though such a formulation did not take into account the continuation (and even the increase) of manufacturing and industrial production in other non-first-world geographical contexts, nor the advent of other nonindustrial types of labor and labor organization (like service), nor that working people still had an historical identity as working people, in some shape or form (that is, that people's working lives still defined their social place, self-conceptions, experience, and worldly relations to a great degree). Feminism's critique of class and the dispersion of its narrative of domination and liberation created a difficulty for making claims or taking action on behalf of working people, even as labor was still being feminized as well as politicized, unions and collective bargaining attacked, benefits cut, credit dried up, jobs made less permanent, wages plateaued, and a series of other draconian maneuvers, including cut-backs in child labor protections in some states and decreases in public educational spending, were unleashed on working people as working people. That is, once women and their working time could be integrated within a Marxist analysis of labor, labor itself would become an unstable or quasi-unusable category.

Marx, Working Time

In *Capital,* the category of class only makes sense within the process of its feminization. The organization of work under capitalism demands a constant pressure to expand unpaid work time[23] while shrinking the historically necessary time for reproducing labor-power. Women's unpaid work time performs those functions within the productive process. Additionally, women's work stores the excess production time, holding it outside of production until the productive cycle is ready again to exchange labor capacity for wages and set labor back into motion. "But if a surplus laboring population is a necessary product of accumulation or of the development of wealth on a capitalist basis," Marx explains, "this surplus-population becomes, conversely, the lever of capitalistic accumulation, nay, a condition of existence of the capitalist mode of production... [I]t creates... a mass of human material always ready for exploitation" (*Capital I,* 592). The features of capital formation that Marx describes in his treatments of circulation can also be found to have been developed through such depictions of women's work. Marx makes visible this comparison in the *Grundrisse,* "It is possible, as we have already indicated earlier, that the capital as well as the living labour capacity set free owing to the increase in productive forces must both lie dormant because they are not present in the proportions in which production must take place on the basis of newly developed productive forces" (444). A formative moment in the maturation of a world market, circulation indicates levels of production that surpass simple exchange, where capital reaches out to mediate and eventually consolidate an array of independent productive circuits. It requires, sometimes, that some units of production finish before others, or take time to be generated into money and then back into machinery and raw materials, and so have to suspend production before beginning work again anew. This means that women's work in reproduction—or surplus production—is, paradoxically and simultaneously, like circulation, both a result of production and its presupposition, its necessary condition. Both literally and metaphorically, women's work as reproduction is the condition, the primary lever, of capitalist accumulation in general—as stored up labor power and value, it is the starting point of production.

Consequently, class can only be constructed as a gendered form. Gender constitutes class by making it a time-relation. In *Capital,* gender works to shrink the labor time historically necessary for labor and capital to reproduce themselves and to realize their value in surplus, and thus reveals the historical dimensions that shape class by shaping time. The gendering of class means that class can only be materialized as it mixes different historical stages and temporal moments in a synchrony. Gender is therefore what makes class impossible to unify, to naturalize, or to stabilize. Gender cannot be thought outside of production, but neither are its meanings determined by one productive phase (and only one), because women's unpaid reproductive time reveals the limits of time accumulated in the historical process, forcing a reconfiguring. Ultimately, women's unpaid labor time serves as a model for time storage as Marx further elaborates on the relation of time storage to profit in the multi-layered systems of industrialized commodity circulation.

In *Capital,* class does not so much represent a pole in an antagonism (as it does in "The Communist Manifesto" and other works) but rather an ongoing historical condition or field of dispossession that alienates the worker's claims to property in his own time. Here, reproduction is a mode of time-capture. In positioning reproduction as a mode of time-capture or time-storage, Marx does not need to decide on a singular relation between production and reproduction. In fact, women's work contains varieties of temporality. Historical time is "punctuated" by the intersections of different but simultaneous phases of the production process—turnover of fixed or circulating capital, cycles of production and rest, etc. Because of the simultaneity of overlapping time processes in *Capital, Capital* cannot rely on the same privileging of the progressive time of stages, the imminent time of the birth of proletariat consciousness, the transcendent time of an inevitable revolution, or the gradually advancing time of developing technology found in Marx's earlier works. Rather, *Capital* gives a snapshot view of contemporeity, where the different historical moments within the current organization of production and reproduction are intersecting and interacting rather than sequencing or replacing the ones prior. *Capital* is a model of time-storage. Even the gradual accumulation of capital and value and the concentration of ever bigger technologies do not follow a linear process, but rather are constantly interrupted, pushed backward by delays, stopped up by money and capital taking holidays, resting, or waiting, idling while the next cycle starts up, and devaluing in the meantime. As Marx summarizes in the *Grundrisse,* "Its [money's] very entry into circulation must be a moment of its staying at home, and its staying at home must be an entry into circulation" (234). The possibility of social organization of the past interacting within machineries of the present (congealed labor) is what makes *Capital* not just a reading of the industrial past, but also a potential explanation of how the industrial past's histories influence and break through configurations of production and profit within the postindustrial present, of production as reproduction. In a nutshell, past relations of production, including the use value of reproduction, when workers were still connected to their own tools of production, enter the present generally as stored time that is eventually realized both in the next phase of production and in profit.

In Volume I of *Capital,* the recruitment of women workers into an increasingly centralized factory system creates the concurrent variances of stored time. The incorporation of women into the industrial workplace does not happen all at once, nor does it happen progressively or gradually. Instead, their assimilation fluctuates, triggered by innovations in production or differing trends in organization, technology, and cooperation, marking moments in the productive cycle when older or newer productive arrangements are assimilating into current normalized practice. The more machinery is amassed, the more labor is brought in, at first in order to increase the surplus, but eventually socially necessary labor time is reduced, and surplus can be made through labor's dispersions, for an interval, with a decrease in the rates of profit leading to a crisis, and then a repeat. For example, the rise of the sewing machine meant the baiting of an army of independent workers into manufacturing (a transitional form between artisanal guilds and the wage labor of industry). Independent workers are out-competed, families break apart, and children "of too tender an age are sent adrift" (*Capital I,* 443). The "poorest of the poor" (*Capital I,* 444), driven from their houses and isolated domestic production, are now cheaper manufacturing hires than those workers with more skills, who compete with the machine. Now, "the new machine hands are exclusively girls and young women" (*Capital I,* 444). Next, manufacturing gains prominence over cottage industries; the distance between branches of trade exhausts labor and absorbs its reserve army; increased mass production of apparel gluts the market; and finally, the steam-engine is invented, becoming "a motive power in the place of muscles" (*Capital I*, 446), and production moves out of the home. More machinery substitutes for labor by "mak[ing] up for the loss of time" (*Capital I*, 446). The capture of women's time occurs at points throughout the historical momentum of capital, sometimes cyclically, sometimes through cresting and shrinking, sometimes sporadically, always governed by the demands of a new technological configuration or organizational structure seeking to profit over the unpaid labor in the preindustrial moment. Women's work appears almost always as an arrangement that is past and present at the same time, dysfunctional, and obsolete, not quite integrated through the wage, below the level of the productive forces with their level of socially necessary paid productive time, but needed to make the current nexus of productive forces viable, progressive, and intensified.

As home or "use value" production is the historical time of reproduction, when the worker owns his own means of production and works to meet his own (and his family's) needs, the capture of women's time parallels primitive accumulation. "Previously," Marx remarks, "the workman sold his own labour-power, which he disposed of nominally as a free agent. Now he sells wife and child. He has become a slave dealer" (*Capital I*, 373). For Marx, the value of labor-power corresponds to the time it takes to produce it, or to produce its subsistence (necessary labor time). This value is paid to the worker as wages. A day's wages pay the cost of the worker's daily reproduction (even if the cost is covered in a half-day's work) in exchange for the labor-power exerted in the worker's entire working day. Wages are what allow the laborer to be alienated from his labor time, that is, to confront his own temporality in objective form, as outside of himself and belonging to others. The hours of the working-day that exceed the time it takes for the laborer to feed, clothe, shelter, and sustain himself are hours that belong to the capitalist who bought the whole day at the exchange value of labor-power, but the capitalist "owns" those undesignated hours without paying for them, as surplus. Much of the middle part of *Capital* recounts the story of struggles over how much of the workers' time should provide for their own maintenance, and how much of it is pure extra. Capitalists can extend the surplus time by extending the length of the working day or shrinking the time spent on producing for the worker's own reproduction (the wage), but there are limits, says Marx. Capitalists view labor-power as pure capital, or profit, but unlike other instances of capital, labor-power is attached to an organic body, a substance. The limits to productive labor time are both natural (the need to eat and to rest) and cultural ("the general state of social advancement" (*Capital I*, 223)).

"Free time" in production, or surplus time—the time of the worker that the capitalist owns without paying for it—, can be extended technologically: "Machinery," says Marx, "is intended to cheapen commodities, and, by shortening that portion of the working-day, in which the labourer works for himself, to lengthen the other portion that he gives without an equivalent, to the capitalist" (*Capital I*, 351). Additionally, the capitalist can extend surplus labor time by cutting the time reserved for the workers' maintenance and reproduction, both of himself from day to day and from generation to generation. Free time makes surplus value, and the capitalist wants to claim as much of it as he can for his own profit. Increases in machine capacity and its rates of productivity squeeze reproductive time out of the time of production. Outside of production, women workers save time; they take care of the reproduction that no longer falls under the wage. By entering industry en masse, they squeeze the working day down to eleven hours, ten, and then eight for moral reasons, reducing reproductive "free time" for all workers. Because wage reduction and unemployment ensued, manufacturers were able then to insist on extended hours back to fifteen, advocating in Parliament "in the name of workpeople" for "friendly" "over-time" (*Capital I*, 270).

Women parallel the circulation of surplus value in *Capital, Volume I*. Circulation constitutes a withdrawal of stored up time, a delay in the realization of its value: capital makes surplus only in production, by increasing the amount of time the worker works beyond what it takes him to maintain itself (reproduction). But the surplus can only be realized once it is circulating, that is, exchanged for money and then passed back—sometimes after travels and suspensions—into the increased capital outlay of the next round, or growth. For Marx, machinery and money are the resting-grounds of the stored up surplus labor time of past labor, waiting to be realized in production. Like machinery. women's work preserves and holds on to value by retaining the surplus time, that is, the dead time of the past, keeping it out of circulation temporarily, and then periodically releasing it as the living time of the present, in a new round of production. As surplus time, reproduction therefore always comes after production—unpaid value from the past that depends on a new round of production to realize its value—in order, paradoxically, to be what precedes production, what allows the cycle of production to begin. Reproduction is the means by which lost or expended time is made productive and resumes value by living again. "It [labor in production] raises," Marx relates, "by mere contact, the means of production from the dead, and makes them living factors of the life-process" (*Capital I*, 194).

Marx frames this transfer of dead time into present objects (production) as when "corpses of machines" (*Capital I,* 197) reappear as the undead, revitalized in the living value of the new product. Like reproduction, production is a (re-)birth: the making-productive-life out of dead and congealed time.

Reproduction is not a set function, a constant factor, or a practice within a specified timeframe within industrial capitalist production. Rather, it is a historical form, politically shifting as past unpaid time that is withdrawn from circulation and then soaked up into it again, at different phases of the productive process. It takes on different forms. Through this transmission of past unpaid time into new objects, histories and forms of life repeat and are preserved as a present that is, at the same time, always in process, consuming them to death. The fact that Marx spends little attention on reproduction in the family unit is testimony to his conviction that the family was a traditional form, and that capital's dependence on it for its reproductive function would eventually dissipate as the project of reproduction through storage and circulation took on new shapes in the changing phases and technologies of capital. I do not read Marx as ever saying that men workers and women workers are the same as abstractions, but rather that reproductive work does not always fall upon women in a particular way. The difference between men and women is a shifting relationship of historically necessary labor time, of paid and unpaid time, rather than a fixed structure of forms or an itemized description of features, positions, and tasks. In fact, for Marx the similarities and differences that institute working lives for men and women are constantly adjusting and readjusting for the benefit of historically situated profit-seeking regimes. Marx believed reproduction was not a singular entity or a trans-historical substance but always setting time awry.

Marx's schematization of productive time within the working day extends as well into the life span of the laboring individual, whose labor-power is consumed in a certain fraction of his lifetime, and then explains the historical movement of industrial centralization and capital intensification. Here Marx makes it quite clear that this historical process of time-capture proceeds through the appropriation of women's domestic time into directly exploitable industrial time, or the time of the machine. "With the help of mechanical force," Marx notes, "they [girls and young women] destroy the monopoly that male labour had of the heavier work, and they drive off from the lighter work numbers of old women and very young children. The overpowering competition crushes the weakest of the manual labourers" (*Capital I,* 444). The increased capital outlay necessary for machinery leads to "[u]nlimited exploitation of cheap labor-power" (*Capital I,* 447), including women and children, in order to compete and an extension of the working day that reduces family life for the laborer. As Marx traces the advance of capitalism from agriculture to handicraft production, cottage industry, manufacture and then to the concentrated factory system of modern industry, he depicts it through the conversion of multiple small workshops housing the labor of one to four women, to large structures bringing more than 30,000 children and 10,000 women in many industries into close proximity for manufacture (*Capital I*, 435), and, as of 1861, 1,024,277 individuals, many women and young children, crowded into apparel and lace factories (*Capital I*, 442). The overwhelming increase in women workers, Marx observes, does not create prosperity for women—on the contrary: "The new machine hands are exclusively girls and young women" (*Capital I*, 444). This large-scale recruitment of women workers prompted regulatory legislation precisely to set controls on women and children's time. Marx scrutinizes the details of public debates over the length of reproductive time, like when and where meals could be taken, whether production would stop for meals to be taken during work, how long meal-time would last, whether schooling would be attended at the worksite or at a separate site, how far workers could travel, and etc., while capitalists fought against such slow-downs.[24] As in primitive accumulation, this squeezing-out of domestic time separates workers from their own means of production and catapults them into the industrial workforce where their labor power is sold to others. Women's work is posited as a history-in-ruins of an already-in-process circulation system that allows productive industry to begin. Domestic work is a first instance of reproduction, a characterization of a circulatory system in its most basic and personalized form.

Domestic reproductive time is destroyed again in each productive phase, to explain the origin and transition of that phase. Domestic reproductive time is destroyed each time by the advent of a new machine so that its excess time can pass into the accumulating surplus of the productive process. Throughout its myriad transitions, reproductive time is both politically debated and technologically manipulated. At one point, "The value of labour-power was determined not only by the labour-time necessary to maintain the individual adult labourer, but also by that necessary to maintain his family" (*Capital I*, 373). Yet, the increased use of machinery changed all that: "Machinery, by throwing every member of that family on to the labour-market, spreads the value of the man's labour-power over this whole family. It thus depreciates his labour-power" (*Capital I*, 373). As Leopoldina Fortunati summarizes this process: "the production of absolute surplus-value signifies the absorption of reproduction—all reproduction—into the realm of surplus labor" (158). In addition, machinery creates a situation where the organic body of the laborer is subordinated to the rhythmic demands of the machine, its uniform motion and consistent time-measure. "In so far as machinery dispenses with muscular power, it becomes a means of employing labourers of slight muscular strength, and those whose bodily development is incomplete, but whose limbs are all the more supple. The labour of women and children was, therefore, the first thing sought for by capitalists" (*Capital I*, 372). Objectifying time in order to remove it from the worker's control, the advent of machines in industry thereby reduces the body to be but an extension of an instrument of labor governed by an external mechanism and a set of skills to be repeated lifelessly in uniform time. The body of the "workpeople" becomes "peculiar," Marx notes, "consisting as it does of individuals of both sexes" (*Capital I*, 399). The growth in the industrial use of machinery is at first a result of accelerated accumulation and an increased field of production "during which machinery conquers its field of action" (*Capital I*, 424). Soon, however, machinery begins to replace workers. As machines concentrate workers under one roof, dispersed handicraft, cottage industries, and manufacturing sites are ruined, "freeing up" families. This is the beginning, says Marx, of the factory system.

In *Capital*, different phases in production are ushered in through different types of management over women's work, from home production to domestic and cottage industries, manufacturing, and the factory system. The cottage industries were homes connected by productive systems, like home-based looms all hooked up to a central engine. They began to lose time once the production of an article demanded disconnected processes rather than sequential ones, so the factory system shrunk the time intervals that separated tasks in space in order to increase the capitalizable time of production. The constant flux between, on the one hand, periods of augmented machinery, accompanied by the absorption of fresh recruits, and, on the other, periods of labor depletion and replacement by machines, creates uncertainty in the conditions of existence, reducing wages and eventually opening labor markets to an ever greater mix of the population: "The workingpeople are thus continually both repelled and attracted, hustled from pillar to post, while, at the same time, constant changes take place in the sex, age, and skill of the levies" (*Capital I*, 428).[25] Machinery "makes its appearance so soon as the human muscles are replaced" (*Capital I*, 433), meaning that work is "entirely emancipated from the restraints of human strength" (*Capital I*, 357), "emancipated from the organic limits" (*Capital I*, 354), "without regard to the question of its execution by human hands" (*Capital I*, 359), abstracting the body into obsolescence, to the point where capital can operate equally well through bodies regardless of shape, size, strength, or sex.

Ironically in as much as the concentration of machinery tends toward erasing gender difference—making muscles obsolete, turning consumption into purchasing, absorbing the domestic sphere into production, destroying the family that constructs gendered roles—, it also insists on the reproduction of gender difference: as women's bodies take on the functionality of men's in relation to the machine and the division of labor, a particularly women's sexuality is then revealed through its connection to the productive process. This overabundance of sexual womanliness results from the "unwholesome influences" that women are subjected to "owing to the long hours" (*Capital I*, 444). Once their time is "freed up" from domestic controls and socializing authorities—once workers have been separated from their own means of production—, women's time is up-for-grabs. Capital's evolving capture of reproductive time from domestic space—from, say, the home to the workroom, from "chambers," "cottages," and "garrets" to the factory—serves to make men fleshless as mechanical appendages, at the same time exposing women and children to irregular habits and greater public contact, often with strangers, that brings out their excesses of fleshliness.

Rather than restricting reproduction to the outside of capital, Marx understands reproduction as a limit that is constantly being absorbed into capital, through the capitalization of social relations and then through the machine: the family dissolves, becoming obsolete as capital takes up its functions. "Since certain family functions, such as nursing and suckling children, cannot be entirely suppressed," Marx describes consumption overtaking family functions, "the mothers confiscated by capital must try substitutes of some sort. Domestic work, such as sewing and mending, must be replaced by the purchase of ready-made articles. Hence, the diminished expenditure of labour in the house is accompanied by an increased expenditure of money" (*Capital I*, 373). The family is a set of relations "based on a purely physiological foundation" (*Capital I*, 332), which is the starting point for precapitalist exchange and a natural division of labor. Yet, as the machines abstract and equalize the body, the body actually changes into a form that is no longer amenable to family life, that actually disparages it and causes its unraveling. "The wretched half-starved parents," Marx describes life in the lace-making factories, "think of nothing but getting as much as possible out of their children. The latter, as soon as they are grown, do not care a farthing, and naturally so, for their parents...Their morality is at the lowest ebb" (*Capital I*, 441). In concert with the machine, the body, now devoid of its own reproductive time, cannot guard itself against the dehumanizing forces that disrupt the types of health and cleanliness, both moral and physical, that keep the family coherent. The body is absorbed into objectified labor time.

The body no longer serves as the origin-point of "natural" or familial relationships between those who worked and traded together, but now the body is an objectivity, abstracted and surrendered to the machine, adopted into its cruelties, its sinfulness, its perversions, and its antihumanism. In particular, the opening of factory production to women workers—by devouring the exterior times of socialization, education, and reproduction—inflicts human relations with "moral degradation," "filthy, indecent, and shameless habits," with "shame," "untidiness," and "contempt" (*Capital I,* 437), the abandonment of "the rules of health, of cleanliness,...of decency" (*Capital I,* 436), the onslaught of "unwholesome influences" (*Capital I,* 444), leading to such unseemly spectacles as "the employment of naked women and girls" in mines (*Capital I,* 371), women who "accompany the men to the public houses" full of "insobriety" (*Capital I,* 437), women who become "rough, foul-mouthed boys,...the legs naked far above the knees, hair and face besmeared with dirt" (*Capital I,* 437), or "the fatal influence of the association of the two sexes by night in the same badly-lighted workshops" (*Capital I,* 284). "A great number of women," reports Marx, "have illegitimate children, and that at such an immature age that even those most conversant with criminal statistics are astounded" (*Capital I,* 441). The sinful and perverted aspect of women in industrial capitalism is that bodies and the time it takes to humanize them no longer belong to them but to an external process, a process producing its own set of objective relations that take the place of physical and familial connections. Reproduction is no longer a family function.

Without the independent time held in family, the realities of the alienated body routs out even the most depraved remnants of a defeated humanism. The human and moral content of literature empties out: "the most loathsome phantasies of our romance writers" (*Capital I,* 437) are as unwholesome, in Marx's evaluation, as behaviors in the workshops. Alienated industrial women workers are central to Marx's sense that alienation is at the crux of capitalism's own depravity, its dehumanization and perversion. To describe this situation for women workers, Marx uses a vocabulary more intensely tinged with tragedy, sensationalist melodrama, religious sermon, and, most palpably, pornography than when he describes ironically the alienated worker confronting his body as labor-power. Similarly though even more corrupted, as commodities that can be placed at the disposal of another person and objectified in units of time, women workers, alienated from the physical and the familial, confront their humanity from a distance, in the inhuman, abstracted, amoral time of the machine.

Reproduction holds time similarly to the way peasants hold land. Marx coins "primitive accumulation" as an intensified reproduction of capitalist relations, both at the beginning of capitalism and as its internal and continuing operational mode: the violent process that capitalist enterprise uses to seize control of the means of production, to alienate workers from their means of subsistence. With improved methods of agricultural cultivation requiring greater concentration of the means of production and greater convergence and magnitude of technological input, peasants are driven off their holdings and set adrift to make room for industry, according to Marx's origin story of capital. This process is what strips away the peasants' means of nourishment, their life-force, explaining why they are driven to sell their labor power as the only remaining value in their possession. By paying the laborer for his labor power, his body, the capitalist turns his unpaid labor time into capital.

In parallel, the use of machinery concentrates production in the factories, bringing about the tendency to "push on the concentration, under one roof, and one management, of previously separated branches of a trade" (*Capital I*, 445), including the dispersed domestic units involved in manufacturing pieces of the commodity. Here, like primitive accumulation, domesticity is but a fiction needed to explain the present of history. As Nancy Hartsock has observed, Marx's treatment of primitive accumulation applies to the present because it is "very clearly and perhaps at its core a gendered set of processes" (2006:183). In its contemporary forms, primitive accumulation can be identified as the underlying mechanism for such contemporary economic reconfigurations as these: 1) agricultural workers are being dispossessed of their land by agribusiness and subsidy policies and forced into migration, thereby disconnecting workers from their means of subsistence, even as the policing of borders and other anti-immigration measures are becoming harsher. This affects women more than men because women are more often than before primary earners for their families; 2) the continual reshaping of governing and state institutions in the interests of big financial players and corporations, and allowing the most wealthy increasingly "to enrich themselves at the expense of the poor" (2006: 181). Cuts in taxation, happening at the global level, and simultaneous cuts in public spending and citizens' benefits (austerity); off-shore savings are examples of such upward redistribution. This tendency includes not only reductions in welfare systems but also structural adjustment agreements promoted and implemented by the International Monetary Fund (IMF) and the World Bank (disproportionately impinging on the lives and livelihoods of women), as well as the Third World debt crisis and the failure of development policies. This redistribution also includes corporate contracting, which transfers public funds into private hands, for example, in the various militarization, reconstruction, and clean-up projects in war zones, natural disaster zones, human-made and ecological disaster zones. All of these trends in the current workings of capitalism extend the capitalization of women and their work. As they turn more nonworkers or under-capitalized-workers into nonwage, temporary, informalized, or extra-legal workers, such factors also reveal that the dispossession of time is replacing the dispossession of space, which Marx underscored as capital's dominant method for creating ever larger populations who, separated from their own means of production, would offer up unpaid labor time for sale.

Marx, Circulating Time

The second volume of *Capital* is all about capturing time. Volume One explored—through stories of women entering into the various developmental phases of the factory system—how work—particularly, women's work—stores time for profit. Volume Two shows how this "work as time-storage" can be understood as the shape of the entire process of capitalist accumulation. Marx's basic question here is how is time reproduced; that is, how does the productive process reinitiate itself and start over after it has consumed all or part of its inputs, and, contingently, how do its profits get stored and then realized. The answer in Volume Two comes in a series of overlapping equations and tangential curves inserted into intersecting narrative circuits. The process of production cannot enter into its second phase until it has passed through circulation where its stored time is consumed in various ways and turned into money and commodities, just like labor power was developed in Volume One. There can be no starting point to production because the congealed labor saved in commodity-machines must always precede the beginning of a cycle: reproduction must always be assumed as first. Capital needs to assume a prior "idle time"—or time that has not yet been capitalized—first for production to occur. The entire process of capital growth is built out of technologies and methods of organization that shrink the prior time of reproduction.

Volume Two sets out to explain the extraction of profit by separating out the different moments in the circuit that link one productive sequence to the next: first how money gets turned into productive capital, then how capital is made to produce commodities of greater value than itself, and then how the increased value is turned back into money. M'—or the amount of the money originally invested in production plus its surplus value in monetary form— "thus appears as the monetary expression of past labour ... [T]he money is throughout the expression of past labour" (*Capital II,* 151). The reproduction of past labor turns into new labor. Since Marx makes it clear that M, or the initial outlay of money in a market, is always M', or the cashed-in surplus of a prior production cycle, production can never be in its first cycle. These phases "are fragmented, and take place at different times" (*Capital II,* 146), say, where money is taken out of the system and hoarded, or spent on luxuries that do not restore value and time back into circulation, or gets delayed in waiting for another productive circuit to begin when needed productive commodities have not yet completed their own cycles in a different productive sphere and do so only in differing speeds. Fixed capital has different rates of turnover than fluid capital, depending on the time duration of a machine or component's life cycle or the time extension of its reproduction. Effective demand might rise or fall, or a reserve of some input might suddenly and unexpectedly expand, causing delays in new purchases. The time length needed for each of the different processes or material investments varies, according to historical conditions, affecting the length of time extending in between productive deployments. "In as much as the greater or lesser length of the turnover period depends on the working period in the strict sense," Marx elaborates, "i.e. the period needed to prepare the product for the market, it depends on the material conditions of production in the various spheres of capital investment, as these are given at the time" (*Capital II*, 391). Periods of stagnation in one area might have to be synchronized with periods of overexcitement in another. The consumption of goods used for production is calculated at different speeds and volumes than the consumption of goods used for reproduction or worker needs, sometimes creating back-ups in one or another sector. Marx instructs that capital "is a movement, a circulatory process through different stages, which itself in turn includes...different forms of the circulatory process...Here value passes through different forms, different movements in which it is both preserved and increases" (*Capital II*, 185). Capital is valorized in the disruptions and delays of moments of production, where future time is temporarily suspended. Volume Two tells multiple stories about how capital needs to store time, how storing time is what makes profit possible. As the reproductive function that it initiated in Volume One actively expands through storing the time of women's work, Volume Two abstracts this time-storage function, expanding it over the whole perverse system.

Whereas in Volume One, the recurrent "punctuation" of women into the workforce meant that the unpaid labor time of reproduction could be captured into greater profit for the capitalist, in Volume Two, time is amassed by delays in both individual and productive consumption, sometimes stored up in the money form, sometimes in commodities that are delayed or do not get reconverted back into money or machines for production. As Marx points out, "it is only within the production process that value laid out in labour-power is transformed (not for the worker, but for the capitalist)...for the first time into self-valorizing value" (*Capital II*, 291). The realization of value has to be suspended until the capital and equipment is ready to be replaced and set back into motion. Starting in precapitalist times, but ongoing and intensifying during industrialization, part of the money capital—the saved time of "past labor"—is removed into hoards, as happens in the regulation of women's unpaid labor time to separate spheres at moments of development into the factory system in Volume I. Money is, says Marx, "stored up, and exists only in the form of a hoard in the process of formation and growth" (*Capital II*, 163). Money, concludes Marx, "figures here as *latent money capital*...lying fallow" (*Capital II*, 164), or stored-up labor time that exists, like women's domestic work, outside of production, that eventually will transform its surplus value into functioning capital. In the meantime, it remains in the form of securities, interest-bearing bank deposits, and bills of exchange, existing "in the actual shape of money which breeds money" (*Capital II*, 164) as a condition for accumulation.

Volume Two goes on to present ever more complicated layers where money or commodities are accumulated as past labor time, held in reserve outside the productive process; or waiting for provision of materials, market conditions, or arrivals in transportation; or becoming fixed in nondepreciated machinery for a time; or forming into reserves of credit or gold, and then shifted back into extended production in a future cycle. "There is a constantly changing distribution of the hoard existing in a society" (*Capital II*, 261). Marx describes a variety of ways where money or commodities are kept outside or alongside the dominant phases of production in reproductive roles. The second volume of *Capital* is only marginally focused on the life history of labor. Instead, the position that labor held in the first volume, where its relation to capital triggered an expansion of free time that translated into profit, serves as the bedrock explanation of the entire capitalist enterprise, its very kernel. The first volume's logic of labor has now been absorbed into the multi-layers of industrial productivity. Within this, the pressure that women's work adds to increase the expansion of unpaid time in Volume One is now exerted through technologies of time accumulation, productive cycles, and finance. In Volume Two, women's reproductive labor moves into new historical situations.

Conclusion

As the economic crisis continues to maintain high levels of unemployment under the new nomenclature of "recovery," many are blaming the budget crisis on working people, and many are claiming that working people's savings and benefits need to make up for public and private shortfalls. The attack on labor is happening at many levels: rights to collective bargaining are being presented in the media as unfair privileges that suck up tax-payer revenues; CEOs are seeing their incomes rise while rates of joblessness have edged upward in some states while remaining stagnant in others; corporations that are awash in unspent and uninvested cash are demanding tax holidays to repatriate off-shore earnings that they say are pivotal to putting money into job creation; finance "instruments" have been designed to bet on mortgage failures. Corporations are "hoarding" about a trillion dollars of cash, and so the productive forces cannot realize the value of past stored surplus time in the continuation of the cycle: labor has again been separated from the means of production through its alienation of control over time, and growth has been reduced virtually to a standstill. This situation has illuminated that the current phase of capitalism is not only about the greedy pursuit of wealth as some maintain, but rather about the organized production of starvation.

Yet, the attack on labor has given labor an identity it did not previously or obviously have; the fact that there is a political demand to repress, marginalize, weaken, and punish labor organization means that labor is being envisioned as some sort of threat that capital sees as important to recognize even to suppress and to vilify it.

The attack on labor is also an attack on women. Even during "recovery," the gender poverty gap has widened, where women's poverty rates have stayed at the lowest level of the recession. The attack on women repeats Marx's narrative of primitive accumulation. In US states whose governments are claiming that public-sector collective bargaining causes treasury depletions and needs to be shut down, fire fighter and police unions are often held exempt, while teachers' and nurses' unions constitute front-line targets. Women are losing pensions and having their healthcare cut as well as losing other contractual protections so that capital can gain increasing control of time. The disassociation between culture and class that is orchestrated in popular culture makes it difficult to understand the scope of the attack on women as related to their work, as much as feminist theory is also reluctant to recognize women's roles as integral to production or as recognizable outside of the domestic sphere of reproduction, affect, experience, and ideology.

The current attack on women as a certain vulnerable set of laborers indicates that labor has been constructed inside of a symbolism that stores value in gender: reproduction is always distributing value through women's role in producing surplus labor time that will be realized in future surplus value. Marx offers the insight that labor is always in the process of feminization because feminization is its means of capturing profit-generating unpaid labor time (within a range of historical variability) for the future. The feminization of labor means that contemporary labor has taken on the form of the reproductive labor formerly attributed to women's work in the industrial age: decentered, service-oriented (producing subjects rather than producing objects), and outside the boundaries of the law, its accountabilities, and its public protections, that is, in outsourced, financed, or entrepreneurial situations, or in de-nationalized zones. The neoliberal attack on labor assists capital's agenda to separate labor again from the means of production by expanding free time and then capturing the excess, in part through its employments of women.

As workers, women in *Capital* are the best positioned to transform distributions of working time. The transformation of working time can go in either of two directions: either toward a future of increased time-objectification and exploitation, on the one hand, or, on the other, of expanded reproductive time, equalizing time—both individually and collectively—for "growth, development, and healthy maintenance of the body." Analyzing how laboring women's relationship to unpaid time makes all labor exploitable, Marx suggests that working time needs to be understood in relation to women's time in order to create a possibility for a radical redistribution of control over working time.[26] Such a redistribution of control over working time is necessary now for countering the neoliberal forces that produce economic inequalities by dispossessing time.

CHAPTER 2

Julia Kristeva's Murders: Neoliberalism and the Labor of the Semiotic

"Gloria was lying in a pool of blood with her head cut off" (1998: 3). So begins the second volume—entitled *Possessions*—of Julia Kristeva's three-volume detective series. Picking up on Kristeva's philosophies of femininity, her parental themes and psychoanalytic orientations, the novel, in its matricidal indulgences, traces how detachment from the mother and its effects on language explain the production of subjects. Matricide, Kristeva has said multiple times—and, most importantly, the beheading of mothers—, explains the origin of representation in the West.[1] Kristeva's emphasis on the production of subjects is a revisionary challenge, along feminist lines, to New Left Marxist and semiotic philosophies that were concerned about the production of objects, or commodities, and signs, or objectified, structured language systems.[2] Anticipating the focus on socialization that would become prominent within neoliberal critique (see chapters 4 and 5), Kristeva's interest in the production of subjects in the novels mixes her discourse on motherhood and on motherhood's loss of its head, on representation and aesthetics, with an incipient narrative of labor's feminization. In contrast to a psychoanalytic reading of maternal language that Kristeva traces in her philosophical work, the novels imply that femininity takes its particular psychical form historically: that the maternal language function is embedded in fields of circulation, not only psychic ones but also economic.

This chapter looks at Julia Kristeva's detective novel *Possessions* in light of her philosophy of the Semiotic, or pre-linguistic bodily thought, and the Symbolic, or the social conventions of language. Kristeva's theory of the Symbolic depends on an original, infantile separation with the mother and her language, a beheading. *Possessions* illustrates this loss in a murder plot where the mother's language—the Semiotic—is replaced by representational intelligibility (though never completely) when the hired language teacher steals her head. By adopting a popular form for her philosophical concepts, Kristeva shows that the necessary resolution of the conflict between the Semiotic and the Symbolic results from a commodifying of the maternal function as paid service: the representation of "women's work" into the money-form, allowing the exchange of signs as universal equivalents or sociality. This chapter indicates how feminist philosophy's work on language and the subject intersects with a narrative of neoliberal labor reorganization, where "women's work" enters into the paid economy but never quite in a form that can be fully comprehended by the economy of symbolic circulation.

Despite her philosophical interest in the place of femininity within artistic revolt, Kristeva's focus on femininity in her novels reveals a fundamental connection between femininity and specifically economic transformation: in this instance, neoliberal ideas—ideas about privatization, immaterial labor, and a weakening of the public's representational authority, for example—are conveyed, partly, by means of a logic of maternity. In other words, as Gloria's death leads into a marketing of maternal and socializing functions, *Possessions* makes legible how Kristeva's philosophical theory of subjective splitting describes and even affirms new forms of alienation that increasingly dominant and exploitative forms of labor, under neoliberalism, are producing. The novel thus divulges an overlapping between femininity and new modes of work that the philosophical and psychoanalytic accounts leave void. This overlapping becomes particularly apparent where femininity is the site of symbolic regeneration and the production of subjects. Feminist critics have addressed how premises of Second Wave feminism—which, as Hester Eisenstein outlines, "emphasized women as self-sufficient individuals" (64), opposed regulated and protected labor markets, dismissed gender roles, insisted "on a changed language" (63), and encouraged women into corporate jobs in the name of "emancipation"—have, as Nancy Fraser says, a "disturbing convergence of some of its ideals with the demands of an emerging new form of capitalism—post-Fordist, 'disorganized', transnational" (2009: 98).

Goodbye, Gloria!

On the surface, Kristeva's fictional writing quite transparently produces narratives adopting her philosophical concepts as characters, plots, settings, themes, resolutions, and descriptive voice. Linking the sign to the violence of primary repression, the beheading of the mother at the start of *Possessions,* for example, does not stray far from the violent beheading of the sacred mother that Kristeva describes in Giovanni Bellini's paintings of sacred mother and child in *Desire in Language,* where "the mother is only partially present (hands and torso), because, from the neck up, the maternal body not covered by draperies—head, face, and eyes—flees the painting" (1980: 247). As she explains in *The Severed Head,* the Judeo-Christian prohibition on images evoked the female body, the void that imprints the image of God in the flesh of the Son, that allows the invisible to become visible, "imprinting the void as a condition for representation and for thought" (2012: 55). The beheading or exclusion of the mother's head gives Kristeva a pictorial allegory of the birth of secular humanism. As in psychoanalysis, the repression of access to the mother prepares the way for the child's entry into culture and language.

Beheading for Kristeva is thus the prerequisite for freedom through the aesthetic, as in the work of Georges Bataille. For Bataille, as human beings have walked erect, the head has become a replacement for the anus as the locus of aesthetic experience, but the anus will often displace the head as its dazzling, repressed discharges come bursting through, letting in the sun: "This part [the anus of the ape]...sent out shoots and flowered in the ape; it turned into a bald protuberance and the most beautiful colors of nature made it dazzling...[T]he metamorphosis of the great ape must be seen as an *inversion,* having as its object...the direction of the discharges thrust back through the head" (1985: 88–89).[3] Kristeva interprets this as a return to the ecstasy of representation, a "liberating utopia" (2012: 130), where the sacrifice of the head turns out not to be a sacrifice after all but instead the unforgotten consciousness of desire and excess, an open wound, an access to the beyond, to the sensory, the erasure of prohibitions. "In seeing that head," Kristeva responds to Bataille, "one can only want it and want to cut it off" (2012: 126).

Likewise, for Kristeva, the primary repression is never complete, and this results in a constant movement of what she calls the Semiotic—or prelinguistic noise, intonations, gestures, rhythms, and gutturals, linked to the drives—within what she calls the Symbolic, or meaning.[4] The Semiotic does not dismantle the Symbolic, nor is it strictly oppositional.[5] It is, as well, never defeated, absorbed, synthesized, mediated, or reconciled; rather, the Semiotic is a motility—a constant coming-up-against the Symbolic's will to unity in representation, its posing of boundaries—that both stabilizes and destabilizes symbolic functioning.[6] It is what the Symbolic produces within itself as the conditions of its functioning. As a shattering inside the social and its authority, the excess of the Semiotic—what is not and cannot be eventually contained in the Symbolic—appears as a pathology, an erotic demand, a manifestation of the sacred, or an aesthetic revolt.[7] Defying both idealist and positivist appropriations, what such a discovery of semiotic language offers theoretically is the necessity of reading representational practices as in constant movement, being constructed and reconstructed, so that the laws and the forms of the social can never be fixed but can, as yet, never be broken. The social can never, therefore, be realized as representing itself, so that the political role of the Symbolic is constantly suspended.

This positioning of the subject through a break, however incomplete, evokes the feminine as the "before," a matter that precedes the origin and complicates it within a process of socialization (and secularization), through a primary alienation. It also implicates the maternal function as rejected but nevertheless persistent within the aesthetic, as its heterogeneity. Critics have debated whether the philosophical concept that disorients the rule of the symbolic is dependent on a projection backwards that is specifically feminine. Toril Moi, for example, citing Jacqueline Rose, suggests that Kristeva concentrates on the feminine in particular because it is "different or other in relation to language and meaning, but nevertheless only thinkable within the symbolic" (11), that is, it stabilizes while destabilizing the Law. Ewa Plonowska Ziarek, meanwhile, understands this version of femininity as crucial to Kristeva as a theorist of radical democracy because sexual difference, like racial difference, blocks the idealization of the "other" by dramatizing internal heterogeneity (2001). Maria Margaroni adds that Kristeva uses the feminine as the generative space that puts origins under question, pushing them back into the primordial, and in this way portraying the *logos* as the process of denial of a prior multiplicity that it still mediates. For this, the maternal body is but a metaphor for "the excess of the oppositional logic in Western metaphysics" (2005: 95) and so cannot be reduced to "actual mothers," but at the same time, "it opens up the process to the embodied experience of 'actual' subjects" (2005: 96). Like the civil society that liberalism depicts as fragments of self-interest, autonomous from authority and yet dependent on it, the maternal is, in other words, itself split between the heterogeneity of experience and the regulation of meaning.

Reading the relationship between the Semiotic and maternity in the form of a mystery, I argue that the feminine is "actual" most forcefully in its relation to work rather than to biology or psychology. That is, in *Possessions,* the "proleterianization" of care-work produces the subject's alienation as integral to subjectivity, much like the Semiotic is integral to the Symbolic, though alienated from it. *Possessions* shows that Kristeva's turn to the subject is based on a commodifying of the maternal function as privatized paid service: the meeting of the Semiotic with the Symbolic of communicative language depends on the absorption of women's priorly unpaid labor time into a money economy, a universal representational equivalence—on the turning of representations of a naturalized function into the emergence of "women's work." The void of the mother's head (the Semiotic) conditions the making-sense of her speech because it allows for speech to circulate as money, as representation within a circulating economy, as paid labor. Allowing a freer circulation of monied service-goods, the death of the mother concedes, as well, the defeat of external or transcendent authority, particularly in the state and the public as a determination of meaning, in favor of intrasubjective disjunction, privatization, and isolation: an erosion of communicability, community, and intersubjective affiliation. For Kristeva, as Joan Brandt points out, "communicative language is a principal vehicle in the preservation of the ideological structures that dominate Western culture" (25). Kristeva disapproves philosophically of such ideological structures which smother the revolt of the aesthetic (the Semiotic) in the economy of language. Such disapproval enters the novels as a disapproval of the public institutions that produce representational narratives of identification, like the police, and their redemption through the birth of singularityin the subject.

For Kristeva, the loss of the attachment to the mother is central to her philosophical challenge, as it performs two functions: 1) it means that the origin of language and the logos is not monolithic but its multitudinous dispersion, though not totally repressed, is still forgotten;[8] and 2) it sets up her insistence that leftist, radical, and feminist thought needs to take into account the subject as a site of production—that is, as produced in struggle—, and that the maternal body is a site of its production. The maternal thus takes over the heterogeneity that Kristeva originally theorized, through Mikhail Bahktin, as the social language of carnival, "the insertion of history" (1980: 68) into text, or the "poetic word, polyvalent and multi-determined" that "adheres to a logic exceeding that of codified discourse and fully comes into being only in the margins of recognized culture" (1980: 65). In Bahktin, Kristeva reads heterogeneity as emergent from vernacular and social practice in everyday dialogic exchange rather than from pre-subjective experience, so that "Carnivalesque discourse breaks through the laws and language censored by grammar and semantics and, at the same time, is a social and political protest" (1980: 65). As this Bahktinian analytic of heterogeneity in popular linguistic usage and the vernacular morphs into the heterogeneity of the Lacanian Imaginary, the mothering function substitutes a dehistoricizing, nonsymbolizable structure of subject-formation onto the diverse historical forms of social struggle, heteroglossia, in Bahktin.

Much as the Semiotic is integral to the Symbolic, though alienated from it, the hiring-out of maternal functions (Pauline)—or the contracting-out of special commodified services to replace the familial, as its reproduction—operates in *Possessions* as what allows the Semiotic to communicate and make sense within the social Symbolic, at the expense of the mother. The money economy—open trade—is the resolution, what restores the integrity of the Symbolic through the sign without repressing the internal, semiotic conflicts and circulations of linguistic material through which the subject continually produces its meaning in representation. The mother is beheaded and dismembered by her hired replacement, and this conditions the son, Jerry's, ability to speak and make sense within the social.

Genre

Possessions assigns Kristeva's critique of language and the family narrative to a particular genre. The choice of writing formulaic genre novels does seem as if it would contradict Kristeva's philosophical devotion to the destruction of signs and signifying systems.[9] The absorption of linguistic heterogeneity and the aesthetic conflict against the sign would not obviously lend itself to a page-turning, gumshoe, psychological thriller, a novel with a sustained plot driven by conventions, or a narrative that follows a linear process to find, with final success, the answer to a question, a discovery. One of the suspects, Larry Smirnoff, a journalist for *Morning Star,* elaborates on how public language closes down the interpretation of crime as he addresses the police chief Northrop Rilsky: "You'd like the truth to be cut and dried, established once and for all, with the criminal identified, the weapon found, and retribution meted out to the hand that dealt the blow and the mind or minds that were behind it all. But that's just the crude logic of the run-of-the-mill detective story" (1998: 85). The novel itself dramatizes this: the police combine their efforts with protagonist Stephanie Delacour who, as a popular journalist, inherits from religion "a kind of absolute power" (1998: 83), a public authority that, through her language, saturates public space with spectacles "exploiting people's basic instincts" (1998: 84), achieving a commonality over the popular aptitude of crime, seeming to stabilize the Symbolic.

However, many critics of modern detection have noted such novels to be the quintessential expression of modern alienation within a culture of late capitalism,[10] and for this, Kristeva's philosophical enterprise could be said to *demand* such generic treatment.[11] Like translation (Gloria's profession), the genre would then stand in the role of an authority or recognizable sign, "the repression of drives beneath language" (1984: 132), the stopping-up—inside the sign—of activities produced by the sign, the generic features in an unending struggle to the death against the Semiotic inside of it. The forward force of the detective plot in *Possessions* is interrupted with descriptions of art objects, flirtations, Jerry's (Gloria's son) language lessons, psychiatric theory, biographical detail of characters (always too late), ruminations, backflashes, gossip, literary allusion, criticism, musical interlude, reflections on the divine, and, in the end, the head of the victim is permanently lost and the culprit never apprehended—the law's resolution remains permanently suspended. The defining features of the detective formula become irresolute under the assault of the literary material that does not quite fit but still, in some sense, is necessary. The form is a type of alienation from the movements and moments of the text. For this, the battle of the form for its own generic definition—against the rhythms of the narrative lines, diversions, and breakages—is reflected in such scenes as when Gloria's deaf son Jerry is first starting his difficult language learning: against his instinctual utterances of sounds, his observations of insulated and disassociated "smell, saliva, color, touch"—the stimuli of a biological process malfunctioning and fragmented through lesions—, Gloria tries to impose enlightened understanding: "a permanent balm for a permanent wound," "the sound-filled light of humanity" (1998: 55). As a result, "Jerry did gradually come to be like everyone else," or "[a]lmost" (1998: 50).

In her comments about *Possessions* in particular, Kristeva has said that she chose the detective genre because "the genre of the detective story seemed obvious to me, for, like Freud (who, at the end of his life, read detective stories), I am convinced that society is founded on crime" (2009: 79). In fact, the figures of crime and murder appear frequently in Kristeva's philosophical works as woven into the sign and the subject, that is, as framing the moment of splitting, when the Semiotic (the attachment to the mother) is sacrificed in order for the Symbolic to form at one level of the social, through a primary repression that founds representation both socially and individually. "In all known archaic societies," she announces sweepingly, early in her career, "this founding break of the symbolic order is represented by murder. Freud reveals this founding break and generalizes from it when he emphasizes that society is founded on a complicity in the common crime" (1984: 70). As well, she continues, art "assumes murder" (1984: 70), as well as sacrifice, because art exposes the limits of the social as constituted through such a signifying process. The detective novel is also, she will say later in her career when she is commenting on *Possessions*, a particularly feminine form: "The detective story is the culmination of the particular feminine genius that is her familiarity with the trauma of killing and grieving... [W]omen prove to be masters of that grating kind of absolute humor that is the desire for knowledge: not the knowledge of where children come from...but the knowledge of where the human desire to kill one's neighbor comes from" (2012: 118).

A typical type of response to Kristeva's fictional turn, then—for example, the one offered by Maria Margaroni—, might see the novels, correctly, as coextensive with her philosophical themes, where "the human body acquires significance only as corpse and murder" (2009: 108) and where the space of murder "has functioned as the repressed, denied Other" or as "lost origin" (2009: 115). However, such a reading does not give enough focus to Kristeva's choice to weave her philosophical analysis through, precisely, the detective fiction genre. The detective novel genre affects Kristeva's philosophical positioning, as a form of literature cannot be reduced to its philosophical content. In this particular case, the conventions of the detective narrative collide against the a-temporalizing stability of the subject in its philosophic treatments. They expose an exodus of the historical similar to the ambiguities in Kristeva's treatment of the archaic—where "primitive culture" stands out anthropologically as its own defined moment in time but also as outside of time, as the universally human. *Possessions* works within the tensions between the formulaic developments of the detective novel and the critique of the sign that Kristeva assigns—in her philosophical treatments—to the psychoanalytic narrative of rejected motherhood.

Ultimately, Gloria's efforts fail. She hires Pauline to make sense of Jerry's stammers, and Pauline ultimately makes off with her head, allowing Jerry speech. The commodification of maternal or affective labor produces the socialized stability of the subject against the guttural language that identification with the mother incited. *Possessions* re-attributes the loss of the mother—or the line between the Semiotic and the Symbolic—to the neoliberal market culture brought into play in the policing plot through the privatization of women's labor. Instead of the threat from the father, the commodification of maternal or affective labor serves as a displacement or repression against the primary identification. Kristeva reformulates the subject as a productive process, that is, as a struggle between Symbolic meaning and its nonlinguistic, bodily, atemporal, experiential, sometimes aesthetic underside that stabilizes it, then undoes it, only to stabilize it again. By understanding the commodification of subjects as conveyed through the feminine, Kristeva assumes a neoliberalism that is carried forward on the backs of women and their work, precisely through the privatization of caregiving.

"Privatization" in this sense means the making-marketable of care-giving services, a capitalization of previously uncommodified human attachments that has been made necessary by a receding welfare state, or what

Kristeva has called, in her enigmatic essay on neoliberalism "Women's Time," "*an interiorization of the fundamental separation of the sociosymbolic contract*" (emphasis hers; 2000: 198). "Women's Time" reorganizes the relationship between the Symbolic and the Semiotic within a much more politicized international scope, a critique of the state and its representations as a prohibitive boundary in the Symbolic. Here, the break that used to be characterized within a process *toward* socialization has been made into its opposite: a break in the identifications between citizens, the state, and its institutions. Kristeva's analysis of neoliberalism displays it as an invitation to split from a politics of identifications and move toward a politics of diversity and disconnectedness, through singularity. As Ceclia Sjöhom notes, "The 'who' [of the political], in other words, appears to be that which disturbs and threatens any socially formed identity in Kristeva's conception...The political is a form of being and speaking, an ongoing process explored in practices that traditional theories of the political regard as too private to really concern them" (74–80). Kristeva praises the new generation of women for accepting that art can demystify "the idea that the community of language is a universal, all inclusive, and equalizing tool" (2000: 198). That is, for Kristeva, art as singularity dismantles the possibility of group identifications, identifications with ideals, collective appeals of any sort, consensus, or agreements.[12]

For Kristeva and her theory of the symbolic, that is, all politics (like genres), as an identification with public life (the Symbolic), is an alienation and a sacrifice, a loss of the sacred. *Possessions* shows that what Kristeva describes as the production of subjects seems to suit neoliberal formations by equating subjective autonomy with sacrificial alienation in new forms of privatized labor exchange and circulation: in specific, the global trade in mothering traits as affective, socializing commodities.

Possessions

Following the progression of the investigation, *Possessions* unravels through a tripartite layering of the murder's solution, where the fictional conventions at first close down the narrative interpretation that the crime demands, but then the fictional conventions themselves are disrupted, reopening alternative interpretive lines and alternative political frames. In a sense, the division-into-three of the narrative sequence replicates the three generations of feminism outlined in "Women's Time," with one alternative dismissed as a relationship of identification and expression,[13] a second dismissed as making demands on the state for public representation and equality.[14] The selected third—the one of the progressive, feminist future—is beyond either identification or representation, an identity constantly separating from itself, both "lethal" (2000: 197) and "untenable" (2000: 198).

Possessions is a "Who Done It" tale where the crime splits into three different criminal acts. The first murderer is discovered to be Michael Fish, Gloria's lover, who strangled her. Mike was an international money launderer with Mafia connections whom Gloria had set up as an art dealer in order to sell off her dead husband's paintings. Jealous of Gloria's attachment to her son, Mike wanted to destroy it by taking possession of her substantial estate. Mike gets caught by the police when he tries to unload a portrait of Gloria with her head severed—a reproduction of Picasso's *Woman with Collar* forged by Gloria's son Jerry that had hung over Gloria's desk—in the Colombian art market, using his Mafia networks. As witnessed by the house-servant Hester Bellini, the murder was a familiar culmination of a romance, a drunken lovers' spat, a conventional dispute over a rich person's inheritance—a traditional affair of the passions, a struggle to the death where "Gloria gave her lover the impression he was merely a laborer in the matter of sex, never the master" (1998: 107) until she stopped breathing. As work takes the form of a sexual position couched in violence, the Kojevian chronicling of the struggle to the death between master and slave[15] tropes into a lovers' dispute: the act of negation is a private affair. Gloria dies of romance, or *jouissance*: "A woman who enjoys sex has made up her mind to die" (1998: 108).

The second line of the crime shows Gloria as a victim of a transfer of public functions into private hands brought about in the globalization of the local economy. Santa Varvara—an island city that is both internal to Europe and its outside[16]—has recently witnessed a series of real estate scandals where the growth of the tourism industry had led to an expropriation and requisition of public hospitals and schools and, then, to the premature expulsion of asylum patients. The psychopathological serial killers Jason X. and Tyson Y.—who possibly had "an obsession with women's necks" (1998: 89)—had been released from St. Ambrose's: as the police lieutenant admits, "They're all guilty, boss, if you ask me [...] The politicians *and* the psychiatrists: the politicians because they cut the funding of public institutions and dispossess the poor..." (1998: 144). The narrator Stephanie Delacour agrees: "Treatment wasn't always all it might be, what with staff shortages, overcrowding and inadequate management" (1998: 148). As one of the witnesses remarks, "Gloria's murder was a collective and thus a fundamentally pathological act" (1998: 88). This diminishment of public supports also explains the cause of the pathology: Jason X. was subject to all the deprivations of "a negligent educational system, rising inflation, an underfunded national health service, suburban violence,[17] and a general decline in civic consciousness" (1998: 150). Despite the witness reports and other evidence that Jason X. and/or Tyson Y. may have had access to Gloria's house on the day in question, Kristeva through Delacour dismisses this explanation of Gloria's stabbing and beheading. It becomes, however, the official police story, a closing of the case, the last nail—so to speak—on the coffin, and, thereby, the shutting down of meaning. "Yes," says police chief Rilsky, "the case *is* closed" (1998: 186).

This stopping-up of storyline movement and narrative interpretation through the final police report repeats throughout the text. The public police often step in as the final arbitrators who dismiss the various streams and impressions, the insinuations of guilt, and aroused suspicions character-istic of detection in novels, deciding which clues fit the total picture—the Symbolic—and which should be dismissed. For example, the housekeeper Hester Bellini's description of the murder suggests alternative—political—frameworks for understanding the events: "Do you think Miss Bellini could have killed Mrs. Harrison in the noble cause of class warfare? ... slaves don't know their place anymore" (1998: 116), or "women always overdo it when they try to rebel, or liberate themselves" (1998: 117). Like the Symbolic, the police weed out sensory or emotional response, fragments, and distortions, in order to make sense and order the disorder of criminality. Outside of the police reading, therefore, the text, like the crime, can be diagnosed as "autistic," according to the research findings of Jerry's therapist Dr. Zorin. A specialist on the cutting-edge of the field, Zorin holds that autism is the result of sensory overload, "a kind of black hole in the psyche made by some tremendous but forgotten event" (1998: 93). Some victims of autism, he says, can compensate through what he calls an "absolute ear," or the ability to diminish "the effects of an overacute and highly painful sensitivity" (1998: 94) by developing the talent for perfect imitation, as Jerry did with Picasso's painting of the headless woman.[18] Likewise, the text of *Possessions* is able to exclude the overabundance of meaning that it creates by simulating generic form. The crime is "the beginning of tragedy" (1998: 117), motivated by money, sex, hatred, and madness, police chief Rilsky announces. In impos-ing a coherent plot generated through the symbolic of literary convention, the police resolution requires the wiping out of politics and heterogeneity. In Kristeva's terms, the solving of the crime for the police thus repeats the crime of killing the mother by repressing the Semiotic.

This is not to say that politics gets extinguished completely. After all, the Semiotic continues its heterogeneous articulations within the unity of the Symbolic as both what sustains it and what shreds it. Kristeva figures it as "the precondition of the symbolic" (1984: 50). The Semiotic has, says Kristeva, a *contract* with the Symbolic (1984: 49), implying a permanent exchange, a regulated circulation, but without substantive effect. The positing of politics as wrapped into the Semiotic insinuates that politics is representation's underbelly that cannot be represented, governed by a rupture or a failure in communications with others, a failure to achieve symbolization. Yet, politics does not fundamentally change the Symbolic. Instead, the police chief acknowledges the fragments in the narrative, the ruptures in the stories of causality, the multiplicities in motivation, and then continues to solidify evidence on the generic line, reasserting the dominance of the Symbolic.

Hello, Pauline!

Kristeva does not stop the narrative with the closing of the case, the official report. Both Jason X. and Tyson Y., Stephanie discovers, have solid alibis. Kristeva does not allow the critique of neoliberalism's assault on the public to become the final resting place of meaning, establishing clarity, shutting down the interruptions of sense, sound, distraction, drive, and affect. The storyline exceeds the police investigation. Once the police have moved on to uncover new incidents of violence unleashed in a Santa Varvara ever more exposed to global forces of corruption, violence, and decay, Stephanie learns by happenstance that Pauline Gadeau, Jerry's speech therapist, stole the head. Pauline herself has a history of melancholia and depression due to the loss of a much-loved brother in a swimming accident, making her susceptible to semiotic play that forces her to surrender pretentions to a career in science and medicine. Her medical talents and tools are revived for the purpose of severing Gloria's head, allowing her to gain back control over the irrational drives caused by her trauma and loss. The resolution between technical reason and its interplay with depressive impulses results in her identification with the autistic child and her success in teaching him language. She returns in the third novel as Jerry's beloved and trustworthy guardian.

Instead of a collective crime instigated by privatization as it opened up the local economy to direct foreign capitalization and increased lawlessness, Kristeva chooses to attribute the crime's last cause to an idiosyncratic speech pathology. Jerry's problem is that his words, like the Semiotic, "had no real content" (1998: 52), did not connect to things, did not communicate, and so he was stuck behind a wall of isolation, sensory trauma, exile, and silence, not able to translate experience into meaningful codes of personality, only binding his emotions to words by citing TV advertisements. Succeeding where Gloria failed, becoming her "synthetic image... in another language" (1998: 195), Pauline turns into the substitute mother-mirror whom Jerry imitates:[19] he models his body impulses into messages and, as Stephanie admits, he is "born anew in another language" (1998: 176), that is, not only copying but also creating, "invent[ing] words" or modestly, says Kristeva, "overhaul[ing] old meanings" (1998: 177). Pauline's treatment opens the Symbolic to its semiotic challenge now in the guise of an economic actor, a purchased service rather than a citizens' contract. Stephanie decides to overlook Pauline's role in the crime, and never reports it.

Kristeva, then, reads neoliberal privatization as the conditions of symbolic meaning and the production of subjects because it breaks apart the generic narrative of representational officialdom in the state apparatus from within. Neoliberalism serves as a gateway for the Semiotic. Pauline herself exceeds the collective crime; she aggressively takes on the caring functions that the public sector has abandoned. In Kristeva's terminology, Pauline assumes the role of the "primary identification," or the "imaginary father"—what "initiates a compensation for the Thing and at the same time secures the subject to another dimension" (1989: 13), or in other words, what allows the attachment to the mother and her unrepresentable language (the "Thing") to be accepted as lost as it is translated into a chain of partial identifications, a symbolic resolution. "Matricide," says Kristeva, "is our vital necessity" (1989: 27). The "imaginary father" is a halfway point, a passageway between the Semiotic and the Symbolic. "'I have lost an essential object,'" Kristeva demonstrates, "'that happens to be, in the final analysis, my mother,' is what the speaking being seems to be saying. 'But no, I have found her again in signs'" (1989: 43). At the same time, this "imaginary father" blends with the father's function of prohibiting the mother's love. For Kristeva, this "imaginary father" guards the maturing child from self-hatred and even from the "putting to death of the self" (1989: 28) by turning away from the drive of the negative, the loss of the self in the unrepresentable revolt of the mother, and toward a positive connection moving toward the Symbolic, where "a person can arrive at a live meaning in the bond with others" (1989: 24). Kelly Oliver sees this connection with the "imaginary father" as formulating "a notion of psychic life that is dependent on social support" (77), that is, as the beginning of a theory of social agency and connection based in individual psychic development and autonomy. However, in contrast, *Possessions* redefines the "imaginary father" as the process of absorbing motherhood into the market, privatizing it, translating it and its productions into "Things," that is, singular objects of exchange.

Care

The centrality of servants and housekeepers in detective fiction dates back to the emergence of the genre in the nineteenth century, in, for instance, such novels as Sheridan LeFanu's 1865 novel *Uncle Silas* and Wilkie Collins's 1868 classic *The Moonstone*. As both insiders and outsiders, servants in these novels have privileged access to the private lives of the landed aristocracy whose properties and positions are missing, concealed, or under threat. Able to delve underneath constructed social appearances, servants often substitute for a police force that represents the municipality or the state authority, out-of-place and ineffectual in the countryside, even sometimes comical in its misguided attempts to solve a crime. This tradition morphs into the early-twentieth-century Golden Age versions, like those of Agatha Christie, where the servant class is replaced by amateurs who are, again, privileged insiders to isolated closed communities like country houses, islands, archaeological sites, trains, or, as in the case of *Possessions,* a dinner party in a mansion, with a specified guest list, all with suspicious secrets circulating around the dead character.

Class structure thus becomes an important device in the tradition: class relations manage the dividing line between the visible and the invisible, between the accessible and the inaccessible, between the public and the private, within tensions of power. In this line of the genre's development, the servant-type—as a holdover of a pre-capitalist land-system and a place-holder for a type of domestic labor not yet absorbed into the systematization of the industrial wage—is therefore a privileged informant who unlocks the case because of its straddling of spheres, its ability to pass from propertied interiors into places of institutional judgment and bureaucratic apprehension. The Victorian servant often appears in its later detective fiction adaptations through a feminization of the detective function, partly because the detective is usually an amateur (Miss Marple) or an aristocrat (Peter Whimsey) and therefore works for free. This construction of "women's work" is necessary to re-write the barrier between private secrets and public scrutiny. This means that "women's work" is a transitional figure between economies, with a privileged position to settle the unsettled line between suspicion and guilt, or between a hidden clue and its revelation as a sign that makes sense or narrative out of the heterogeneous pieces of a crime. In other words, the figure of femininity in such texts translates "use value"— or unrepresentable heterogeneous singularities—into "exchange value"—or social meaning. The detective form, therefore, shares in envisioning "women's work" as the carrier of one economic identity into the next, tracing the fragments of the old into a new symbolic sense, a socially recognized symbolic equivalence. The economy—synchronized, for Kristeva, into an icon-omy: the transition between the invisible, nonsymbolizable in terms of equivalence (*chora*), and unpaid into the representational, language functions, and social belonging—absorbs the socializing functions of the mother by killing her. In Kristeva's sense, the resolution of the Semiotic within the Symbolic requires the death of the mother that opens into the circulation of signs. The market for "women's work" takes over where she left off, as representation.

The detective genre thus depends on this transitional figure of "women's work" to be defined in relation to care. *Possessions,* too, feminizes detection by revealing that the crime resulted from a shift in economies of care, from public to private. Kristeva's taking up of the problem of care in a detective form shows how her philosophical treatment of care is a screen for an economic problem. According to Kristeva, the phenomenological tradition (particularly with Heidegger) envisions care as a method for reifying the subject, stopping up its mobilities and circulations, and denying that it is always in production. The idea of care is a "patching-up" (1984: 129) through first-aid—as does "the wet-nurse, the mother, or the nurse" (1984: 129)[20]—a subject already formed, opaque, and unified. This, she says, is a type of regression, reducing the production of the subject "to anxiety and social work" (1984: 129)[21] rather than understanding it as fragmented through negativities, ruptures, and splittings and always in process, as semiotic challenges lead to its constant dismantling and reformulation. Care in a Heideggerian sense thus resembles desire for it assumes the subject as essentially lacking: it denies that the subject coordinates with "the heterogeneous process that questions the psychosomatic orders" (1984: 131). Phenomenology's framing of care, she concludes, colludes with capitalism in hypostasizing the subject of productivity (like genre), smothering its creativity, and thereby taming the subject in a role suitable to its automized mechanizations, "slave of his own mastery" (1984: 130), cut off from the socio-historical process of continuous signifying.

Kristeva has here again killed the mother. Her type of care takes the place of the paternal prohibition, denying access to the mother's language. Kristeva ties her critique of capitalism to a critique of the work of mothers. Mothers through their work, like social machines, turn care into first aid, repairing an already formed subject, teaching—as Gloria teaches Jerry—"the secret of imitating ordinary attitudes: how to behave, how to stand up straight, to be correct, honorable, considerate, charming" (1998: 55). The social norms constituted by mother's work appear as in parallel to public authority, group identifications, and collective appeals. In opposition to Kristeva's reading of Heideggerian phenomenologies of care, *Possessions* indicates, however, that the capitalization of care in the form of "women's work" (the death of the mother) frees the sacrificial object, allowing it to slide within the social in order to destabilize the articulation of the social, its dispersements, alienations, fragmentations, shifts, circulations, within the endless and conflictual process of its production. The end of the politics of representation—the end of reification or identification with a politics—unleashes multiplicities within the social (multiplicities linked to the market): on the one hand, pathologies, killers, delinquency, and violence but, on the other, the production of Jerry as the artistic subject, redemption from death in the symbolic, and, contingently, a formative account of revolutionary creativity.

Conclusion

Julia Kristeva can be said to be one of the inaugural thinkers of poststructuralism. For her, Marxism had made the mistake of focusing too much on the production of objects at the expense of any consideration of the production of subjects. On the one hand, this insight led to a greater attention to questions concerning femininity within theoretical inquiry, not only in terms of revisiting psychoanalysis and reassessing language, in all its fluidity, but also in situating femininity, its reproductions and socialization processes within spheres of production rather than outside of them. On the other hand, however, critics have faulted her turn to the subject for separating the subject from the social, dehistoricizing it, depoliticizing it, isolating it, or interiorizing its relations, including relations of power, turning subject formation and language formation into a problem of coping, and alienation into a diagnostics of depression or melancholia. These are not far-fetched conclusions considering some of her statements on politics in a neoliberal age that appear in her later work. In *Hannah Arendt,* for example, Kristeva lauds Arendt for her heroic insistence on defending an Aristotelian perspective that narrating lives has the "potential to be a political action, unlimited and dehiscent" (2001: 95), reducing the public's role in politics by equating politics to the production of heroic subjectivity via language and the singularity of genius. Similarly, in *Strangers to Ourselves,* relationships between people and powers across national borders turns into a linguistic or psychic split that destructures the self, like translation, a sign whose linguistic barrier gets opened up to its own internal strangeness, its incongruousness with itself, and its latencies: "How could one tolerate a foreigner if one did not know one was a stranger to oneself?" (1991: 182).[22] The reduction of the foreigner to interiority has been seen as a reduction of politics, particularly the politics of immigration and the effects of colonization and decolonization in France. As Fiona Barclay points out, "The threat posed by the uncanniness of the foreigner to those borders which constitute identity is commonly seen in terms of national boundaries. However, here Kristeva figures the challenge in individual terms" (5). As Kristeva skirts an acknowledgement of power in skirting the objective, institutional, or ideological order of states and nations, or of states and their citizens—translating these into psychoanalytic problems and discomforts—, national borders have no other resistances besides psychic ones.[23] The linguistic critique that Kristeva makes about the incomplete repression of maternal language seems to parallel indirectly a critique of the symbolic in its function, for Kristeva, as state-like: an institutional body that needs to be avoided because its only task is repression and control of subjective production in symbolic forms, or genres.[24] Kristeva's critique of Marxism, meant to radicalize its inquiry, ended up invigorating a rejection of economic and political explanations and public power which returned to what Jacquline Rose suggests Kristeva wanted to avoid: "to the very order which revolutionary practice seeks to change" (140).

The critics have been divided on how to read Kristeva's challenges to the political, particularly in its relation to the politics of the state, representation, and its public authority. Cecilia Sjöhom, for example, reads Kristeva's turn to the subject as a move that dangerously redefines the political as private: "The inability to focus on the subject, rather than the mechanisms that determine the object, makes Kristeva leave Marxism behind...What psychoanalysis has shown is that the important conflicts do not take place in the social sphere, but rather in the subject itself, which will interiorize these conflicts" (15). Likewise, Rosemary Hennessy has worried about Kristeva blunting the radicality of language as difference: "As many of Kristeva's critics have indicated, corporealizing the transgressive force of signification closes off any possible treatment of the relation between the symbolic features of subjection and other functions. It reduces the social to an interplay between individual drives and symbolic functions" (1993: 51). Jacqueline Rose has revealed limitations in using Kristeva's work for political critique on the basis of its avowed separation from traditional Marxist perspectives. For her, Kristeva's focus on the processes that unsettle identity have disassociated her analysis from institutional or state critique, depoliticizing the unconscious, discarding her earlier revolutionary project, and thereby favoring "a highly individualistic conception of dissidence and worth" (150) that inadequately poses "her appeal to semiotic heterogeneity in terms of social practice" (147). For such critics, the emphasis on internalization and the psyche sets in place a firm border that separates subjectivity from the social and the state increasingly, particularly in terms of action. As Sara Beardsworth, for example, has remarked, as the theory starts to stress revolt over revolution, "the destabilization of the subject" is "invoked by the reactivation of nonsymbolizable drives" that "encloses negativity within the confines of an ego" (42).[25] Destabilization appears as mental illness rather than as social or political critique.

I argue here that the seeming insularity of the Kristevan subject is not a defense against the social nor a total interiorization of its conflicts. Rather, the bordering-off of the subject—the staging of conflict *within* the subject—performs the very political task of marginalizing the public as authority. The public, as a point of contractual identification with socio-symbolic representations (and repression), is marginal, even suspect, while politics, as the messy mobility of interpretation and meaning, never manages to find symbolic form. On the one hand, Gloria's beheading makes visible the expansion of foreign and private control of economic culture, that is, the taking over of local lifeforms by market forces. On the other hand, the violent death of public life (the beheading)—necessary in the fiction for the interiorization of the subject and the celebration of creative personalities—appears in the philosophy as a resistance that is never realized or realizable.

In the meantime, the loss of the public in the novels—like the loss of the mother—figures paid, working women as its reproduction, performing its functions. That is, with the end of the mother comes the end of the translation of bodily impulses and political articulation into the language of citizenship (e.g., the end of repression of the Semiotic in the Symbolic), and the beginning of its projection into a disturbed and exploited, privatized field of labor (e.g., free expression as an aesthetics of liberation). A mother's work that used to convert bodily drives into symbolic form, but inadequately and never completely and without ever really effecting the symbolic function, is annihilated and replaced by a type of paid care that lets those drives speak without such regulations, singularly, heterogeneously, but outside of symbolic identifications. Kristeva's interest in language, in the disruptions of the unconscious, and in the fundamental unraveling of identity that femininity evokes, discloses an antipublic neoliberal ethic that can be read and critiqued through her emergent poststructuralist aesthetics. Kristeva's is a philosophy of contingency that sees freedom as the freedom from representation.[26]

The translation of this type of subject into fictional genre narrative reveals how the terms and contours can slide into a new vision of the social where the institutions where people have traditionally sought to exercise power and demand representation are unraveling violently so that citizens have diminishing effect on the socio-symbolic determinants of social action. In the novels, however, Kristeva's revolutionary insight is that the dominance of the production of subjects and processes of socialization in the new economy indicates a transformation in relations of "women's work" that, by opening up the social to an explosion of imagination, disrupts the system violently. As I elaborate in chapter 5, this insight awaits further development.

CHAPTER 3

Feminist Theory's Itinerant Legacy: From Language Feminism to Labor Feminism

In the late 1980s and early 1990s, feminist theory was booming, even hegemonic. In a particularly potent position for activating and further developing many of poststructuralism's most vibrant insights, particularly in its engagement with the production of subjects, feminist theory was in the front-line of paradigm-shifting narratives being constructed about how language worked, what was the relationship between language and subjectivity, how language and subjectivity engaged with the social and the symbolic, and how language produced new identities in its encounters with new needs, broader recognition, and redistributive claims. Feminist theory was a project that bridged academic thought and activism by integrating humanities' practices and social science research (and also, at times, the hard sciences and the history of science) while focusing on how to construct new rationalities and consciousness with a view to emancipation. Many of its innovations emerged out of a critical theory tradition as it intersected with psychoanalysis and language theory (structural linguistics and ordinary language theory, in particular), and so it was principally concerned with a critique of philosophical systems and a moving-beyond them on the tailspin of literary experimentalism.[1]

By the late 1990s, one could say that the energy behind this collective effort had largely dissipated.[2] One could also say that this slow-down in the production of feminist theory coincided with a consolidation of a neoliberalism that began in the 1970s and expanded. Even though works in feminist theory were still being produced and ideas applied, the great movement forward, the advances in thinking, were no longer formative, and many of feminist theory's stars had moved on to other topics of inquiry where gender was marginalized: other related content-areas where the politics of language and debates over ethics were playing out—with feminist theory's key techniques and abstract categories redirected, say, toward opposition to terror policies, Zionism, the Greek crisis, the corporatization of the genome, or the politics of pets in prisons. One could justifiably wonder if the field of feminist thinking, as a field with a somewhat defined object and a canon of ideas, had disappeared and dispersed for good, had become hegemonic to the extent that it was no longer distinguishable from criticism in general, had seeped into all critical inquiry to the point where it no longer was distinguishable as an item of inquiry in itself, or if it would reappear in a form that was not yet recognizable to its former adherents and practitioners.

This chapter suggests that the anthropologist Aihwa Ong represents the next step of the critical conversation that culminated, for the most part, in the generation of Judith Butler and Donna Haraway, but mostly in Butler's work. In this development, feminist theory, as it moves away from methodologies mostly connected with fields in the Humanities, also defines its project of accounting for sex and gender in reference to "work" rather than to "language": "work" sets the Symbolic in place. This development is connected as well to a development in the constitutional site of gender, where "women's work"—or the work of socialization—moves further away from a naturalized domesticity and toward a more bureaucratic or commercial sense of the social, referencing more directly extended fields of exchange. For Butler, the main location for gender production is the Symbolic, which in itself is outside any particular grounding or moment of materialization, but still is borrowing from Kristeva and other prior feminist thought, as well as poststructuralist analytical frameworks, a narrative of primary language acquisition. [3] Butler's rendition of the Symbolic as indicating a primary alienation opens up a path for Ong to depict "women's work" of socialization as it carries the organizational rules, the incentives and disincentives motivating the meanings of work, and the division of labor within transnational negotiations over value. Though still basically engaged with a metaphorics of maternity and primary care, "women's work" for Ong (as for Butler) does not originate in family relationships, blood-sharing kinship, natural affect, organic bonding, or an initiating entry into language. For Ong, "women's work" is called upon in places where economic need is produced through unequal corporate infiltration across nations: "motherhood"—care, service, affect, and socialization—is primarily an economic relationship and a market function and exists quite apart from any particular body who might inhabit that Symbolic for a time, and kinship is shown to be arbitrary, its terms transformable through differential placement in biopolitical networks operating transnationally. In fact, the economic, in Ong, is defined through this transnationalization of motherhood and socialization. Though Aihwa Ong seems friendlier toward, even nostalgic for liberalism than either Butler or Haraway, I believe that Ong adopts some basic tenants of feminist thought developed particularly by Butler but also by Haraway in their critique of liberalism, specifically, the conceptualization of the body and identity as itinerant and, in their itinerancy, as calling subjects into existence. What Ong relinquishes in situating feminist theory's Symbolic of gender in the transnational exchange of work is the creativity that Marx attributed to work in general and feminist theorists like Kristeva, Butler, and Haraway identify as inherent in "women's work" because "women's work" is tied to production and socialization in language.

Butler's, Haraway's, and Ong's philosophical positions share a vision of the body as at the node of a wide range of social, institutional, and discursive networks that produce and stabilize the sense of an underlying cause, meaning, interiority, nature, or even "soul," which Butler might call "sex," Haraway might call "the human," and Ong might call "ethnicity" or "culture." "[T]he subject," notes Butler, as early as 1987, "can only be understood in its movement" (1987: 18); it is a "romantic traveler" (1987: 22), "in exile" (1987: 25), "always beyond itself" (1987: 31), in "estrangement" (1987: 36), "[e]xperiencing itself as an essential poverty" (1987: 37). "[D]isturbingly lively" (152) and expelled from their origins, Haraway's cyborgs, she says, are also "floating signifiers moving in pickup trucks across Europe" (153). Like Butler and Haraway, Ong believes that subjectivity is a product of "travel and displacement," "practices favoring flexibility, mobility, and repositioning" (1999: 6); an apt figure to represent contemporary life is "[t]he multiple passport holder" (1999: 2). As they assume various positions within a field of market values and governing strategies, these new mobile relations that produce subjectivities, then, are understood as shifting the "structures of meaning about family, gender, nationality, class mobility, and social power" (1999: 6), or identity.

Where Butler and Haraway believe that such fluidity in identity and consciousness is caused by its structure in language and its place in a chain of signification, work—as a category of bodily identity—becomes for them a problem of desire.[4] Because work—in Butler's reading of the tradition of the Hegelian subject—becomes the self-focused, inventive creation of the self out of language (in a variety of situations and in response to a variety of demands), "historical action is possible within the spheres of interaction and production alike" (1987: 68)—in both production and reproduction—as overlapping functions, constituting consciousness, and staged through desire: the social and the economic are interchangeable because they both operate according to the linguistic principles of signification that shape their existence. Production itself is an instance of language, and language is one of the circulating tools or logics—the main one—through which it invents and reinvents itself, similarly to other instances that require social inputs. Much as in Kristeva, language here operates in ways that overlap with means of production—where its meanings can be fixed and congealed by power—but it also exceeds the means of production—it cannot be fixed or owned permanently or all-inclusively, because it is a moment in a chain of signification and difference that circulates through it, contradicts it, and struggles within it, resisting stabilization.

Ong, on the other hand, presumes work as the primary social lever that places value onto bodies from the outside as it is manipulated through a series of historical reconfigurations of relations between institutions, market interests, and governing forms in globalization processes. In other words, as the main concepts of feminist theory move the Humanities toward a dominant basis in the social sciences, work comes to function like a language, instead of language. Socialization processes, the production of subjects, and the formation of the Symbolic, with maternity at the helm, merge increasingly into institutions of power. Such perspectives share with poststructuralism a sense of language as arbitrary and inessential. Yet, the Symbolic now appears partly as ethnographic, or described through discursive formations occurring across cultures, in response to the internationalization of labor markets and domestic service demands. That is, the idea of what a gendered person is, of how that person acquires that gender, and what that gender is in relation to that person, has shifted away from its core poststructuralist understanding in Semiotics—with language as underlying the structure of self-construction and difference in its intersections with the social—to one in work, where work serves as a quasi-linguistic "flow" of meaning between first and third worlds, corporate governance and state sovereignty, national citizenship and postnational, "deterritorialized" rights regimes.

As Butler and Haraway try to think of the body outside of assumed biological determinism,[5] other types of determinism come to seem less crushing or imposing, or even become invisible. Ong, on the other hand, makes visible how market or economic determinism in particular foregrounds a way of understanding the body as de-essentialized, or as made flexible through price fluctuations, fluid circuits of exchange, local needs, ethical action, transport, and, most fervently, the overlapping of state, market, and civil governance and practices of sovereignty. For Ong, the distribution and circulation of work across geographical areas challenges the metaphysics of identity and the politics of presence. Yet, even as Ong's emphasis on the mobility of global work offers a version of the subject that breaks out of the instrasubjectivity of, say, Butler's performative monad traveling along on its merry way, it also surrenders the separation (or autonomy) of certain elements of subjectivity from preexisting or overarching social determinants—that is, it surrenders itself to market determinism, without excess (that is, in Kristeva's terms, without the Semiotic): actors become wholly coextensive with the powers and interests that define them (the Symbolic, as Kristeva would have it), without recourse to resignification through the plays of signifiers or any other sort of linguistic remainders or rebellions. Whereas Haraway turns to science fiction to experiment imaginatively with the radicality of cyborg transformations, and Butler understands the subject's travels as "a study in fiction-making" (1987: 23) with the subject constantly disengaging itself from its regulative world of naturalized substance, Ong sees culture as produced in response to political economy, where workplace demands, state institutions, and corporate networks take a hold over cultural identities, institutions, and local practice.[6] With the intensification of neoliberal practices and systems from the 1990s and after, the concept of identity, even as it is presented by its critics, has become increasingly instrumentalized as an inalienable extension of market cultures.[7] Though feminist theory benefits from a vision of how gender is being manufactured and manipulated as an economic lever that eases into place neoliberal relations of exploitation, its project will be stymied in as much as it adopts a terminology that is complicit in such enterprising.

The End of Feminism

There is a reason that Judith Butler and Donna Haraway herald, in some sort of way, a block in the forward trajectory of feminist theory. One might remark, for example, that Haraway announced a "post-gender world" (150), a world where identity had become so fragmented and uprooted that "being 'female'" no longer provided an "'essential' unity" that "binds women" (155). In *Gender Trouble,* Judith Butler agrees that "The very subject of women is no longer understood in stable or abiding terms [...] There is very little agreement after all on what it is that constitutes, or ought to constitute, the category of women" (1990: 2). "The identity of the feminist subject ought not to be the foundation of feminist politics" (1990: 8), she continues. Even more fundamentally, *Gender Trouble* tries to open up a new field of possibilities for the study of gender by showing how feminist theory itself is caught up in heterosexualizing normative assumptions that it, at the same time, wants to oppose: it cannot get out of replicating the very paradigms that it understands as its objects of critique.

In addition, such gender theory has made gender identity seem not only impossible, an invitation to failure, but also painful and destructive. Butler reads identity as fundamentally caught up in a logic of exclusion: any claim to recognition through stable signification, because it establishes, through language, "the ontological field in which bodies may be given legitimate expression" (1990: xxv)—that is, by producing the "real"—, forecloses on other possibilities, often violently. Butler indicates how all practices of gender, including feminist practices, reawaken and stabilize "specific formation[s] of power" (1990: xxxi) because they exclude certain subjects as illegible, illegitimate, tenuous, or false within the given structures of reality. There, the outside to the logic of identity is incoherent, unrecognizable. Most allusions to the gendered body are caught in such a reified system of referentiality where meanings are predetermined and inescapable. The one option against the force of language—the performance of gendered acts that dramatize the falsity of gender in the body—has "clearly punitive consequences" as "we regularly punish those who fail to do their gender right" (1990: 190). Additionally, such a performative politics is mostly described as an individual act, with the outcome being that the individual might succeed in pushing the symbolic form ever so slightly in a direction over which the performer has no control. The act of resymbolizing painfully demonstrates the impossibility of symbolization altogether, and so the impossibility of identity. The ultimate result of the performance of identity is to show that the doer of the deed—the intention—does not and cannot exist before the deed: the social codes that have projected themselves as the doer's preexisting nature, its soul or internal depth, its "person"-ness, are but *effects* of language rather than causes of being (as they are projected to seem). As much as such poststructuralist theorizing seems to open up gender to theory and to agency—to show that the construction of gender is something we all do as we reconstruct, manipulate, and change the social—, it also stomps out primary conceptual tools for advancing theory. In other words, as such radical antifoundational thinking is exciting for inciting a creative approach to what seems entrenched in social existence, it also leaves us without foundations.

Feminism and Neoliberalism

Such projects that radically question philosophical foundationalism and ontology do not necessarily put a block on liberationist advances in political thought and theory, as the history of philosophy since Hegel clearly demonstrates. Rather, at that period of the late 1980s and early 1990s, such a dismantling of identity would inadvertently dovetail with an ascension of corporate governance that was, ideologically, emptying out the sovereign governance of the subject required by liberalism and democracy. Certain poststructuralist tendencies reflect this process: from an idea of that borders of identity are tenuous and arbitrary, assumed in signification with its metonymic chains, to a sense of power where no wizard seems to be behind the curtain, and power is projected as governed by laws and desires rather than interventions, controls, or regulations. By immersing political possibility within the movement of the sign, both Butler and Haraway espouse a vision of the political with precarious agency,[8] or an agency with a precarious relationship to consciousness or decision, a politics that happens outside of the traditional areas of political practice, an idea of the political that marginalizes the state and looks to exchange—the Symbolic—as the main space where political action stakes its claims. As the "linguistic turn" brings the status of the referent into question, such a politics that are based on it are instigated primarily within a context of primordial loss, lack, and failure.[9] This primordial loss, lack, or failure has taken a very particular shape within the formation of neoliberalism, with poverty either on the rise or stagnant, many losing their savings, precarity more the norm than the exception, cuts to long-time benefits like pensions and healthcare, salaries leveling out or dropping, and unemployment high. The democratic power that was supposed to fuel the state ends up empty: the power of the state itself is dispersed inside of various networks of exchange that seek to escape control.

Butler's version of poststructuralism—with language as embodied performance—allows for a central consideration of production and therefore work, though much of the Marxian vocabulary that she uses to talk about production has, instead, moved away from its Marxist context. Production happens, in Butler, when subjects inhabit the Symbolic, (re)producing the Symbolic and becoming subjects through that embodiment. Language produces worlds through embodiments rather than workers through commodity production. Though accepting a Marxist premise that production is creative and world transformative, many Marxist concepts used to critique production would contradict Butler's Foucaultian framing of production, where the sovereign no longer weilds repressive power and so power is productive. In adopting a Foucaultian critique, Butler makes words familiar within Marxism mean differently. This tendency cuts the claws off a vocabulary for economic or class critique. Like Marx, Butler understands that meaning and power are negotiated in social relations. Meanwhile, however, within Butler's rhetoric, "production" no longer refers to a command economy, material production, or an alienation caused by the separation of workers from the means of production, but rather to categories of being, identity, consumption, or self-fashioning. "Regulation" would no longer be what a state did to control territorial borders or to offset capitalism's excesses;

rather, "regulation" refers to an exclusionary meaning-function asserted by linguistic rules and designations, a granting of coherence through descriptive features of normative types of personhood.[10] Closer to the logic of desire than to the coding of the juridical, Butler's "law" is not repressive as in police action or state control; rather, the "law" in Butler corresponds closer to a circulating but productive mode, like a market: "[T]he attribution of universality to a law," Butler elaborates, "may simply imply that it operates as a dominant framework within which social relations take place" (1990: 103). As she points out in *Undoing Gender,* the state does not "monopolize" "the norms of recognition" (2004: 114) via the law, but rather "[a]re there not other ways of feeling possible, intelligible, even real?" (2004: 114). "Law" has separated from its sense of a general standard of conduct enforced by agencies of state, or of its defense of person and property through a contract with the state, and becomes instead—as in the Lacanian narrative—a "*literalizing fantasy*" (1990: 95), a "normative ideal" (1990: 95), or a congealing of cultural expectations that sidelines certain categories of identity as prohibited, inexpressible, unknowable, or unnamable. The centrality of language as agency brought out in the Butlerian imaginary suggests that language functions are taking over a series of governing actions. Language does not need anyone at the controls, but just speaks itself.

In Butler as in Lacan, language sets out the conditions and the possibilities of life on its own, circulating, making decisions, determining distributions of value, creating sensuous worlds, at a time when, as Aihwa Ong says, "financial flows" are being "unregulated" (2006: 1) and "economic zones" are "imposing market criteria" on citizenship identities (2006: 1). That is, such poststructuralist theories imagine language as governing itself, freed from external authorization and reference, just when the sphere of citizen action is being severely limited by its subsumption in deregulated market-based categories claiming that deregulation means an absence of authoritative decision and controls. As Nancy Fraser characterizes this strand in feminism, "Rejecting both Marxism's exclusive focus on political economy and liberalism's exclusive focus on law, they unveiled injustices located elsewhere—in the family and in cultural traditions, in civil society and in everyday life" (2009: 103). Fraser interprets these developments as intentionally critical of state-centered capitalism and economism while promoting the democratization of power. Yet, neoliberalism was able to "change the terrain" which gave meaning to a countercultural mass-based social movement oriented toward ending social injustices. She goes on: "With the benefit of hindsight, we can now see that the rise of second-wave feminism coincided with a historical shift in the character of capitalism, from the state-organized variant [...] to neoliberalism. Reversing the previous formula, which sought to 'use politics to tame markets', proponents of this new form of capitalism proposed to use markets to tame politics [...] The effect, I shall argue here, was to resignify feminist ideals. Aspirations that had a clear emancipatory thrust in the context of state-organized capitalism assumed a far more ambiguous meaning in the neoliberal era" (2009: 107–108). In other words, theories such as Butler's are oppositional in their attempts to rethink power in other terms besides in those of state and sovereignty, of force and coersion, of the consciousness and decision of self-defining, autonomous individuals. Yet, Butler's radicalism loses its edge because it arises at a time when reactionary economic forces are also putting the screws on the credibility of sovereign democratic power residing in the state. Deliberately shying away from Marxist analysis for its reduction of subjectivity to class and its under-theorized assumption of sovereignty (among other problems), Butler still espouses economic vocabularies but iterates them outside of traditional, recognizable economic or political contexts. She names the problem she focuses on, rather, as a problem of "representation" without directly addressing the implications for political representation as the political field is increasingly emptied of agency, with no doer behind the deed, just a set of self-operating regulatory forces, markets, and laws. Yet, as Butler reimagines economic activity as taking on linguistic form and capacities, she also is able to show how such economic identities (work) assume creative action (the action of self-invention), or the movement of language, signification in the form of productive bodies.

Though it seems like the Marxist meanings attached to production are repressed by their poststructuralist reappropriations, they might, at times, reveal themselves inside. Donna Haraway's work makes visible the linkage between poststructuralist theories of language like Butler's and "women's work." Haraway remarks that a cyborg is "a creature of social reality as well as a creature of fiction" (149), a hybrid form that links fiction to facts, or rather fuses the two designations. Nevertheless, cyborg creatures draw their constitutions from the defense industry, and later from the "informatics of domination," which reimagines work in terms of information, codes and frequencies, communications technologies and biotechnologies, and the "homework economy," which "broadly has the characteristics formerly ascribed to female jobs, jobs literally done only by women" (166). This latter category includes the types of work that emerged in relation to the electronics and information economy that Haraway identifies as ascendant, demanding superexploitative conditions, with workers from poor countries. The home is integrated into the workplace, and profits are sustained through high personal responsibility, new technologies, and their privatization. Lacking protections and benefits, such jobs are linked to the demise of the welfare economy.

Yet, even though work, in part, constitutes the identity of the cyborg, work does not travel, as it does for Ong, bringing into play identities as the product of its mobilities. Instead, work for Haraway secures subjects at junctures within communications circuits: in other words, work is an interruption of language functions, a temporary system breakdown, linked to positivist traditions and systemic stress. It stops the flow. What brings circulation back is not work but rather work's linguistic under-belly: imaginative reflections and narratives that are born as a cybernetic outgrowth of the possibilities created through mixing technologies with organic forms. The technologization of work does not, Haraway says, end black poverty by creating more opportunities for black women outside of domestic service, but rather places women in jobs that impoverishes them *with* employment, just as Third World women working in industrial zones end up more deeply integrated within their families who now depend on their wages. Work constitutes a type of stability of the subject. The fact of work is only ruptured in the fiction that constitutes political action.[11] The work of the cyborg is the cyborg's site of oppression, its existence as "fact." Work grounds the cyborg in defining relations of exploitation, impover-ishing the cyborg's culture specifically by ontologizing it in opposition to the mobility of capital.

The last section of "The Cyborg Manifesto" on science fiction, however, shows how the cyborg form is also, like a language, in "luminal transforma-tion" (177), outside of the dream of origins, holism, individuation, rooted-ness, and fixedness like in the intergalactic adventures of the heroes in TV's *Star Trek* series. Though Haraway insists on the breakdown between fiction and fact, it seems that fiction and fact compose different sections of the manifesto and acquire separate functions within the matrices of an emergent cyborg capitalism: fact is where work happens, while fiction is the future of nonidentity and nongender, of transformative possibilities. The culture of capitalism is detached from the essentializing fact of work. Unlike in Ong, where work itself is itinerant, work in Haraway—as "fact"—blocks travel, places people solidly within immobile technological systems, and only fic-tion offers such displacement and border-crossings that Ong sees as undoing reified subjective forms and the metaphysics of identity.

Butler's hesitancy to acknowledge debts or reductions to neoliberal mar-ket orientations[12]—or her hesitancy to posit any (determining) causality between economic history and social practices—allows her theory—and also Haraway's—to exceed economic determination. Whereas Ong believes that culture has to be considered locked down by the definitions given to it by geopolitical economy, the opposing idea that the subject is caught up in making itself as signifier means that Butler as well as Haraway could see identity as—in part or provisionally—escaping from its economic, instrumentalizing terms through self-innovations.

In Butler's understanding, in fact, signification has two modes: one is repetition, where culture is congealed as fact, regulated in order "to produce the appearance of substance" (1990: 45), to create a sense of "factuality" in the body; the other side of signification for Butler is the failure of repetition, the idea of a set of acts that do not cohere to an original and so expose facticity—the appearance of the natural—as contingent, displaced, unresolved, unnecessary, artificial, comedic, distorted, arbitrary, dissonant, and parodic. The place of the literary is the place where repetition breaks down. Citing Monique Wittig, where she finds more linguistic and sexual mobility in the novels than in the other works, Butler notes that though literature "is a war machine" (1990: 162), congealing power through discourse and making power "real," its linguistic-ness also seeps through the edge of this consolidated construction, maintaining "a privileged access to this primary field of ontological abundance" (1990: 162) as excess. Embedded inside every iteration of the Symbolic code, literary language spills out illegibly over the repetitions of the "war machine," allowing each repetition to be different than its parent. Indeed, in the preface to the new edition, Butler defends the difficulty of her style of writing by defending its loss of intelligibility, the way her readers find political possibility in its challenge to "the rules that govern intelligible speech" or "normalized language" (1990: xix). Butler's constant interruptions of her own analysis with a series of questions—some rhetorical and others not and most with multiple possible answers, sometimes contradictory ones—exude a linguistic overabundance, in literary-like scenes of dramatic dialogue with her critical interlocutors. Often, within this dramatization of rhetoric, it becomes impossible to tell who is doing the speaking, or where Judith Butler's critique begins or ends—where she agrees or differentiates herself from her predecessors whom she cites—as her own perspective merges into the critiques that are her critical objects, as she internalizes—both desires and identifies (in even an almost-romantic fashion) with—those she loses, reviles, even mourns[13] and yet cannot reconcile completely. Sometimes dramatically, Butler dresses in the drag of those she criticizes. *Gender Trouble* could easily be read novelistically, where each of the wandering "Butler's" iterations incorporate their irreconcilable antagonist, allowing "Butler" to change toward its next identity-form in its next critical adventure: it takes in Freud, and uses that Oedipal moment of identification as its entryway into a critique of Freud, and so with Lacan, Kristeva, Wittig, and Foucault, where none of these interlocutors end up dead in her path but rather lost, mourned, and then newly speaking as a scene in "Butler's" own metonymic projection of its subjectivity-in-process.

"Butler" as subject is born through her inability to repeat well her antecedents but repeats them nonetheless. While Kristeva situates poetic language as revolutionary in its endless disruptions of a Symbolic that eventually asserts back its power, Butler shows the Symbolic itself as refashioned in its donning of the literary on its margins, exhibiting how the Symbolic cannot hold onto itself as the real.

This chapter proceeds by addressing the similarities and differences between the ways Aihwa Ong, on the one hand, and, on the other, Butler take up the idea of civil society and governmentality, and in particular, how they take up the biopoliticization of civil society that Foucault describes in his lectures. I then trace how norms work to form and mobilize identities in each of the theories, how moral or civil production substitutes for sovereign state rule, and how consciousness has become a primary commodity. I end by considering the implications for feminism of Ong's "sociological turn," or a longing for "the real" that Butler criticizes as a repression of the politics of desire.

Homo Oeconomicus

For Aihwa Ong, the "human" is a nexus where markets, states, and systems of value temporarily stake their claims, intersecting temporarily and then moving on, asserting their techniques of management variously: "[T]he nation-state—along with its juridical-legislative systems, bureaucratic apparatuses, economic entities, modes of governmentality, and war-making capacities—continues to define, discipline, control, and regulate all kinds of populations" (1999: 15). What Ong adds to the critical literature on neoliberalism is that such intersections of (international and national) economic governance institutions, management, and norms take form predominantly through the production of gendered subjects. In other words, the control and regulation of population that Foucault labeled "biopolitics" is a strategy for constructing gender traits as "effects" of circulation, distributing them according to the dynamics of global capitalist demand, and effectively humanizing them.

For Ong, the large forces of global capitalism call into play specific cultural characteristics and values based on technical, ethical, and productive needs. Specified populations are called in to serve the symbolic needs of a capitalism in constant transition. For example, Filipino or Indonesian maids, hired in answer to the needs of domestic settings in other, more rapidly industrializing parts of Southeast Asia (Malaysia, Singapore, Hong Kong), are feminized by, for instance, "self-managing techniques that instill proper attitude and conduct" (2009: 162). To encourage the export of their surplus labor, both Indonesia and the Philippines have promoted themselves as labor-exporting nations by putting symbolic moral value of their women on sale internationally. Such women are solicited into choosing such employment by Non-Governmental Organizations (NGOs), state agencies, and labor syndicates who teach them to espouse a form of femininity bound to exercising a "free choice" that is both moral and "empowering." As with Haraway's cyborg economy, the concrete circulation of Southeast Asian women responds to the need for foreign domestic labor in geographical spaces where the technological level of production has risen. They reproduce the socialization process by embodying the humanistic values that the domestic sphere has traditionally inculcated. Detached from bodies, the traits of womanhood, therefore, get called in to service the symbolic and abstract needs of accumulation and exchange.

In Ong's analysis, through constructing a specifically gendered ideal of work as moral essence and national duty, these women are nonetheless brought in to an increasingly disciplinary social structure based on an expanding logic of incarceration: workers are subjected to a variety of surveillance practices, their passports and working papers held from them, their days-off limited, and their access to protections from employer sexual advances insecure, at best. Though maids are lured into service based on their moral exemplarity as capitalizable traits, their detachment from ethical and national communities makes them vulnerable to impositions of immoral meanings. Filipino or Indonesian femininity often translates, within the context of the foreign household, into a transgression of ethical norms, a security threat, a potential "marriage wrecker" (2009: 170), or an exotic perversion, for whom sex is defensively prohibited, along with marriage to a local citizen, with transgressions punished by the suspension of working rights, and pregnancy leading to automatic expulsion, regardless of circumstances. As women's citizenship identities, as constructed through the interests of their nation-state, are turned into national value for working identities abroad, often what gets erased are the gendered moral attachments given in their citizenship or familial identities. This situation is what Ong foregrounds as the "biopolitical."[14]

Ong's adoption of Foucault's term "biopolitics" in this context foregrounds an element of Foucault's reading of governmentality that often gets neglected. Foucault's analysis of "biopolitics" gets interpreted predominantly as more or less a theory about the management of race and populations. Though certainly central to Foucault's narrative, this perspective tends to minimize a parallel analysis that Ong hooks on to, where "biopolitics" is a theory about the management of gender as well. As, for example, Achille Mbembe reads it, for Foucault "biopolitics" was the sovereign power to decide life and death. The power to decide life and death is coterminous with the expansion of technologies for implementing death—like the concentration camp (12)—which Mbembe links to both industrialization and imperialism. Constructed in accordance with distributions of productive labor needs as well as with the administrative imperative to integrate a territory, the power to decide life and death was dispersed in unequal ways across population divisions within the biological field that Foucault, according to Mbembe, labels as "racism." Mbembe says, "That *race* (or for that matter *racism*) figures so prominently in the calculus of biopower is entirely justifiable. After all, more so than class-thinking (the ideology that defines history as an economic struggle of classes), race has been the ever present shadow in Western political thought and practice, especially when it comes to imagining the inhumanity of, or rule over, foreign peoples" (17). Further, he adds, the development of productive technologies and their contingent technologies of death leading up to the death camp "was aided in part by racist stereotypes and the flourishing of a class-based racism" (18). Mbembe disregards how gender inhabits the frame of racist stereotypes, even in Foucault.

Published in French a year after Mbembe's critique and in English in 2008, Foucault's lectures on "biopolitics" do not start by addressing the growth of administrative power as filling nonproductive space with technological equipment and factories on the backs of racial stereotypes and imperialist expansion. Rather, Foucault's preamble to this development of "biopolitics" is in his analysis of the tradition of liberalism, as the power of the liberal state starts to be thought through an investigation into its limits (Foucault makes no distinction between liberalism and neoliberalism). "But what does 'the self-limitation of governmental reason' mean?" asks Foucault. "What is this new type of rationality in the art of government, this new type of calculation that consists in saying and telling government: I accept, wish, plan, and calculate that all this should be left alone? I think that this is broadly what is called 'liberalism'" (20). Limiting government meant that sovereignty would take the form of "the economy, economic development, and economic growth" (84). As price, according to the philosophies of liberalism, reveals a system of veridiction that idealistically enables a naturalized correction of error (if understood without an analysis of power)—and as, therefore, the reason of the sovereign in affairs of governing begins to seem an imposition or an excess—, the problem of governing becomes how best to enable economic decisions to be independent of political interventions. This theorizing of government through theorizing its limitations modeled individuals who played its game as "enterprises," or "*homo oeconomicus*" (147). An "enterprise" was an object of government that dispersed government, turning smaller and smaller units into productive industries rather than proleterianizing the population, forming residential units into productive units through narrowing specialization and the division of labor, and, broadly speaking, "shifting the center of gravity of governmental action downwards" (148) toward individual responsibility. In Foucault's assessment, the principle of government limitation, as defined through the liberal tradition, allows for the globalization of markets, that is, the realization that European countries could only have a mutual benefit in exchange if the field of goods and products was constantly unfolding into larger geographical spaces: "Nature intended the entire world, the whole of its surface, to be given over to the economic activity of production and exchange" (57).

Ong uses Foucault's insights on "biopolitics" to show how "women's work" stands in for the "natural balance" of price and responsibility that substitute for the governmentality of the state: its limits. For Ong, the chore of gender is to carry forward the political agenda of the state while limiting its direct interventions,[15] just as for Foucault, "The new governmental reason needs freedom[;] therefore, the new art of government consumes freedom. It consumes freedom, which means that it must produce it" (63). For Ong, governing institutions are using moral incentives to mobilize young female migrants to "choose" labor in overseas labor markets, inducing them to expose themselves to situations of danger and violence through appealing to their "responsibility" (2009: 163). Expressing free economic agency, "free choice," NGO guardianship, according to Ong, consists in choosing to use their constructed "natural abilities" as female workers to perform their moral function and patriotic duty as "modern-day heroes" (2009: 162) in attending foreign homes. Like what Foucault describes as governmentality, Ong's national labor distributing mechansisms appeal to the woman worker as "capital" (224), and gender as a "worker's skill" turned into "a machine that produces" (224), an ability that can be turned into an income, an income that cannot be separated from the person who possesses it, or, in other words, an "entrepreneur" (226)—a maker of herself.

As Mbembe cites, Foucault does bring up the role of genetics in the value of human capital (228) and calls it "racism" (228), narrating how risk calculation then gets posed within ideas about, for example, the choice of reproductive partner. However, Foucault then concludes, perhaps scandalously, "this does not seem to me to be the major political issue at the moment" (229). Instead, Foucault privileges, like Ong, "educational investments" (229) and, particularly, the role of mothering, the time the mother spends with the child, the investments in feeding, stimulation, and affection, that contribute to the formation of human capital. Within his acknowledgement of the role of race and racism in the analysis of the value of human capital, Foucault foregrounds "women's work" and socialization as a machine of freedom-production and character management motoring imperialism forward on the principle of the making of human capital, that is, the making of selves as the limits of state governance. What Ong does is to imagine mothering as an enterprise or a strategy. What Foucault labels as discourse gets translated in Ong's analysis into an outsourced manufacturing of human traits, skills, and aspects of personhood. *Homo oeconomicus* is in drag.

The system of migrant maid and childcare mobilities adheres, says Ong, to Foucault's ideas about "economic rationality of governmental techniques" (2006: 76), a specific set of techniques that is applied from multiple political spaces to a varied terrain and that overrides the national territory as an operative field: "Especially in emerging, postcolonial contexts, varied techniques of government rely on controlling and regulating populations in relationship to differentiated spaces of governance" (2006: 77). To be sure, Aihwa Ong's descriptions of neoliberalism follow a similar path to Foucault's: "It is important," she remarks, "to trace neoliberal technology to a biopolitical mode of governing that centers on the capacity and potential of individuals and the population as living resources that may be harnessed and managed by governing regimes... *Technologies of subjectivity* rely on an array of knowledge and expert systems to induce self-animation and self-government so that citizens can optimize choices, efficiency, and competitiveness in turbulent market conditions" (2006: 6). That is, governance works by means of specialized institutions designating some individuals as "useful" lives because they allow the thinking of the limit of the sovereign power of the state. As she characterizes it, "In contemporary times, neoliberal rationality informs actions by many regimes and furnishes the concepts that inform the government of free individuals who are then induced to self-manage according to market principles of discipline, efficiency, and competitiveness" (2006: 4). The movement of capital calls workers to identify into the traits of solicited human capital, to become "enterprises" or "entrepreneurs." Ong calls this "culture," by which she means that "Chinese personalities, even 'souls,' must be 'reengineered' like computers 'for the global age'" (2006: 222). Business manuals and management workshops train local managers of foreign corporations by focusing on internalizing self-governing practices—for example, for developing "team spirit" (2006: 223)—that were contrary to Chinese cultural values of calculative self-interest, but still called these manufactured traits Chinese indigenous. Ong is saying that "culture" is the referent or the call for which selves are made as itinerant human capital, through "educational investments" and the investigation of the sovereign state's limits, for the purpose of filling itinerant capital's needs. In effect, she has reduced all production of subjectivities to this role. She does not offer a judgment on this, this positivist ethnographic method not demanding a normative or ethical position but rather an objective descriptiveness that repeats culture as "fact."

As is well-known, the process of assuming an identity for Butler is similarly a process of interiorizing scripts, or the Symbolic. "Gender," she writes, for example, "is the repeated stylization of the body, a set of repeated acts within a highly rigid regulatory frame that congeal over time to produce the appearance of substance, of a natural sort of being" (1990: 45). Butler, like Ong, takes Foucault to be saying that the "soul" (the inner core or substance)—or the body's interiority—is an imaginary effect of power on the body: "The figure of the interior soul understood as 'within' the body is signified through its inscription *on* the body[...] The effect of structuring inner space is produced through the signification of a body as a vital and sacred enclosure" (1990: 184). Where Ong posits the figuring of the interior "ethnicity" or "culture" as an effect of the mobile needs of capital, Butler recognizes the place of interiority as an effect of regulatory linguistic practices and the movement of difference that produce norms in the body as the prefigurative or "the real": "if that reality is fabricated as an interior essence, that very interiority is an effect and function of a decidedly public and social discourse" (1990: 185).

For Ong unlike for Butler, the state changes its articulation of the symbolic of gender when capital changes direction, and this symbolic becomes real when gendered bodies come to inhabit the state's new symbolic call. For Butler, the gendered body is an effect that rearticulates the Symbolic but the gendered body can never make the Symbolic real: there is always a remainder, an illegibility caused by the disjuncture between the symbolic and its substance. The very stringent possibility—even inevitability—that Butler's subject would repeat the given forms badly, or fail to reproduce and reinforce them,[16] leads on the one hand to a censure or violent punishment—though Butler does not specify who the faceless torturer might be outside of a social estrangement (there is no wizard behind the curtain, no doer behind the deed)—and, on the other, to a subversion that reveals the symbolic coding of identity as contingent, artificial, and inessential. For Butler, the subject loses its sovereign subjectness when the system of referentiality falls short or falls apart, that is, when the relationship between the signifier and the signified is wrenched open; there is a dislocation, a gap between the social-symbolic, on the one hand, and, on the other the bodily forms it assumes and the subjectivities it calls into being.[17] Butler's conclusion that most subjects do not fit well within their symbolic forms, that most fail to assume their identities appropriately, might not bother a capitalism that prides itself on its flexibility, absorbing differentials rather than losing stability in them, and still meets its goals.[18] Butler does not specify, as Ong does, that a failure to adhere to the appropriate ideological constructs might land the subject not only in a place of desolation and loneliness but out of work.

Civil Society

Foucault follows Althusser in understanding institutions as dispersed productions of ideology—or what he calls "discourse"—that reproduce relationships between the needs of power and the conduct of its subjects. For Foucault, there is no real difference between civil society and power, as the power of the state to set limits on itself saturates those limits. "Biopolitics" is when economic reason constructs identities as bodies at the limits of governmentality, when subjects perform on their own the projects of governmentality, carrying power on their shoulders. For Foucault, civil society is constructed as a subject of right—the person who forsakes his or her natural right for the right of the political bond—that occupies an overlapping conceptual space with the subject of interest: "[h]omo oeconomicus and civil society are therefore two inseparable elements" (296). The theory of the invisible hand premised that individual pursuits of interest would engender a nontotalizable multiplicity that presented itself as a limit to sovereign knowledge and government rationality. Civil society is, for Fouault, a combination of what he calls its "disinterested interests" (301), or relatively autonomous, localized feelings, instincts, sentiments, cultures, languages, and sympathies.

By addressing women's work and socialization as model capitalizable activities—or "enterprises"—Ong, in essence, furthers Foucault's observations about the overlaps between civil society and *homo oeconomicus* as producing a rationality on the limits of government, but through gender. In her defining of neoliberalism, Ong calls "ethical" those local practices that adopt and then adapt the universals of state, citizen, and human rights, and that show such universals to be diverse in their multiple interpretations and applications: "[C]omponents of citizenship have developed separate links to new spaces, become rearticulated, redefined, and reimagined in relation to diverse locations and ethical situations" (2006: 7). The "ethical" is the exception that marks out where the sovereign state has not yet assigned value, the outside or the limit of legal and juridical representation.

Similarly in agreement with Foucault, Butler, on the other hand, depicts the civil sphere as largely made coherent through linguistic categories stabilized and then destabilized through the abstract functions of power. This power sets the normative framework and, as such, largely works through nonstate-enforced regulations, norms, and prohibitions. For Butler, this linguistified civil society is where the limits of representation and representability are set in place, exceeding the state. Reading Hegel and Lacan's interpretation of *Antigone*, for example, Butler notes, "A social order is based [...] on a structure of communicability and intelligibility understood as symbolic" (2000: 12), and later reiterates that "the distinction between the symbolic and social law cannot finally hold" because the Symbolic is itself "the sedimentation of social practices" (2000: 19). The civil is an effect of language and discourse that is naturalized in its repetitions. The configuration of power in the civil results from the struggles of language within itself: the signified falls in with its signifier but then wrenches itself away, undoing the hold of the social bond (like "interest" in Foucault's "biopolitical" civil sphere, or the Semiotic in Kristeva). In other words, the struggle of the representational function of language to do the impossible—that is, to represent what it externalizes—destabilizes the whole system: "the subject desires to be identical with the signifier, and yet such an identification is precluded by language itself" (1987: 193). For Butler, the civil must be imagined as a perpetual face-off—a bar or a prohibition—between the Symbolic and its seeming foundations, or substance. This is what she calls norming, or the law.

Ong, then, interprets gender norms as produced through the reproduction of the limits the state sets for itself in the economic production of civil society through the subjectification of gender in labor. Gender is the mechanism articulating the relationships between the needs of power and the conduct of its subjects, particularly as a strategy for limiting the power of the state. Through its connections to currents and tensions within work, its distributions, and its displacements, gender norms participate in an alliance with other social forces to detach citizenship identities from the state and reattach its traits and features to nonstate apparatuses, social and economic forces.

Ong's analysis of how norms work in the place of state enforcement reveals how it is possible to read a poststructuralist theory like Butler's as inflected within neoliberal culture. For Butler, the norming of gender is not a strategy of the state, a mode of its legitimation, or a structure of articulation for the economic interests that gain power or lose power in relation to it. Rather, as in Ong, gender is where the state is not: gender is the marginalization of the state. As frequently noted, Butler envisions norms as effects of the interactions of institutions, enactments, and practices that cannot be traced to singular causes, centralized origins, or sovereign systems of control.[19] Without enforcement bodies, norms are not enforced. Norms are rather inscribed through structures of intelligibility, linguistic modes that operate at the limits of sovereignty: "Power, rather than the law, encompasses both the juridical (prohibitive and regulatory) and the productive (inadvertently generative) functions of differential relations. Hence, the sexuality that emerges within the matrix of power relations is not a simple replication or copy of the law itself, a uniform repetition of a masculinist economy of identity" (1990: 40). Composed of linguistic fragments, gender is a substrate composed of almost recognizable traits and characteristics that delineate the constructed coherence of the interiority of the "person," or the "core" (or "interest" in Foucaultian terms) of the subject, an articulation in language that never quite coheres to itself. Butler is challenging the philosophical approach that assumes the person as a category prior to external impositions and social involvements. As these mobile and changeable fragments of gender expose the absence, limits, or falsity of a sovereign subject, Butler's challenge to personhood splits citizenship apart.

The state in Butler functions in accordance with the rules of language by creating zones of intelligibility and unintelligibility: "the state presupposes modes of juridical belonging, at least minimally, but since the state can be precisely what expels and suspends modes of legal protection, the state can put us, some of us, in quite a state. It can signify the source of non-belonging, even produce that non-belonging as a quasi-permanent state" (2007: 3–4). The state works like the Symbolic, often stand in the place of the Symbolic. What Ong sees as exceptions to modes of citizenship that creates new and multiple "economic possibilities, spaces and techniques for governing the population" (2006: 7) and reveals sovereignty to be "graduated or variegated" (2006: 7), Butler understands as an absence, "the phantasmatic effect of... a politically tenuous construction" (1990: 192), a challenge to representation itself and thus to the logic of state. Foucaultian discourse and social fields in structures of governmentality are congealed in the Symbolic and then displaced by Kristeva's Semiotic or Derridian "play."

The difference between Ong's sense of civil society—as fragments of the real in working citizens' bodies—and Butler's—as breaks and illegibilities at the limits of the Symbolic—resembles the gap between positivism and the antipositivisms of Sassurian and Lacanian-based philosophies. Modeling civil society on a split and slippery concept of language gives a way out of the imposition of the real that sovereign power enforces. Based on its authority to rule through prohibitions, the power of the state, for Butler, coincides with the power of the Symbolic to designate categories of recognition, to mandate forms of "cultural familiarity" and "common belonging" (2007: 25). States exercise power, like language, by repeating a system of differences that establishes and secures boundaries between the conceivable and the inconceivable, the legitimate and the illegitimate: "the state both produces and presupposes certain operations of power that work primarily through establishing a set of 'ontological givens.' Among these givens are precisely notions of subject, culture, identity, and religion whose versions remain uncontested and incontestable within particular normative frameworks" (149). In this context, the "economic" principally works as an invisible force expelling from civil society those who miss the mark of its ontologizing representation, a "lack" or illegibility inhabiting, for example, the status of refugees: *"the exemplary moment of sovereignty is the act of deportation"* (2007: 102). Like language and like the law, states therefore exercise their sovereign operations principally through an act of reading: by framing some bodies as subjects of appeal, identification, and sympathy and others as "bare life" or difference without ontological status.[20] As such, they are constantly pushing the Symbolic up against its inability to set down the terms of the real. Ong, in contrast, interprets "bare life" in a liberal vein as bodies situated outside political normativity, perhaps as the next line of appeal: "There is the Schmittian exception that abandons certain populations and places them outside political normativity. But articulations between neoliberal exceptions and exceptions to neoliberalism have multiplied possibilities for moral claims and values assigned to various human categories, so that different degrees of protection can be negotiated for the politically excluded" (2006: 5–6). Ong cannot imagine the limits of the state as a limit to the capacities of the Symbolic; for her, the real of representation is ultimately accessible in the extension of markets and their institutions.

For Ong as for Butler, civil society is composed of representations that do not exactly articulate the Symbolic, creating disjunctions between subjects and their symbolic place within the system. With Ong, too, the principle act of state sovereignty is in the designation of the refugee as the limit through which sovereign states exercises power, but now the refugee has been granted an economic status of value and utility—of enterprise—by its expulsion. A combination of state actions, business interests, technological configurations, and international strategies fashions knowledge about health, skills, self-care, and entrepreneurial character—or "living systems" (2006: 180)— as mobile models in connection to which potential adherents can reinvent themselves and become real by becoming economically viable. As state functions are fragmented into disparate units, the contents of citizenship are dispersed into skills and traits, including feelings and sentiments, that can be produced in shifting territories, across borders—what she calls "transnational biotechnicity" (2006: 181) or "sovereign flexibility" (2006: 7)—even as commodities: "In short, components of citizenship have developed separate links to new spaces, becoming rearticulated, redefined, and reimagined in relation to diverse locations and ethical situations. Such de- and relinking of citizenship elements, actors, and spaces have been occasioned by the dispersion and realignment of market strategies, resources, and actors" (2006 7).

For Ong, state functions and citizenship conventions are cut apart, fragmented, recombined, realigned, and dispersed into a variety of elements occasioned by chains of economic value. Ong uses Singapore as an example, where a stringent policy of restricting births gave way to a policy to increase birthrates in order to attract global biotech and biomedical laboratories and companies to relocate in the new economy. The promotion of Singapore to foreign scientists was carried out in a campaign that needed to change the religious constitution of citizenship status in Singapore—in fact, to disengage citizens from deeply held religious beliefs. New citizenship identities had to conform to new ethical norms that allowed experimentation on embryos and stem cells as well as the deregulation of trade in human tissue. Ong calls this "biosociality" (2006: 184): the ability of the state to encourage families to become enterprises by socializing children to adopt "biovalues" (2006 185)—that is, to manufacture value in forms of the human, to "manufacture people" (2006: 186) and their sympathies in order to "adjust [...] the population mix" (2006: 186) strategically—that are attractive to foreign knowledge and capital. Citizenship becomes a project of socializing and resocializing, of articulating and rearticulating oneself within the identities produced in the motions of state and market forces, as human capital. While Ong would agree with Butler that the invention of the self requires the suspension of "natural" kinship systems, their singular production of the Symbolic, and their laws and prohibitions, Ong understands civil society as producing and reconfiguring norms through the transformation of human beings, their characters and their cultures into assets for extra-state cross-border capitalization. While Butler understands the social bond as ultimately disconnected because of the principle of difference in the linguistic agency on which it is composed, Ong's focus brings to light, in line with Foucault, how economic interest is currently forcing state sovereignty to resymbolize its governing functions through the calculation of its limits.[21]

For Ong, this constant give-and-take between state, corporate, civil, and global forces articulates itself through the construction of a new reality—a new humanity—with new social norms: "Transnational forms, norms, and practices were conditioned, configured, and transformed within the overlapping spaces of modern capitalism" (2006: 58). For instance, the incursion of transnational capital into Malaysia has led to increasing occurrences of "Muslim women [working] alongside non-Muslims and under the supervision of foreign men" (2006: 36). The traditional local authorities then sought to reclaim lost power to counter the breakdown in the public/private divide that had already taken place with the influx of secular ethics into everyday life. A vigorous pro-Islamic campaign arose that insisted on bringing back local Islamic (*sharia'a*) courts, with religious judges and the implementation of Islamic laws. These were meant to restore the power of the Islamic community—or the "*ulama*"—as a new bureaucratic power that would redomesticate women, restricting their access to participation in the public sphere mostly by reinstalling the practice of polygamy and its moral control over women. In response to this, the government cultivated a "Moderate Islam" (2006: 36) naturalized as "authentic" and indigenous to Malaysia, a "corporatist Islam" (2006: 49), which promoted "its ideal of two-career families [as] the foundation of a technocratic future" (2006: 40) with an eye to attracting foreign capital. For this, it supported a professional women's feminist social movement that developed a vigorous reinterpretation of Islamic texts and their moral grounding, including themselves in argumentation over ethical norms. In this scenario, the norms of gender are reconstructed in response to the changing norms of citizenship, through a struggle between different forces within and between the state, the economy, and civil society to limit the state. Women become newly real as the state changes what it recognizes as real women. Gender identity norms come about as a calculated strategy, an *effect* of power, marshaled between the state and other forces in order to limit the state's own powers in the exercise of market rights.

Whereas Butler recognizes that the Symbolic in civil society fails to secure the ontology of bodies and identities, envisioning a linguistified civil society as freeing subjects—for bad and for good—from their stakes in the real, Ong sets a flexible, transnational economic power to the task of putting the limits on the power of the state to produce the real. The terms of legibility change in response to corporate economic needs calling the state into its service by producing new terms of citizenship. Butler also sees the Symbolic's limits in civil society as escaping controls and set concepts but empties out the terminology of production that she uses to describe this process. However, at the margins of civil society, where Butler witnesses illegible bodies produced and reproduced at the limits of sovereign symbolic power, Ong reveals an invisible corporate power producing subjectivities as exceptions, in the same apparent absence of soverign power to set the real.

The Literary and Intellectual Labor

Alongside social movements, religion, and family structure, civil society for Ong is also about the historical generation of ideas and consciousness, as well as their institutionalization. In this she also parallels Butler, though with some contrast. Like Ong, Butler reads consciousness as an effect or appearance of interiority or substance, regulated by social norms embedded in language and operating according to the signifying process of language. Ong, too, presents knowledge and intelligence itself as effects of global circuits of exchange that produce internalized identities in accordance with a cross-section of capital's fluctuating needs and the state's constant refashioning of the limits of its public power. For Ong, markets in this system are not just tied to manufacturing and material goods (manual labor) but also to the linking of national goals to the commodification and circulation of the production of ideas (mental labor). Ong calls this process "arbitrage," where knowledge is split into small, standardizable, computerizable, and tradable units that are more easily repeated and transmitted as trainable skills.

Behind this conclusion that the productive process of intellectual labor is exportable, Ong traces a change in the conditions of gender: whereas US masculinity had once claimed leadership in skilled labor markets, the transfer of technocrat-class jobs into developing nations at lower salaries and wages—along with the relocation of US university campuses, training facilities, and education budgets into closer proximity to new technological and industrial zones in developing nations—has led to a loss of US competitive advantage. As well, rising third world professionals, service personnel, operators and technicians have adopted US interpersonal protocols, mannerisms, and even local cultural references. This has resulted in a loss in the view of US citizenship as naturally tied to superior innovative capabilities and technological creativity in men and a devaluation of intellectual labor as "women's work" because of its loss of US identification: "Thus labor arbitrage not only finds substitutable but cheaper labor overseas, it also requires Asia-Based workers to assume virtual American personalities[...T]he South Asian knowledge worker comes to represent the disarticulation of citizenship entitlement from its territorialized base and its connection with tradable skills as deterritorialized claims in a spectrum of market zones" (2006: 169).

As I argue further in chapter 5, the transformation of intellectual work into "women's work" in the information economy—through shipping such jobs to the "Third World," hiring Asian women with "nimble fingers" in the electronics industry, and "massifying" creative production, etc.—forms a gap between the Symbolic of the job and the bodies that answer to its call. Yet, in Ong, work becomes a complete superimposition, a new order of the real, through gender, of value, substance, and ideas onto the body, with no meaning outside of its relational position in an international flow of itemizable productive tasks. Bodies *are* the economy, and only that. Like the detached fragments of citizenship, bodies and brains acquire shape, flesh, culture, materiality *and gender* only as instruments (even if Symbolic ones), and internal form only through immediate usefulness. Though Ong is quite articulate about the problems of neoliberalism—how it substitutes market rights for civil rights, how it dilutes politics, how it includes only "a primitive, narrow vision of citizenship" (2006: 2) as those who own property, how it creates inequalities, it assaults communities and their values, and etc.— she still sees hope and possibility in the specific readjustments people can remake of themselves to align with these new modes of management. She believes that neoliberalism will open up possibilities for becoming real, new and more diverse forms of inhabiting the human, because of the ways that market forces break down and multiply articulations of sovereignty.[22]

Though Butler likewise understands the embodiments of ideas as always in circulation, the process of embodiment that she describes as the active principle of civil society is detached from work. Butler borrows from Hegel the understanding that consciousness approaches the world through desire and work, that desire and work confirm inner certainty and eventually give rise to self-consciousness (in the paradigm of the lord and the bondsman, for instance), and that desire and work are how the world is brought into relationship with both the individual subject and the subject of history. Yet, Butler emphasizes the primacy of desire as a function of language that operates as difference, and then accordingly reframes "work" as desire, as self-fashioning or self-invention. For example, with drag, the intention would be to expose the "reality" of gender as unreal (even "literary" or "figurative" (1990: 174)) and thus expose gender norms as both tenuous and violent. Fiction, artificiality and construction play a central part in this process, as the flesh itself becomes a "style" (1990: 190). Describing the configuration of gender as an injunction to fit into symbolic and cultural roles that are never finally appropriate, always somewhat fictional, and always failing, Butler declares, "There is only a taking up of the tools where they lie, where the very 'taking up' is enabled by the tool lying there" (1990: 199). The activity of (Heideggerian) construction here is not, as in Ong, a transnational trade-off that uses gender identity to pose limits to the state in order to wedge a labor market into various national and international economies, as needed. For Butler, rather, each subsequent performance proves itself falsely naturalized or displaced, irreconcilably. There is, she says, a gap between the instrument and the body (1990: 199). This gap appears when the Symbolic is revealed as at "play" with itself, as falsified, as artificial, as mocking, as errant, like the Semiotic: in short, as fiction. "From Hegel through Foucault," she concludes, "it appears that desire makes us into strangely fictive beings" (1987: 238). As the practice that converts work into desire, the literary inhabits the gap that prevents total instrumentalization within the embodiments of power. The literary here holds a similar constitutional space as does the economic exploitation of flexible sovereign citizenship in Ong—it is what invents identities, inscribes them as interiorities, distributes them, attributes them, and all in the service of marking its own limits. Yet, the literary does not find itself always and everywhere in the service of furthering global markets and instrumentalizing citizenship, norms, ideas, and bodies to that end. The aims of sovereign power become outside of the Symbolic, unreadable.

Ong uses realist ethnographic technique to show a direct line of intention between state policy and citizen self-representations in a poststatist work world. The signifying power of dispersing state sovereignties and value is complete and seamless, leading to a certain sense that the progress of economic accumulation is endless, inevitable, and inside of all of us: in fact, the economy *is* our inside. Capital flow *does* provide the only possibility of assuming subjectivity, reducing value to commodity exchange, and reason to calculation. Ong does not leave room for maneuver: for instance, she makes it seem that universities and civil societies are necessarily in the service of enhancing production through training local management, demasculinizing labor markets, and so it would be unreasonable to make an argument for investing in public higher education at a national level or in the service of other possibilities besides competition in global exchange. Ong's positivist realism leaves nothing but "what is" as the sense of capital, and then affirms that. For example, she concludes lamentingly, "Seldom is there an attempt to analytically link actual institutions of state power, capitalism, and transnational networks to such forms of cultural reproduction, inventiveness, and possibilities" (1999: 15). Her own realist analytic here depends on a description of capitalism that has a myriad of both positive and negative impacts, so that the exploitative nature of capitalism itself becomes coterminous with dramas of inventiveness and celebrated cultural difference. She can see no alternative.

In contrast, Butler, by focusing on language—like Haraway in her use of science fiction as a biotechnological escape-valve—, omits crucial intersections between language and the economy, of how accumulation and need often congeal into naturalized fixed meanings, including identity formations, without granting individuals opportunities for refashioning themselves. Nevertheless, she points to places where power's signifying function breaks down, where its referential projection onto identity fails. Though it would benefit from a more in-depth analysis about how the work of language and culture overlaps with work in a broader economic sense, this perspective invites us to theorize through a nonconceptual imaginary, where we are more than what we do within the global productive matrix and its enterprises. Feminist theory needs to articulate intersections between these two accounts of gender formation: neither can the economy be sidelined, because then feminism itself loses its historical and political connections to the ways gender is being institutionalized for profit, nor can its paradigms, narratives, and analytical frameworks be wholly determined by its placements within the value systems and class struggles of the global market economy, because this would mean that feminism was abandoning its projects of emancipation and, therefore, its legacies. Developing this conjunction is the project that the next two chapters begin.

CHAPTER 4

Girls in School: The "Girls' School" Genre at the New Frontier

In April, 2011, the news hit the wires that Greg Mortenson, the author of the celebrated *Three Cups of Tea* and *Stones Into Schools,* had not described his adventures building schools in Pakistan and Afghanistan with full accuracy. *Three Cups of Tea* and *Stones Into Schools* are both feel-good memoirs that chronicle Greg Mortenson's heroic travel exploits in an unfamiliar and often hostile environment to bring learning to Muslim girls. In a number of TV exposés and other mainstream outlets, including a dialogue with Jon Krakauer on *Sixty Minutes,* Mortenson's credibility was interrogated: evidence had surfaced that his stay in the village of Korphe, and his promise to build a school there, did not directly follow from his failed attempt to climb the Himalayan mountain K2 in 1993 and getting lost on the descent as he had written, and he was not really kidnapped by the Taliban.[1] Krakauer is explicit about the questionable accounting practices that Mortenson practiced and later claimed as but instances of a naïve guy who suddenly and miraculously finds himself at the head of a large business enterprise, unawares. Not only did many of the members of the CAI charity's Board of Trustees resign due to Mortenson's inadequate reporting of expenses—for example, he was using expensive private jets to travel to speaking engagements—but also money that was collected from schoolchildren in the United States to pay for "teachers' salaries, student scholarships, school supplies, basic operating expenses" (41) was not spent in these designated ways. The total 2009 outlay for such school support amounted to "$612,000" (Krakauer, 41). "Most teachers...have never received any training from CAI" and "a significant number of CAI schools only exist on paper" (48). Most poignantly, observers and researchers either could not find the schools that Mortenson claimed to have built or did find the buildings but converted to other uses, like storage for produce, or in various phases of deterioration due to neglect.[2]

I am not so concerned here with the authenticity or veracity of Mortenson's texts but rather with questioning the desire for authenticity that the texts elicit. After all, as Henry Louis Gates, for example, amply demonstrated, memoirs have often historically played various tricks with the truth and authenticity, particularly when they are being called upon to represent a certain set of ideas, national or ethnic identities: "However truthful you set out to be," he notes, "your autobiography is never unmediated by literary structures of expression" (29). In keeping, neither *Three Cups of Tea* nor *Stones Into Schools* demands to be read as a reflection of the real. Though certainly referring to real world historical events, they also participate in a literary tradition carried forward, for example, by such writers of imperialism as Rider Haggard and Joseph Conrad, where the Western imperial subject penetrates into the heart of darkness to find a horrific reflection of his own inner being. Contingently, they cite a tradition of rugged American individualism where, like Jack Kerouac, the solitary Mortenson starts to build his enterprise, against all odds, from a beat-up car which becomes his only lonely abode as he faces the savagery of the "wild west" of the east. Though Mortenson eventually marries, his saintly wife and kids completely understand why he needs to abandon them for six months or more every year in order to go off with his club of male buddies and warlords in the dangerous game of saving the women of Pakistan and Afghanistan, putting the needs of the world above their own.

Additionally, while referring to himself in the third person, Mortenson's exploits, unrelenting drive, overcoming all obstacles and maintaining substantial control, his adorable irony, and his hypermasculine bravura are embellished in superlative, self-congratulatory metaphors that constantly and fundamentally challenge credibility: for example, "Perhaps it was his experience with solitude, being the lone American child among hundreds of Africans, or the nights he spent bivouacked three thousand feet up Yosemite's Half Dome in the middle of a multiday climb, but Mortenson felt at ease" (*Three Cups,* 12). Mortenson's self-aggrandizing anecdotes often verge on the comical. For example, in *Stones Into Schools,* when Mortenson's daughter, after reading *Where the Wild Things Are,* advises him to "get those kids some jump ropes" (199), Mortenson dashes out to Gold's Gym, and eventually adds playgrounds to his schools in highland Afghanistan. One day, a Taliban fighter arrives, puts down his weapons, and along with his companions "gleefully sampled the swings, the slide, and the seesaw" (201).

Smiling widely, the Taliban warrior then decides that he likes the idea of educating girls after all "but [the schools] absolutely must have playgrounds" (201). Immediately seduced upon first contact with US consumer products, the terrorist throws away local traditions, religious beliefs, and historical resentment for the sake of a friendly romp in the sandbox.

Given that Mortenson's tale is both so familiar and so preposterous, what is surprising is precisely the surprise with which the pundits responded to the revelation that the stories are fiction. Jon Krakauer asks, "How could those of us who enabled his fraud—and we are legion—have been so gullible?" (68), and Katha Pollitt adds, "How did Mortenson enchant so many, including knowledgeable people...?" (9). Pollitt's conjectured answer is that Mortenson is telling his readers a tale that they believe because they like to hear it: "We've gotten used to a certain kind of NGO fairy tale...: Heifer International gives a family a farm animal, and in a dozen years, the profits send a daughter to college" (9). Certainly the imperialist clichés and promises saturate Mortenson's prose throughout, making US military ventures in Afghanistan into miraculous acts of care, competence, benevolence, and democracy-promotion (Mortenson eventually connects with the US military command who offers him material support and transport to promote his work). Mortenson's "follow-up" on his ventures entailed taking the most academically successful girls out of their local communities and away from their family obligations and family economic structures in order to send them away to high-schools for professional training in cities: "We would channel a portion of our resources into this cadre of elite girls, and they would serve as a vanguard for others. Slowly but surely, we would prepared our young graduates for careers of all sorts" (*Stones,* 231). With the particular girl in question, Ghosia, the father, Sabir, did not want to grant permission because, as the oldest sibling, she was his primary caretaker, so Mortenson offered to hire a nurse for him (even though, as Mortenson admits earlier, in this Islamic culture, women must not interact with men outside their family). As a result, Mortenson boasts, he will break the cycle of generations of women who have tended their fields and families while observing local customs that Mortenson finds stagnant. The school ends up being the crucial pivot through which the old culture can be broken and the new, American-friendly one can be inserted.

The idea of spreading education to girls promises the success of the imperialist dream while shadowing the nightmare of continued extremist attacks on girls and their schools, including insurgents throwing acid on the schoolgirls' faces, high dropout and low attendance rates, and low quality of curriculum and instruction[3] (in contrast to his vilifying of madrassas for teaching extremism, Mortenson never mentions these problematic aspects of his own schools and, in contrast to his depictions of unattended and decrepit public schools, Mortenson's only acknowledgement of his own schools collapsing, being abandoned, or failing is on account of natural disasters). In response to Katha Pollit's question, this chapter argues that girls' schools give an additional meaning to imperialistic enterprises than a heifer: girls' school narratives, as Angela McRobbie recognizes, position girls as the carriers of new economic rationalities:

> The girl emerges across a range of social and cultural spaces as a subject truly worthy of investment... [T]he girl who has benefitted from the equal opportunities now available to her, can be mobilized as the embodiment of the values of the new meritocracy... Nowadays the young woman's success seems to promise economic prosperity on the basis of her enthusiasm for work and having a career. (721–722)

For McRobbie, the girl under neoliberalism is "now a social category understood primarily as being endowed with capacity" (722) or "motivation and aptitude" (728); she is, domestically, the celebrated outcome of the success of the education system as a whole and, on the international plane, the strategic and compelling target of worthwhile investment aid in the form of educational aid for the production of "the ideal... subject of the new international division of labour" (729): in other words, "gender training to the long term benefit of the global corporations" (729). "The restructuring of flexible global capitalism," she concludes, "now relies heavily on the willing labour of girls and women... but this... coincides with the fading away of feminism and the women's movement" (719).

Mortenson's "feel good" narrative of girls' emancipation through girls' education builds on a prior positioning of girls' schools as the crux of the struggle between colonizers and nationalist movements in other postcolonial renditions. For example, in his famous chapter on women revolutionaries "Algeria Unveiled," Frantz Fanon interprets girls' schools as methodologically destroying the indigenous national culture. Fanon's description of girls' schools have an uncanny similarity to many of the celebratory descriptions that Mortenson, too, constructs: "Much is made of the young student's prodigious intelligence, her maturity," remarks Fanon. "A picture is painted of the brilliant future that awaits those eager young creatures, and it is none too subtly hinted that it would be criminal if the child's schooling were interrupted. The shortcomings of colonized society are conceded, and it is proposed that the young student be sent to boarding school in order to spare the parents the criticism of 'narrow-minded neighbors'" (fn. 39).[4] In keeping, Mortenson promotes the girls' school as the crux of social change in

Afghanistan and Pakistan, but the culture that the schools are instituting is constantly extolled as a new economic culture, in this instance as the culture of the sweatshop: "In a disused room at the back of Hafi Ali's home, Korphe's women gathered each afternoon, learning to use the four new Singer hand-crank sewing machines Mortenson purchased, under the tutelage of Fida, a master Skardu tailor... 'Balti already had a rich tradition of sewing and weaving," Mortenson says. 'They just needed some help to revive the dying practice" (2006: 193). Mortenson uses the schools and the girls they are meant to benefit as praise-worthy examples not only of such overcoming of indigenous culture, traditions, and practices, imposing in their place technological rationality and the temporality of the machine. Mortenson's girls' schools also establish a transformation into neoliberal economic relations: public sphere destruction, military benevolence,[5] and private initiative. Every instance of public involvement, for Mortenson, ends in tragedy that Mortenson's heroic construction of schools will alleviate: for example, "the few permanent government school buildings that had been reconstructed were inappropriate, having been raised directly over the foot-prints of the old schools, and with the same techniques that were responsible for the structural failures that had killed so many children" (*Stones,* 219). Girls in schools come to represent a naturalized relationality and coopera-tive ethic that exist as an alternative to indigenous cultural values, outside of external state controls and systems' regulations, or, as Krakauer cites Mortenson, outside of "government scrutiny into our operation" (57), at the limts of sovereignty as unmediated market potential.

Mortenson's construction of girls' education as the cornerstone of impe-rialist policy participates in a literary tradition of a girls' school genre that develops an economic rationality through displaying a common sense about girls. The girls' school trope has functioned first as a nervous plot about female employment that turns into a disruption of the symbolic order, a chal-lenge to tradition, or a transgressive or transformative principle that needs to be expelled for symbolic health. The girls' school narratives have exhibited a social and symbolic unease with their mainstay plot of linking women and their work with markets and institutions of economic circulation. This unease has taken various forms. Since the nineteenth century, the symbolic break ushered in by the girls' school genre has evolved from gothic-like domestic romance in Charlotte Bronte's *Villette,* into a site of play and erotic transgression in Modernism (e.g., Foucault's *Herculine Barbin*, Hellman's *The Children's Hour,* Sayers's *Gaudy Night,* Stein's *Fernhurst,* Richardson's *Pointed Roofs* and *Backwater,* Colette's *Claudine in School*[6]), and finally into a postcolonial phase where girls' schools take up their role as the symbolic carriers of global power. Mortenson's intervention, then, is in revising the girls' school trope of the broken Symbolic to be allied with the economic and institutional order and its production of conformable subjects of labor. That is, for Mortenson, imperialism is itself transgressive because of its alliance with girls' schools and their symbolic connection to aesthetic disruption. In its early twentieth-century form, as Patricia Tilburg notes, girls' school narratives "became...a kind of shorthand for feminine success" with the girls' school depicted "as a powerfully modern and powerfully female public space" (77). I show here how imperialist culture has co-opted the figure of rebellion that girls' school narratives developed to represent the problem of the marketability of women's work. As imperialist narratives merge into the girls' school trope, "women's work" turns from being a social anxiety and a transgression to being a display of women's compliance with regimes of capitalization. Allied with the girls' school, capital becomes the transgressor. This change in the literary role of women's work for the imperialist context has migrated into the social scientific justification in policy debates over girls' education, separate schooling, "achievement," and "choice."

Girls' Schools in the Social Sciences

The US has witnessed a renewed policy interest in gender segregated schooling mainly for two reasons: (1) race and racial desegregation have become political nonstarters for addressing equity issues after bussing was abandoned; and (2) gender segregation stands as "difference," that is, as an individuated "choice" that turns parents into consumers of aesthetic, stylistic, or conspicuous products or expressions, in ideological line with neoliberal policies of public school privatization. The social scientific literature is consistent in finding a lack of evidence for the effectivity of gender segregated schooling or in constructing a consensual methodology for demonstrating such an effectivity. Yet, what the social science literature consistently does assume is that educational difference must be located essentially in the body, and so inequalities can be remedied only by taking into account the educational differences literalized in the gendered body, that is, by treating differently gendered bodies with different pedagogical methods and tools. This sociological literalizing of educational differences in the gendered body evolves out of a historical construction of girls' schooling that extends beyond the contemporary context. The sociological sedimentation of educational differences in the gendered body participates in a reemergence of anxieties about working women's bodies in relation to changing labor markets in the industrial age, anxieties made visible in literary imaginings of girls' schools. What Greg Mortenson accomplishes is to reproduce such girls' school narratives as narratives of imperial conquest, projecting anxieties over commodifying women's labor in the industrial age onto imperialized subjects as a form of neoliberal hegemonic governance in the developing world.

Though, in industrialized nations, private women's colleges and some high schools would in earlier parts of the twentieth century allow women access to equipment and instruction in areas where they were subordinated or altogether excluded in coeducational or all-male environments, increasingly in the eighties and after, feminists came to see gender segregation in schooling as inherently unequal. Single-sex schooling, such opponents expounded, perpetuates and reinforces harmful gender stereotypes and opens the possibility for an unfair allocation of resources. As cited in the American Association of University Women's (AAUW) statement about Title IX[7], for example, "Historically, public single-sex education has often harmed girls by depriving them of equal educational opportunities. Where programs are established separately for both boys and girls, they have tended to be distinctly unequal with fewer resources allocated for girls' programs and stereotypical notions limiting vocational options." The negative stereotypes sometimes lead to girls getting different treatment by teachers, teachers having different expectations in subject areas like math and science, girls being called on less often, and the ensuing low self-esteem, as Peggy Orenstein notes particularly about girls' performance in math and science classes,[8] in her acclaimed 1994 ethnography *SchoolGirls,* sponsored by the AAUW.[9]

Yet, public single-sex schooling and single-sex classroom options were resurrected and reinvigorated in the school choice rhetoric of the "No Child Left Behind" era. Under the premise that public schools were failing, single-sex schools were championed as one option that might improve achievement levels for some children. I show here how the debates over single-sex schooling serve to call upon and preserve the nature of the gendered body as underscoring the division of labor under neoliberalism, and to entrench the division of labor in the pledge of advancing prosperity.[10]

Though single-sex schooling has no discernable or believable scientific defense, 400 public schools have arisen in 37 states and the District of Columbia (McNeil)[11] along with 445 sex-segregated classrooms for the purpose of solving "sagging test scores and behavioral problems" (Medina).[12] This trend continues despite a 1991 Supreme Court decision in *Garrett v. Board of Education* where the court decided that single-sex classrooms violated the Fourteenth Amendment and a 1996 decision in *United States v. Virginia* that commanded the Virginia Military Institute (VMI) to accept women.[13] Much of the movement to create single-sex public schools has followed on the end of desegregation policies like busing and the resulting racial resegregation of many public schools. As Andrew J. McCreary remarks," The rise in single-sex programs came with the fall of race-linked integration policies" (462) because they opened more diverse options to counter discrimination and imbalances as well as special programs to offset economic disadvantages. The 1991 decision in *Garrett,* for example, ended a Detroit initiative to found all-boys schools with Afro-Centric curriculum. The initiative to provide such schools came out of a sense that African-American boys were being ill-served by their schools because all their teachers were women, and these new schools would give Africa-American boys the opportunity to "come into contact with positive male role models" (Salomone, 129). The National Association for the Advancement of Colored People (NAACP) opposed the measure, fearing resegregation. Yet, McCreary continues, "The inability to treat racial disparities in achievement with race-conscious policy led to broad new permissions in sex-conscious education... The new generation of single-sex schools emerged as a remedy for low-income, black males falling behind similarly situated female in all-black districts" (164). The *Virginia* decision, then, forced a military institute to open its doors to women students on the basis of educational "appropriateness" and the right of access to "substantially equal" facilities: women could not be excluded categorically simply because most women were not "capable of all the individual activities required of VMI cadets" (Salome, 162). Even as it clearly prohibited justifications that perpetuated harmful stereotypes, *Virginia,* however, left open the possibility that same-sex schools could be justified as "appropriate," "diverse" (based on needs) and "voluntary" (based on the provision of choice: e.g., women should be given the option of becoming cadets) and carrying forward a government interest. Instead of correcting for inequality, "choice" came to be, as McCreary concludes, what "mattered most" (490).

Though Title IX of the 1964 Civil Rights Act, enacted in 1972, explicitly denies federal funding to institutions that discriminate on the basis of sex, the George W. Bush administration in 2006 loosened its provisions, allowing the expansion of single-sex classrooms and schools in order to create alternative possibilities for raising achievement and competition. The reformers claimed that there was no substantial research done and so single-sex classroom examples had to be provisionally allowed in order to discover whether they "worked," though there was no real discussion about what they "worked" for, nor what "working" might look like. Advocates allege that single-sex schools grant independent spaces for "voice" and expression, improving self-esteem and discipline, removing distractions, empowering students, building community, and improving discipline. "A space targeted specifically for young women," rhapsodize Lois Weis and Craig Centrie, for example, in a study about an abstinence-only program in Buffalo, New

York, "can encourage a political project around gender that enables them to 'speak their own name' and hold together for collective health and safety" (31). Other proponents see the loosening of legal controls over the interpretation of "substantial equality" as necessary for the expansion of charter schools: as Salomone, for example, explains this position, "The charter school concept allows school districts as well as outside groups to organize schools that are essentially public but freed from many of the usual hiring restrictions and other state local regulations" (180). In other words, the litigation on same-sex public schooling eases into place the transfer of public schools into private or privatizing hands that are beyond accountability or public scrutiny and that can therefore avoid rules that were formed to protect equality measures as well as other protections like unions, worker benefits, and curriculum oversight. Meanwhile, critics claimed that the focus on achievement through testing in schools disallowed the possibility that what "success" for single-sex schools should mean is reducing sexism not adapting safely into it.

The research routinely shows that single-sex classrooms have no proven or provable effect on educational "success." "There remains no strong evidence," McCreary states, "for the concurrent or long-term effects of these policies and no federal structure for uniformly studying those effects" (492). A 1998 study by the American Association of University Women (AAUW) found that sex-segregated classrooms did not make education "better." "There is no evidence," the researchers conclude, "that single-sex education in general 'works' or is 'better' than coeducation. The 'success' or 'failure' of any K-12 single-sex initiative is relative to a particular group of students in a particular setting and a given set of academic social objects. Claims that single-sex education is inherently 'better' or 'worse' than coeducation beg the questions: What constitutes a 'good' education? And for whom?" Furthermore, they add the obvious, "No learning environment, single-sex or coed, provides a sure escape from sexism."

In fact, researchers on either side agree on just this one issue: that the research on the effectiveness and benefits of single-sex public education is inconclusive, anecdotal at best. "Educational research on single-sex classes and schooling," Herr and Arms indicate, "is inconclusive and controversial" (529). Single-sex schooling expanded at the same time as high-stakes testing and accountability regimes were also expanding, blending together the effects of each. "There are no guarantees," they go on, analyzing existing empirical data, "that simply separating the sexes creates an equitable learning environment or one that interrupts stereotypical and racial arrangements" (548). Jennifer Friend also finds little proof in the empirical studies: "The effectiveness of same-gender schools and classrooms as a strategy to promote gains in student achievement is debatable. Some research findings related to same-gender education have documented higher academic achievement and more positive student attitudes, especially for female students and male students who are from low socio-economic or racially/ethnically diverse backgrounds...Other studies have found that same-gender grouping makes no difference academically...In addition, there may be unmeasured consequences" (56). Wendy Kaminer also observes, "Studies do not show that girls fare better in single-sex schools," and there is absolutely "no consensus" among psychologists that there are cognitive differences between the sexes that would lead to different learning behaviors or needs. Gerald Bracey asserts, "It is hard to see, currently, how any such schools could be justified by the weak and contradictory research evidence which now exists" (26). The US Department of Education's report from its "Policy and Program Studies Service" sums up," Any positive effects of SS [single-sex] schooling on longer-term indicators of academic achievement are not readily apparent. No differences were found for postsecondary test scores, college graduation rates, or graduate school attendance rates" (xv). Even researchers looking into the historical evidence for the benefits of same-sex schooling have found scant support. For example, E. Thomas Ewing reads through Stalin-era Soviet documents before the regime ended the policy in 1954 and discovers that "claims of significant advantages are rarely supported by measurable educational outcomes" (638).

Likewise, though supporting single-sex schooling, Rosemary C. Salomone contests that "research efforts to determine the precise magnitude and source of gender differences in cognitive abilities are still much of a 'work in progress'" (114). Though Salomone claims unequivocally that "girls and boys interact with the educational environment in different ways" (102), her reviewing of the research record reveals a substantial amount of variability, with girls significantly more likely to learn through social interaction except that boys show greater gains from engaging in such interactive social activities (97), and boys are more visually and spatially oriented, learning best through activity and movement, but are really trained to do so by playing video games. In fact, Salomone pronounces that most of the disparities measured between girls' and boys' performance often can be said to be disparities due to race or economic disadvantage since "the data make clear that the convergence of race, culture, and class present a complex set of social factors that reach well beyond the conventional girl-boy argument" (113). The empirical reports repeat perennially that their results do not definitively prove same-sex education as educationally optimal.

Part of the problem in the social science perspectives is, throughout, a lack of clear articulation of the intentions of single-sex schooling and what would count as "success": whether what is sought is higher "achievement" or equality. Because of this indistinctness in outcomes, what counts as inputs often also seems variable and arbitrary, as well as how such inputs are to be isolated from other potential influences. As Saeeda Shah and Catherine Conchar summarize, "Assessments of single-sex education's success or failure are linked to multiple factors such as institutional goals or ethos, indicators of success used, historical context and status of school, student selection processes, and others" (197), including cultural and religious factors, particularly in gender socialization. As well, in studies over time, the evidence that single-sex schooling increases job-market opportunities is insubstantial: "We find no impact of single-sex schooling [in a 1958 cohort]," report Alice Sullivan and her co-researchers, "on the chances of being employed in 2000, nor on the horizontal or social class segregation of mid-life occupations" (311). Though the research does not give a definitive sense of the benefits, there is substantial concern over how such programs reaffirm harmful stereotypes. As Diane F. Halpern notes in *Science,* "Research has demonstrated that, when environments label individuals and segregate along some characteristic (e.g., gender, eye color or randomly assigned t-shirt groups), children infer that the groups differ in important ways and develop increased intergroup biases" (1707).

In order to literalize these education differences in the sexed body as grounded in material fact even with the ambivalence in empirical findings, researchers often turn to the body. As Munira Moon Charania notes, anxiety about all girls' schooling resonates with a "public anxiety surrounding girls' bodies" (306), situating girls' bodies as "the symbols of both cultural continuity and cultural crisis" (307). Often through medicine, neurology, chemistry or psychology, researchers have sought scientific proofs that the differences in how boys and girls learn is hard-wired in the brain. As Juliet A. Williams observes, "The rhetoric of science has been foregrounded as the basis for segregationist policies. In claiming a scientific basis for sex-segregation in K-12 public schools, proponents of single-sex education have adroitly circumnavigated constitutional anti-stereotyping norms by rallying purported facts of nature to argue for judicial reconsideration of where the line between a stereotype and legitimate generalization about males and females should be drawn" (557). The impetus is to show that though segregation by race is inherently unequal, segregation by gender does not need to be. Summarizing for this context what she has learned about antiessentialism from the history of feminism—from Mary Wollstonecraft and John Stuart Mills to Carol Gilligan and Catherine MacKinnon—, Rosemary C. Salomone declares, "Race is a social construct; sex is irreducibly biological with an overlay of social considerations that define gender" (120).

This frequent recourse to the "truth" of the gendered body in the social science literature most often passes through a reference to the writings of Leonard Sax, M.D., Ph.D. Sax's thesis is that "Girls and boys behave differently" and learn differently "because their brains are wired differently" (28). In his book *Why Gender Matters,* Dr. Sax gives multiple examples. The first example is that girls have better hearing than boys because of the configuration of their ears. Though the variation in hearing is clearly greater within genders than between genders—as are most of the differences that Sax encounters—, Sax does not then recommend separating children on the basis of hearing ability, or providing variable curriculum content in specifically, say, music class, but rather he advocates a wholesale embrace of gendered classrooms on the basis that girls are more easily distracted by soft noises. Eyes also operate differently, where girls' retinas transmit through "P cells" that are wired to accept information on texture and color, while boys' through "M cells," spatially oriented for movement and direction. Boys' emotions get stuck in the part of the brain called the amygdala, from where they cannot be communicated, while girls' emotional activity works through the cerebral cortex, where they affect higher functioning like reasoning and language. This makes girls more skillful at language activities like reading and group work, while boys can better understand and navigate through space.

Girls and boys, Sax concludes, have different ways of learning: girls learn better through talking while boys learn better through doing. From these brain-wired differences, Dr. Sax is able to determine not only that girls like playing with Barbie while boys like playing with G. I. Joe, that girls like fiction while boys like nonfiction, that girls are better at reading and boys better at math and Grand Theft Auto, that girls like math problems that apply to the real world while boys like abstract mathematics, but also that men like pornography more than women do, and that men are more prone to raping women than women are to raping men. Dr. Sax goes on to explain that these brain-determined differences in eyesight, hearing, and brain processing of emotions translate somehow into irreparable differences in risk-taking, attention, self-esteem, and income. The gender differences that Dr. Sax spots in his learning bodies amount to a core understanding that boys move and girls do not.

In response to Dr. Sax's conclusions that physical and neurological differences justify same-sex schooling, a 2011 study in *Science* has found that his recommendations are based on misinformation, debunked science, and stereotypes: "Certain sex differences," the research team maintains, "have been reported (e.g., in brain activation patterns, auditory thresholds, memory performance), but none are substantial enough to justify different educational methods... [F]unds spent on training teachers in nonexistent 'gender-specific learning styles' could be better spent on training them to teach science, mathematics, and reading, or to integrate boys and girls more completely in the learning environment" (Halpern: 1706–1707). Gerald Bracey also criticizes Sax's allegations: "Unfortunately, he [Sax] often grossly distorts the data to make a point. Modest correlations in a single study become universally deterministic, causal effects" (24). Yet, following on Dr. Sax's findings, the sexed body continues to be called upon to make educational difference visible in the same-sex schooling debates. Many advocates, for example, claim that students are less distracted in single-sex settings,[14] implying not only that members of the opposite sex are the only cause of distraction for school-age kids, teenagers, and college-goers, but also that members of the "opposite sex" (presumably the only ones that could arouse desire) have to be physically present in order to be distractions. Such perspectives assume that sexual desire can be expelled from the classroom with the simple act of barring physical, heterosexual direct eye-contact during class hours.

The single-sex schooling debates make the body visible in a particular way. As McRobbie underscores, such visibility of the sexed-body produces an understanding of sexed bodies and subjectivities as carriers of economic capacity in ways that suit the economic layout of the present. McRobbie contends that with the decline in radical sexual politics and feminist political culture, gender has been transformed to where "young women are allocated a pivotal role in the new global labour market" as the global economy depends "on the willing labour of girls and women" (719). This process, says McRobbie, is partly accomplished through schooling, that is, in the way that such debates about schooling in a postfeminist era figure girls as the passionate promise of economic prosperity by understanding their bodies as laboring effectively. I argue that the global economy captures the girl's body as capacity by displaying its difference, that is, "ensuring," in McRobbie's words, "appropriate modalities of female economic participation" (729).

Though the social scientific record is ambivalent about the validity of calling upon the sexed body to account for educational variability, some still insist that certain features of the sexed body are capacious, that is, educatively relevant because productive of future value. Boys learn by actively moving, the anecdotes insist, while girls learn by sitting still and talking. In its mainstream renditions, stereotypes used to defend cognitive sex differences more than often focus on boys as moving bodies. Jennifer Medina begins her *New York Times* article, for instance, with the basketball coach telling his math class in the Bronx to move faster. "Mr. Cannon had experimented with after-school tutoring," reports *The New York Times* about an all-boys' public school in Manhattan, "playing sports with students and their fathers on weekends[...] Test scores improved enough" (Medina) When asked why he favored his single-sex learning environment, one 11-year old student responded, "I like learning how to be a man," and then explained by commenting, "To put on deodorant" (Medina). Anna Scott in the Florida *Sun-Sentinal* also recaps, "'Boys learn differently,' said Wise, a former teacher. 'They like to move around.'" "'Boys,'" says 5th grade teacher James Hearn from South Carolina's Beech Hill Elementary School to Michele McNeil of *Education Week,* "Are always wanting to move around...[T]hey're into sports." The need for separate classrooms results from boys needing to move and girls needing to sit still, even while this stillness and social skills in girls' bodies is a recent invention. As Patricia Tilburg notes, discourses of physical fitness, linking morality with gym classes and exercises in school, were vitalized in early twentieth century girls' schooling policy.

The metaphor of boys' bodies expressing a wildness—played out in physical games and running around—that would, through education, be gradually brought under the control of reason remains here as part of the construction of masculinity that Gail Bederman has analyzed. For Bederman, turn-of-the-twentieth-century progressive boys' schooling advocates understood boys as needing to pass through primitive stages of development, to express the violence and savagery of their untamed, unconscious, ancestral nature on the pathway to white civilization:

> Children's primitivism was the 'light and hope' of the overcivilized world...because children's reliving of their evolutionary past provided an unfailing guide toward man's true evolutionary destiny...By encouraging small boys to embrace their primitive passions instead of repressing them, educators could 'inoculate' boys with the primitive strength they would need...As adults they could be safely civilized, refined, and cultured—but only if they had fully lived and outgrown a temporary case of savagery as small boys. (96–97)

The (boys') moving body appears in the educational setting as moving toward mastery, like manual labor—in Marx's sense—taking control over nature. As, in contrast, immobilized, the girl's body indicates, on the one hand, a lack of forward motion or advancement—in other words, a site of need, an unrealized capacity, a productive delay, even a momentum destroyed, awaiting inputs; on the other hand, the girl's body is in perfect submission, inactive but ready for service: the girl learns through talking, relating, cooperating, collaborating, not acting. As accounts of differential aptitudes, the contrast between the moving body of boys and the still body of girls reappears in Greg Mortenson's justifications for why girls make for good educational investments. Mortenson imagines the state school as a site of devastation in a way that parallels the devastation of the public school that advocates for single-sex schooling assume when they address the need for choice through segregation. In October of 2005, an earthquake hit the northeastern region of Pakistan: "the vast majority of those dead school-children were girls...While the boys had tended to race to safety by bolting out the windows and doors, most of the girls had instinctively huddled together and perished" (*Stones*, 156). Girls' still bodies merge into the devastated public schools, making the schools into a call for intervention or, as Mortenson himself professes, "a potent symbol of progress" (*Stones*, 159), a potential and an underrealized capacity.

The Literary Record: Bronte's Villette

Though the scientific treatment of single-sex schooling cannot credibly explain its constant recourse to the body as final justification and cause of educational difference, the literary tradition does offer a way of reading the body as the source of educational difference. In other words, fiction is where historical ideologies are drawn through the gendered body in ways that the social sciences tend to literalize. The literary analysis of girls' schooling allows for breaks and discontinuities in the direct observation that sediments as what seems to be the self-evident stability of the sociological real. In contrast, "It is self-evident," Theodor Adorno begins his polemic on aesthetics, "that nothing concerning art is self-evident anymore" (1). In its uncertain "relation to the world," art through reflection opens an "infinitide of new possibilities" (1). Art's purpose is to be different than what is. "Artworks," he continues, "detach themselves from the empirical world and bring forth another world, one opposed to the empirical world as if this other world too were an autonomous entity" (1). Adorno's point is that art is in conflict with its own affirmation of the world; it exposes from within the empirical its "nonidentity" with the empirical. For Adorno, within art, the empirical affirmation is, at the same time, an affirmation of another world in contrast to what exists. As Fredric Jameson interprets this: "is the text a free-floating object in its own right, or does it 'reflect' some context or ground, and in that case does it simply replicate the latter ideologically, or does it possess some autonomous force in which it could also be seen as negating that context?" (1981: 38). Whereas the social scientific literature observes and measures "what is," not reflecting on how empiricism itself conspires in the creation of the "what is," literary language traces the opposition within the "what is," what does not quite fit. In the framing of a genre that could be called a "girls' school" genre, the possibilities offered in this tradition knock up against the current moment of its articulation. As it moves from the Victorian through to the modernist, the "girls' school" genre can be said to register, within the representational framing of an institution, a transgression of the sexualized body at the moment when "women's work" is uncomfortably adapted into a new economic capacity as a commodified form.

Girls' education became important to the history of the novel already in the eighteenth century. Jean-Jacques Rousseau called on girls' education to challenge John Locke's liberalism, speculating that girls' education would be necessary to the formation of the republic. In Rousseau's fictive reconstruction of what such an education would look like in *Emile*, girls were not supposed to be educated in parallel to boys who were meant to experiment, inquire, and travel; instead, the girl would be educated "to please and to be subjugated," that is, "to make herself agreeable to man instead of arousing him" (532), to be pregnant, to raise children, to love them, and to serve as the link between her husband and his offspring. The fiction here replicated the project of educating girls by providing ideal lessons in domestic conduct through example.

Rather than supposing that girls fit comfortably within domestic roles, however, the nineteenth century girls' school genre started to weave anxious plots around women's bodies in relation to the prospects of women's paid work. For example, in the early twentieth century, Virginia Woolf— reflecting back on the nineteenth century—famously isolated women's literature and education outside of labor, as though labor was the death of autonomous knowledge and creativity:

> Before that [my aunt died, leaving me five hundred pounds a year] I had made my living by cadging odd jobs from newspapers, by reporting a donkey show here or a wedding there; I had earned a few pounds by addressing envelopes, reading to old ladies, making artificial flowers, teaching the alphabet to small children in kindergarten. Such were the chief occupations that were open to women before 1918…To being with, always to be doing work, and to do it like a slave, flattering and fawning,…and then the thought of that one gift which it was death to hide…perishing and with it myself, my soul. (37–38)

Likewise, though with a different rationale, the famous French feminist Madeleine Pelletier, in her 1914 *L'éducation féministe des filles* (translated as "The Feminist Education of Girls"), described the practice of girls' education as anxiously defending the girl from paid employment. Except for in cases where "the parents want to assure an honorable position when, without a sufficient dowry, they do not find a way to marry her off" (my translation;

96), the science and math lessons let the girl "reach the conclusion that she only needs to know very few of the general laws of science and many of their applications towards managing the household" (my translation; 98).

The girls' school genre made visible that the "natural" relation between women and domestic work was a construction and not comfortably stable. According to Anita Levy, early twentieth century literary productions wove literary scenes out of the nineteenth century's "household as emptied of female labor" (51). Not only were women in greater numbers employed increasingly outside the home, but also the home itself was being newly occupied by technologies, scientific expertise, professionals, and specialists for hire, including teachers. What Mary Poovey says of the role of governesses in Victorian literature—that they naturalize gender traits emphasized in domesticity and socialization but also exhibit such traits as manufacturable and marketable products—would also apply to women as teachers:

> The governess is also significant... because of the proximity she bears to two of the most important Victorian representations of woman: the figure who epitomized the domestic ideal, and the figure who threatened to destroy it. Because the governess was like the middle-class mother in the work she performed, but like both a working-class woman and man in the wages she received, the very figure who theoretically should have defended the naturalness of separate spheres threatened to collapse the difference between them. (127)

The girl's school symptomatized the insecure line between women's domestic, reproductive work, on the one hand, and, on the other, their inclusion in the productive economy.

Cultural historians have also noted that girls' schools were a site where domesticity was both defended and challenged by new market relations. Girls schools would give women the increasingly complicated knowledge they needed to run a household but, on the other hand, also provide examples of settings for women and their work that were not domestic. Christina de Bellaigue, for example, explains, "One reason for the proliferation of girls' boarding-schools was that in a context in which work for pay was constructed as a male prerogative and femininity predicated on domesticity, teaching—as an extension of the maternal role—was the only occupation a middle-class woman could undertake without losing caste... The fluidity of boundaries between the family schoolroom and educational establishments bolstered this domestic conception of the school" (15–17). In France, the Napoleonic administration was particularly interested in bringing the girls' school into the purview of the secularizing state in order to offset the power of the Church that had previously organized education for girls in convent and charity schools. The religiosity of women in their function of socializing children was a problem for the secularizing state. As Bellaigue continues, in the later part of the nineteenth century, "The Revolution had made female education a public issue, had strengthened and politicized a potentially valorizing notion of feminine domesticity, and had underlined the need for women to develop skills which would prepare them to respond to fluctuating circumstances" (29). In England, girls' schools, in contrast, were meant to be replications of home and familial life, kept outside of governmental influence, with even the architecture and interior arrangements modeled as closely as possible on the family drawing room. Nevertheless, schools were not families, and teaching was becoming increasingly professionalized. As Baillaigue concludes, for both England and France, "It could be argued that the treatises underscoring women's domestic role were a response to the sense that women were increasingly stepping outside the bounds of their feminine sphere" (41). Rebecca Rogers agrees that nineteenth century schooling marked a changing definition of femininity open to economic influence: "Pedagogues might argue for women's natural religiosity but they also emphasized the need for rational study. This rational study could take the form of examinations and emulation that point to the importance of work and the work ethic in evolving female identities" (255).

In defining the line between religious custom and independent, secular reasoning that Q. D. Leavis has identified as central to *Villette*'s narrative structure, the girls' school becomes integral to how economic realities are newly entering symbolic form and affecting identities.[15] The incursions of external market relations into what was supposed to be an autonomous or private natural feminine identity are marked by a defensiveness about domesticity in accounts of girls' schooling. In *Villette*, the architecture of the school itself maintains central plot distinctions between English Protestant free-thinking and Beligan-French Catholic submission to a culture of faith and traditional domesticity: with its narrow, darkened conclaves, leafy seclusions, obscure alleys, a dusty attic, and vague reliquary shapes, the school hides away a resident ghost of a nun, interpreted by the locals as a hold-over of a past offense. Lucy, however, is not tricked into "the inheritance of a ghost story" (117), "rousing fear and inflicting horror" (117), but rather deciphers the specter as "romantic rubbish" (118) and independently researches its empirical origin. What in Q. D. Leavis's analysis appears as "English" or secular is the construction of autonomous personhood in contrast to an outmoded French traditionalism tied not only to locally grown irrational beliefs but also, through domesticity, to social and moral control.[16] "The continental 'female,'" notices Lucy, "is a quite different being to the insular 'female' of the same age and class" (87). As "English" and therefore free of the hold of legend, family resignation, archaic community knowledge, or moral regulation, the character of Lucy Snowe is, then, where femininity forms into an autonomous social category that can freely give and take of itself and its labor.

However, the differences between "England" and "Belgium" to which Leavis alludes do not only refer to an archaic religiosity but also to social elements that arise partly in response to the supernatural and to the growing sense of exterior forces encroaching on the domestic interior. As it turns out, the "nun" was a disguise that colonel Alfred de Hamal—a foreign count—donned, cunningly, to enter the girls' school citadel and court one of its English inhabitants. What Leavis remarks as "English probity" in conflict with "French *surveillance*" and "callous self-interest" translates into a semi-acknowledged penetration of the "English" familial by what is an emergent momentum of bureaucratic objectification and competitive, bourgeois individuation that Bronte attaches to "Belgium." Jennifer Ruth has demonstrated that Bronte's depiction of the proto-profession of teaching—which in both *Jane Eyre* and *Villette* develops as women's work—exhibits an ambivalent attempt to represent in marketable form a type of labor that had heretofore not been marketable. For Ruth, intellectual work like teaching in the nineteenth century had to be considered outside of the quantifiability of manual labor because of its irreducibility to time measurement and calculability, but, with the demise of a patronage system for art, intellectual products had to "embrace commerce" (284): intellectual work had to remain ungoverned by capital's determinants but still appropriable into capital's value system.[17]

The position of women's intellectual work as conflicted between the "natural" sensibility of household care and its production by circulating capital does affect women's bodies. In *The Professor*—Bronte's first novel, written in 1845–6 but only published posthumously in 1857, which many critics, including Leavis and Ruth, acknowledge as the rough draft of *Villette*—, the professor's love interest, Frances, changes from inaction and a docile corporeality—"a corpse-like lack of animation" (89)—in a state of ignorance to an absolute mobility—"wakened to life, . . . she . . . could move with vivacity and alertness" (109)—when engaged in learning, to the point of eroticizing her acquisition of knowledge. Such active bodily stimulation would instigate her potential for work: "The exquisite turning of waist, wrist, hand, foot, and ankle satisfied completely my notions of symmetry, and allowed a lightness and freedom of movement which corresponded with my ideas of grace" (109). Visibly revealing Frances's talents, these physical tensions between her domestic "quiescence" (89)—resistant to or even failing at market appropriations—and the physical energy of her marketable knowledge, propelled the girl's body into motion, indicating her potential as a teacher. In *Villette,* Lucy is similarly afflicted. Left alone at school, with no employment or intellectual engagement over the holidays, Lucy's body literally becomes "lifeless" (173), "wasting and wearing" (174), without strength and compared to death and burial. Consumed with depression, Lucy wanders around until her body becomes immobilized, stilled in sickness, and collapses.

In *Villette,* the contradiction between nonmarketable and marketable forms of work is constructed into Lucy's femininity through her relation to her work in the girls' school. In the middle of the novel, Lucy reencounters in Belgium some of her English relations. Now a count, M. de Bassompierre, formerly Mr. Home, considers sending his daughter Polly to the school where Lucy teaches. M. de Bassompierre praises Lucy for the way working affects her character and physicality, making her "one who had to guard and not be guarded; to act and not be served" (317). As Lucy herself reflects, work gives her independence: "I am spared the pain of being a burden to anybody" (317). M. de Bassompierre even admits that he would aspire to the same for his own daughter if she were ever afflicted by a sudden change in circumstance, due to economic fluctuation. Polly, on the other hand, clearly surprised that she saw no visible sign on Lucy to distinguish her as a working person, again surprised that Lucy works for income rather than philanthropy, quite openly pities Lucy for having to work.

The scene recognizes a historical shift in the relationship between women's work and marketability woven into a plotting of girls' education. By constructing women's work in a calculable form, the girls' school stages the development of service as labor. The school shows women's paid labor resulting from economic instabilities and need but also, more substantially, from character, and so shows the girls' school as producing a character—women's character in particular—*for* the market.

By indicating that women's skills need to be learned and acquired rather than just naturally assumed, by divulging that femininity is a set of particularized, variable, nation-based cultural forms that are physically embodied, girls' education exposes women's work, even when intended for training in domesticity and marriage, as made "visible," in Ruth's terms, "as productive labor" (280). Anxious about leaving her job as caretaker of the headmistress' children in order to give classes, Lucy's employment as a teacher demonstrates the fallacy of believing that intellectual engagement could not be subsumed in the calculus of labor (or even that it was not already subsumed): "I seemed to hold two lives," she notes to herself as she hesitates to enter the classroom, "—the life of thought, and that of reality; and, provided the former was nourished with a sufficiency of the strange necromantic joys of fancy, the privileges of the latter might remain limited to daily bread, hourly work, and a roof of shelter" (85). Her entry into the classroom proves her wrong, establishing that the work of the caretaker as well as the work of the thinker overlapped, and could be rendered countable in commodity form.

The Girls' School as Transgression

Modernism found in the girls' school a screen on which to project its break with the Symbolic. The girls' school would be a temporary transgressive disruption to institutional practice, usually indicated by a type of female sexuality that fell out with convention. The girls' school contained a secret world of girls, and its literary representation would reveal the titillating contents of its secrecy and pleasure only, by the end, for the institution to re-insert itself, ejecting or absorbing the nonconforming aspect. The girls' school thus resembles the Semiotic, the infantile corporeal fragmentation in Julia Kristeva's poetic language, where modern literature "attests to a 'crisis' of social structures and their ideological, coercive, and necrophilic manifestations" (1984: 15), a shattering of symbolic cohesion brought about through the "unceasing operation of the drives" (1984: 17) and primary processes. Both the girls' bodies and the consciousness developed in the girls' schools were thus external and even antagonistic to normalization. In Modernism, this antagonism disclosed the opening of the Symbolic, the places where representation unraveled and meaning-making was contested. The "outsider" status that the girls' school invoked was treated as a capacity for strategic calculation that contradicted institutional domestication. Because of their link to autonomous agency and economic potential, girls in these accounts are anything but "relational," impossible to silence or to still, and certainly not cooperative.

This excessiveness of girls' bodies and sexualities in girls' school plots arises when women's bodies refuse the symbolic economy of women in the division of labor. One might consider, for example, Michel Foucault's 1978 "retrieved memoir" *Herculine Barbin,* where once allowed to see inside the hidden fortress of the mid-nineteenth century convent school—or, as Barbin writes, with "the password for penetrating into the sanctuary" (106), "initiated into all those secret little details that are exchanged among persons of the same sex!!" (73)—, the reader learns its true secret to be that the headmistress has a penis. Once the girls' school reveals this secret, all sorts of unexpected misreadings and moral reversals ensue, as when, during a storm, Herculine, in shock from a clap of thunder, jumps out of bed into the palliative embrace of her teacher-nun Marie-des-Anges, only to find herself completely naked and visibly aroused. In the end, *Herculine Barbin* turns out to be a symbolic tragedy, where the institutional apparatuses of education, religion, law, and medicine are set in turmoil because the symbolic was wrongly assigned. This mis-assignation entailed, as one of its discomforts, "the prospect of being a *working woman*" (Barbin's emphasis; 20). Only when the designation "man" would be restored its functionality, in its proper body and for its proper job, is the convent institution again made secure.

Though such temporary suspension of sexual conventions seems stock-narrative for the Modernist girls' school plot, the sexual, symbolic, and physical disorientation is often a cover-narrative for a deeper symbolic disturbance caused by the challenge of women's productive work to the sexual division between paid and unpaid of labor-time. Often, the sexual-symbolic problem of the girls' school plot erupts in the uneasy intersections between girls and economic capacity, that is, through the merging of women's work with professional labor or, rather, of domestic, maternal socialization and caring functions with market value. In Lillian Hellman's classic 1934 play *The Children's Hour,* the young student Mary accuses her two teachers of "sinful sexual knowledge of one another" (58) and doing "bad things" (37) that can be read about in books, things she saw through a keyhole that delegitimate the women and their knowledge as teachers. Dorothy Sayers's 1936 mystery-thriller *Gaudy Night* takes place in the moment between the initial romantic encounter in *Strong Poison* and heroine Harriet Vane's final acceptance of Lord Peter Wimsey's proposal of marriage. Harriet returns to her *alma mater,* the women's college at Oxford, only to find herself the recipient of anonymous poison-pen letters and threatened with murder. The crime motive is eventually revealed to be the murderess' resentment over the loss of conjugal domesticity caused by the professionalization of women's labor where a woman took a man's place and got him fired: that "you must be expected to be thought a womanly woman" but "I fear the illusion was destroyed when you informed me that personal attachments must come second to public duties" (480) and that "it's women like you who take the work away from the men" (486).

In her girls' school novella *Fernhurst* (first written in 1904–5, revised in 1909, and published in 1925), Gertrude Stein makes clear the connection between the Modernist challenge to representational systems and anxieties over gendered bodies that changing gendered work roles make visible. The contradiction of the girls' school, Stein insinuates, is that women can acquire the learning of men without acquiring their economic capacity: "I am for having women learn what they can," the narrator voices-over, untrustworthily, "but not to mistake learning for action nor to believe that a man's work is suited to them because they have mastered a boy's education" (4). As women and men's working identities increasingly overlap despite the efforts of the narrative voice-over to keep them apart, the language of the telling, like desire, becomes increasingly unable to name the thing it is to reference.

It reverts often to flighty metaphors and allegoric phrasing. The characters themselves become phantasmal-seeming, with, for example, the main love interest Miss Bruce reflecting an "utter indifference to worldly matters" (20), a "dreamy detached nature" (20), and "a strange incapacity to touch the lives of others" (20). The story of a cerebral-minded chair of Philosophy who meets this cerebral-minded chair of English over coffee and a conversation about naïve realism unfolds into a cerebral language that never quite touches on sex but never quite gets away from it either. Their affair is announced through an evasion of the real: "The happiest period of their life was this. This worn ardent man and this worn ardent woman talked, thought, felt and deepened together" (34). The dean learns of the affair through the students' gossip, where the language of revelation self-consciously obscures and twists what it simultaneously reveals and does not reveal: "While the pair filled with desire and love of life were teaching each other new meanings day by day and the dean always with them her mind engaged with her many duties saw nothing of all this ardent life the whole story had become the gossip of the college" (35). What rescues the school from scandal is the dean's repeated assertion of authority that returns the English professor to her place while sending the Philosophy professor away to pursue a career of letters so that "Fernhurst"—the name of both the novella and the school—"was itself again" (49): reference was restored.

Such girls' schools narratives insinuate girls' sexuality to suggest that girls cannot identify with the symbolic or representational economy, that they are alienated, disjointed. The mismatching of school girls' sexualities with the symbolic economy brings into view the incongruities and temporal shifts between girls' bodies and subjectivities on the one hand and, on the other, gendered forms of labor. Dorothy Richardson's 1915 novel *Pointed Roofs* explores a subjective narrative of a British girl, Miriam, who, in face of her family's bankruptcy, is forced to take a position as a governess in a girls' school in Germany. The coming-of-age novel here is quintessentially a novel of exile, but the exile narrative is paralleled with a narrative exit of women's labor from the home. As Anita Levy points out, "the novel marshals all the elements of the nineteenth-century domestic novel [particularly those of the Brontes] to persuade us such fiction is no longer adequate to portray the nuances of female consciousness" (63). The novel presents the school as a social forum where domestic relations are replicated but only to show them, ultimately, as absent, symbolically empty: "She could only think that somehow she must be 'different'" (123), she muses upon learning that all the German girls were preparing for marriage, had, in fact, "already a complete outfit of house-linen" (123). The novel, Levy continues, represents domesticity in modernity as "deprived of the power to reproduce subjects fit to inhabit the world" (65). The novel ends when the French governess Mademoiselle is driven from the school because of some illicit sexuality that is referred to but never explicated.

In the second volume of *Pilgrimage, Backwater* (1916), Miriam quits her job and leaves the North London school where she has been teaching at the same time as she decides not to pursue amorous possibilities with a series of family acquaintances. The scenes of outings with groups of her sisters and friends that provide romantic openings slide between scenes at the school, suggesting a correspondence or an interweaving of the two roles, though Miriam's consciousness remains securely outside either, noting physical details or sensory impressions that break from the narrative of development expected in a coming-of-age thematic: "Sitting there, in the Perne boat, still an oar and determined to fling herself into the sea" (329), she dreams as she waits for her employers to respond to her announced departure, or "I must be going away from them" (287) she muses when she is supposed to be teaching, "The sunlight in this little schoolroom was telling her of other sunlights" (287). Miriam's consciousness is often overtaken by details, sounds and fragments of images, objects whose descriptions disrupt the forward motion of narrative time—distractions that separate her from events and objects in her objective surroundings, distractions that move, metonymically, toward others. What is important to Miriam, she says, is independence: "to get them to think for themselves, and that's much more important than whether they know facts" (333). In her final scenes at the school, Miriam develops an intimate interest in a student-teacher, Julia, whose musical talents, revealing her "alone with life and death" (345), were scorned by the girls. Miriam's departure from the school, like Mademoiselle's before her, reiterates her distance from the sexual and symbolic drama of family as it shapes girls' self-projections.

Colette is the writer who captures fundamentally the formation of girls' consciousness as economic capacity precisely in its resistance to institutional appropriation and regimentation. *Claudine in School* was published in 1900, under the assigned authorship of both Colette and her husband Willy (with Willy receiving the royalties), but written two years before by Colette alone. Colette's quasi-autobiographical *Claudine in School* imagines the girls' school as unambiguously and unabashedly in the business of training girls for the teaching profession, not predominantly for domestic or conjugal prospects. "Mother sent me to boarding-school," a student confesses, "father he didn't want it, he said I'd do best looking after the house like my sisters, and doing the washing and digging the garden" (143). Claudine's fellow students are not middle-class—since generally those families, she stipulates, send their daughters away to school—but rural working-class, "the daughters of grocers, farmers, policemen and, for the most part, of labourers; all of them none too well washed" (4). The meandering series of school-time adventures, comic pranks, and pointed caricatures, which Claudine calls a "diary" (5), progresses toward the teacher certification exams and, though, unlike her companions, Claudine has no intention of ever becoming a teacher, the exam becomes her chief mechanism for demonstrating her difference from the institution that controls and prepares her proper socialization unsuccessfully; like capital, Claudine cannot be regulated.

Much of the criticism on Colette has focused on Colette's version of transgressive sexuality and, in particular, her homoeroticism, as when she manipulates and secretly caresses her English tutor, the sensitive Aimée Lanthenay and then her sister Luce. The critics question if Colette contributes to what might be understood as "lesbian literature," as Claudine takes so much pleasure in sexual play with women, or if, as Elisabeth Ladenson disapprovingly reads in the prior criticism, "The schoolgirl homoeroticism of *Claudine à l'école* is, according to Colette's own account, the product of a marriage between her own imagination and Willy's imprecations to spice up her original text" (31), especially when the "lesbian content" is followed by other sexual capers that do not involve women. The critical impulse toward integrating identity formation and salacious content takes as a given that Colette's intention is to solidify an identity defined through sex and social place, when the texts ride on the cultural and class displacements that the educational context for girls demands. "I had immense pleasure," Claudine characterizes her impressions of a dictation, "in hearing these daughters of grocers, cobblers and policemen meekly reciting and writing down parodies of the Romantic School" (37). Behind Claudine's sexual escapades and impish tricks, the girls' school upsets the expected correspondence between knowledge, language, and class identity.

In fact, what makes Claudine exude sexuality and pleasure, even as she does not engage in direct sexual acts beyond playful kissing, is that she seems always to know more than she should and more than either the other characters or the reader. Claudine *uses* knowledge against its intended usage and its established value, like when she totes her mathematical aptitude, evading Mlle. Aimée's questions about square roots—"Give me fractions to reduce to the same denomination, similar triangles to construct... *cracks to verify*... anything, anything at all. But not that, oh *not* square roots" (77)—in order to get Aimée to leave the classroom in frustration and flee into the corridor where she could be fondled. Claudine makes clear that girls, when they acquire certain kinds of school knowledge, also acquire capacities that cannot be domestically restricted: "She's not a girl you'd overlook," Claudine hears Rabastens, one of the schoolmasters, characterize her, "with that hair flowing down her back and all around her and those very naughty brown eyes! My dear chap, I believe that girl knows more things she oughtn't to know than she does about geography!" (23). Patricia Tilburg sees the main intention behind Colette's capriciousness as a way of defining as "labor" certain knowledge-practices (particularly in relation to immaterial and aesthetic production) that had not, before, found such currency or acceptance, especially for women. Claudine's creativity could not be classified in the categories of value and calculation available. According to Tilburg, the girls' school during the Third Republic taught its students, including Colette, "a profound valorization of physical fitness and wage-paying craft labor that pushed uncomfortably against cultural dicta encouraging women to find moral contentment within the confines of a respectable marriage and home" (15). Colette was looking for new ways to capitalize her knowledge. What was counted as paid labor for women did not include craftwork or performance entertainment, the kind of intellectual work that Colette would later engage and try to legitimize as part of a paid economy.

The break between identity and knowledge that the girls' school plot provides creates out of Claudine the character of an autonomous thinker, aware of conventions of identity only to strategize an escape from them, to use them otherwise. "I know we shall be just as absurd in twenty years' time," laughs one of her examiners at her response to a question about troubadours, "but that idea of a troubadour with a helmet and a lyre!...Run away quick, child, you'll get a good mark" (147). Having an excess of knowledge, including sexual and artistic knowledge, lets Claudine play with accepted knowledge. This play sets young Claudine in opposition to the social identity of "woman," particularly in relation to the work that women of her class can do, and so also, therefore, in opposition to her class identity. As in *Fernhurst, Gaudy Night,* and *Herculine Barbin,* the break from the institutional and symbolic apparatus constructs her as a mobile economic variable, a working potential. Girls' school literature tied Modernism's symbolic breaks to the maturing of girls' economic rationality beyond domesticity, the formation of women's bodies and consciousnesses defined as autonomous interest.

Into the Wild

Greg Mortenson re-imagines the girls' school as participating in the work of exporting knowledge in order to defeat the impulse to violence erupting in Central Asia as "the terrorist threat."[18] For Mortenson, "Young women are the single biggest potential agents of change in the developing world— a phenomenon that is sometimes referred to as the Girl Effect...In military parlance, girls' education is a 'force multiplier...[T]he ripple effects of female literacy can be profound" (*Stones,* 13).[19] Mortenson is orchestrating a reversal in the girls' school genre. Now the home is the site of degeneracy, tragedy, and downfall for girls and a challenge to their potential as women rather than, as in *Villette,* the working life: "Unless that girl can land a job outside her home," Mortenson interprets the situation, "it is unlikely that her skills will translate into a substantial boost in her family's income…Aside from become a teacher, there are almost no jobs available for rural women outside the home" (*Stones,* 231). The girl in the process of getting educated is no longer oppositional as an expression of autonomous interest in a break of symbolic and institutional form. Rather, the girls' school is revamped as the symbolic form of imperial state power. The girls' school is what marches into the heart of darkness to tame the wilderness and bring the violent savages into the light of civilization. By releasing girls into the productive landscape, the girls' school is able to move the heretofore unproductive developing world into capitalizability. Merging into the girls' school narrative, imperialism appears as the heroic breaker of local conventions, like Colette.

In his attempts to build schools for girls in Pakistan and Afghanistan, Mortenson is—like capital—constantly coming up against obstacles, *fatwas,* Taliban attacks, local traditions, and resistances—just as Claudine comes up against teacher rules, examiners, and government superintendents—and mostly outsmarts them, avoids them, seduces them, or moves on. The goal of his efforts is made particularly clear when he returns to the village of Hushe in Pakistan and visits with Shakeela, one of the graduates of the Hushe School that Mortenson built, now attending the Government Girl's High School in Khaplu. This is one of the very few examples that Mortenson gives of his encounters with the students who did or would benefit from the schools he built, as most of his tales address the difficulties—physically, financially, and politically—of his own heroic exploits in the construction process. Shielding her face behind a shawl as her father compliments her, Shakeela is "poised and pretty at fifteen" (*Three Cups,* 207), and, smiling "confidently" (*Three Cups,* 207), informs the interviewer that she plans on attending medical school and becoming a doctor, though she is better in reading and language skills than in physics. As a doctor, Shakeela plans on going "to work wherever I am needed" (*Three Cups,* 208), being an "honor to the village" (*Three Cups,* 208) by serving others' needs. Mortenson's girls' schools are poised on the brink of the same cultural divisions faced by Lucy Snowe—between religious traditionalism and secular free-thought—and Harriet Vane—between women's professional, artistic, paid labor and family obligations, including care of the home. However, instead of women's capacity for professionalism appearing in the body as physical fitness and sexuality, as in Claudine, or as uncontrollable urges and protrusions, as for Herculine, it materializes as an immobile, retiring, and obedient body, both docile and inviting. The use of girls' school tropes in *Three Cups of Tea* and

Stones Into Schools invites expectations of literary themes relating to professional women who market their intellectual labor and then twists them into feel-good "success" stories of women who compliantly market their service labor for imperialism. That is, though taking its cue from historical literary representations of women's professionalism and its anxiously divided consciousness, Shakeela's inactive and retreating body—through which her role as "good student" and "nonterrorist" is attributed—extends the formulation of gender differences as learning differences-in-the-body through which the social scientific literature affirms help and cooperation in calculable terms as gendered labor-in-service.

The social scientific rendition of girls' bodies as exuding educational difference constructs girls' education as a site of intervention. Absorbed into imperialist narratives, such difference has a particular message: that girls educated for work marshal the economic capacity of imperialism's global power. The suggestion that developing countries are places of expanding girls' schooling carries with it the sense, from its literary legacy, that educated girls are poised between autonomous domestic economies and work that can be quantified as capital for imperialists: that is, that imperialism advances by capitalizing on girls' work and capacities, thereby making productive a heretofore unproductive and uncommodified territory. In the guise of girls' schools, imperialism's upsetting of traditions in the name of instituting its own Symbolic and division of labor looks like adventure and good, solid boys' play. The image of girls in schools redesigns ideologically the imperialist mission as adventurous men encountering helpless, eager, willing, docile, and compliant potential female laborers. Feminists have been right to air concerns that single-sex education could potentially perpetuate stereotypes that, in turn, promote inequalities and the unfair distribution of educational resources. Katha Pollit remarks that Mortenson's deception disappoints his Western readership who wants to think of US war policies as rescuing the peoples of the developing world from ignorance and deprivation. Mortenson's lie also keys into a desire that girls' difference makes visible the potential extension of markets into the heretofore unpaid working time of women globally. The adoption of such educational policy stereotypes—as feel-good success stories—into narratives about masculinity taming nature and violence in developing countries serves to make appealing and even comforting imperialism's expanding labor markets despite the cultural destruction, alienation, violence, and disenfranchisement such markets may and do cause to women.

CHAPTER 5

Gender Work: Feminism after Neoliberalism

In prior chapters, I have pointed to elements of the current organization of capital that depend on expanding paradigms of "women's work." By "women's work," I mean a type of labor that in the industrial age was considered domestic, affective, immaterial, or reproductive, and having to do with functions of "care" and socialization. Designated as a "separate sphere" outside of production, such sets of productive tasks were, traditionally in the twentieth century, represented as outside of public concern, not organized by the wage, not protected by the rights and privacy discourse of the liberal state (e.g., labor, security, safety, health, environmental, educative, etc.), formulated as "autonomous," and not connected to a package of guaranteed protections and benefits. Instead, they added "free time" to the productive process—time for which capital did not need to make an exchange, that in capital's terms was separate: pure excess or "surplus" that capital got for free. Currently, capital is demanding that all work fit such paradigms.[1]

As such forms of work have become increasingly prevalent as a structural tendency (even if not quite a statistical "norm"), transformations have taken place, as well, in cultural spheres. As capital has approached the limits of the universal expansion that Marx imagined for it, "women's work" has become one of the most viable sites where primitive accumulation can still operate by creating new zones for robust capitalizability and exploitation. As Angela McRobbie has remarked, "[I]t does not make sense to interrogate the post-Fordist field of immaterial labour without foregrounding gender" (2010: 69). To place "women's work" at the center of neoliberal globalization means to start to imagine femininity in particular as the framework for understanding processes of universalization under new forms of capital accumulation. In other words, the feminization of capital *is* its universalization.

Recently, philosophers Michael Hardt and Antonio Negri have described the current nexus of primitive accumulation through corporate growth and consolidation as expanding in ways that capitalize on the types of work women have done in private, and they also understand that women's work offers a particularly rich symbolic setting for thinking through biopolitical life-in-common. A "major trend," they write, in the composition of labor is the "so-called feminization of work," including "the rapid increase in the proportion of women in the wage market," but indicating "how 'women's work,' such as affective, emotional, and relationship tasks, is becoming increasingly central in all sectors of labor, albeit in different forms in different parts of the world" (2009: 133). This trend, they note, marks a "qualitative shift in the working day" (2009: 133), in jobs that are more temporally flexible, irregular, and informal while spatially more varied, mobile, and migratory, but also symptomizes a change in the content and type of work, toward greater focus on the production of bodies, subjects, communications, ideas, interactions, relationships, services, and types of socialization: "As the temporal division between work time and the time of life is becoming confused, the productive power of labor is being transformed into a power to generate social life. We can accept the term 'feminization' to indicate these changes as long as it is said with a bitter irony, since it has not resulted in gender equality or destroyed the gender division of labor" (2009: 133–134). This model suggests that all work tends toward a political frame appropriated from the private side of industrialization's separate spheres, maintaining its focus on the contents of a formerly reproductive and domestic production, becoming calculable so as to enter into relation with the wage. Such a relation to the wage impoverishes the work, in order to suck it of surplus. The perspective puts work formations like sweatshop labor and migrant domestic help at the conceptual center as these exemplify a form of work organization toward which all work is headed. All work, regardless of its demographics (that is the race, ethnicity, gender, sexual orientation, age, ability, etc. of its dominant practitioners) is equally abstracted in ways that direct it toward adapting to the formerly most privatized forms.[2]

What makes Hardt and Negri's work provocative for feminism is this: they understand class formations in the late twentieth and into the twenty-first centuries as tied to a process of economic feminization, and thus put to the forefront the indispensible claim that thinking femininity entails thinking class. With women making 78 cents on the dollar globally (and even lower for minority women and women on the margins), gender alone is an entrenched source of surplus. Furthermore, as well as understanding femininity as a mechanism whereby the new division of labor under neoliberalism can be organized to extract surplus, Hardt and Negri also put economic feminization at the forefront of envisioning and theorizing the force of resistance against capital presently. I therefore disagree with Lee Quinby's assessment that Hardt and Negri's philosophical enterprise exhibits "gender-blindness" (240), or that its subjects of resistance are "masquerading as a gender-free embodiment of universal values" (242), in its centralizing of violence, its romanticization of opposition, and its insistence that revolutionary change must be total. On the contrary. Hardt and Negri's work first emphasizes that neoliberalism is a violent system precisely because it has built class discourse from gender in different ways than industrialism's separate spheres did, in part by flattening the differences between production and reproduction, and turning what was once the free work of labor socialization in the private sphere into a serviceable principle of exploitation: the production of surplus time. Hardt and Negri then project a liberated future by projecting a total liberation of "women's work" (though Quinby is right to remark that repressive power is more marked and intense against women and their work, she is not right that things as they are determine things as they have to be: the "pressing and quite particular needs of women" (241) underlie Hardt and Negri's construction of a future that is better). By reinserting labor into poststructuralism's theories of difference, Hardt and Negri reveal some of the contradictions and vital, productive questions that arise in suturing class onto gender in a neoliberal age, questions that differ substantially from those surfacing in response to the interweaving of class and gender evident under the assumptions of Fordist culture analyzed in chapter 1.

Hardt and Negri's idea that left philosophies need to concentrate on the production of subjects as much as, if not more than, the production and commodification of objects, evolved out of a feminist interest in the 1960s, in such writers as Julia Kristeva, on socialization and language as increasingly integral to the construction of identities, social, symbolic, and economic relations. They also relied on contributions, from such feminist thinkers as Mariarosa Dalla Costa, Silvia Federici, and Selma James (for example), on social reproduction. They promote a radical transformation of the times, processes, and organization of work as contingent on a radical transformation in the work relations of the traditional family and the traditionally gendered body: "These barbaric deployments work on human relations in general, but we can recognize them today first and foremost in corporeal relations and configurations of gender and sexuality. Conventional norms of corporeal and sexual relations between and within genders are increasingly open to challenge and transformation... The will to be against really needs a body that is completely incapable of submitting to command. It needs a body that is incapable of adapting to family life, to factory discipline, to the regulations of the traditional sex life, and so forth" (2000: 215–216). Hardt and Negri attribute to second-wave feminist theory their interest in collective bodies, bodies in revolt, and "the theme of life itself on . . . center stage" (2009: 26): "[o]nly the standpoint of bodies and their power," they conclude from the lessons they glean from feminism, "can challenge the discipline and control wielded by the republic of property" (2006: 27).

In fact, Hardt and Negri's analysis of capital draws on a construction of time and value as separable from the political domination of the means of production and circulation, but still internal to them, in a way that is indebted to feminist critiques of the private sphere. Negri's earlier philosophical contributions, for example, have theorized a split or an event where an emergent form of "use value"—formerly attributed to work in precapitalist, domestic, and traditional settings that capital later subsumed—and "surplus value"—or work-time appropriated by capital "for free"—explode production from within. This happens when "living labor," or the processes of the production of life, revolts against "dead labor," or the accumulated productive forces that give it power. "[U]se value is nothing other than the radicality of the labor opposition, than the subjective and abstract potentiality of all wealth, the source of all human possibility . . . [T]he workers' opposition, the proletarian struggle, tries continually to broaden *the sphere of non-work,* that is, the sphere of their own needs" (1991: 70–71)—that is, of worker reproduction and "women's work." As this "sphere" of "radicality"— of "nonwork"—takes on features autonomous to production and to the wage, it becomes the hinge or transition between intensified exploitation and an opening toward difference.

Ironically, perhaps, given that women's labor seems so central to this picture Hardt and Negri give of "use value" in neoliberal labor regimes and so integral to the antagonism against capital that arises in capitalism's historical course, it is worth remarking that there has been a relative scarcity of feminist interest in Hardt and Negri's critique of globalization.[3] Notably, Angela McRobbie reads in Hardt and Negri "a failure to foreground gender, or indeed to knit gender and ethnicity into prevailing concerns with class and class struggle" (2010: 60). McRobbie understands Hardt and Negri as permitting "no space at all for reflecting on the centrality of gender and sexuality in the post-Fordist era" (2010: 62) as a result of their assuming that "gender is no longer a 'problem'" (62). Whereas they abstract relations of everyday life outside the workplace as the new site for relations of production, they favor describing class itself as envisioned through urban disenchantment or shallow creativity, marginalizing the question of gender within the formation of political subjectivities. Though the multitude seems like a broader, less nationally based rendition of what an older left called "class," it shares, for McRobbie, the white masculinist privilege of this older form of class, drawing its roots through industrial militancy and other conflicts within the purview of the factory. Women become subordinated to or invisible within this larger abstraction. Though I agree with this critique, it assumes women as always and only the particular whereas Hardt and Negri, in their methods of abstraction, experiment with the idea that all workers are women now. That is, neoliberalism abstracts labor to the point where it becomes only woman (again, this would be a direction where the social is headed rather than a present reality, a tendency rather than a norm). This does not necessarily disregard gender or fail to foreground it as much as it reconfigures gender along new axes of difference: the body that becomes new in neoliberalism is sexed as woman. There are definite problems in this perspective, some of which I hope to draw out, but I also think there might be value found in giving Hardt and Negri their day in court and trying to imagine how this plays out.

An industry of criticism has developed responding to other aspects of Hardt and Negri's oeuvre. Many have discerned that Hardt and Negri's prognostications about the contemporary developments of capital did not exactly come to pass, or that Hardt and Negri have neglected vital components of the contemporary economic situation, and many others have detected that Hardt and Negri's readings of their philosophical progenitors have often taken quite a bit of license. Their omissions, expound their critics, distort their views of the North-South divide, the population of the workforce, and the histories of oppositional political activity. Giovanni Arrighi accurately reproaches Hardt and Negri for foretelling the smoothing out of global power differentials into one immanent plane of production, and consequently, against the empirical record, the narrowing of the Third World/First World income divide: "Indeed, all available evidence shows an extraordinary persistence of the North-South income gap as measured by GNP per capita" (32). Ellen Meiksins Wood chides Hardt and Negri for proposing that the cure for the ills of capitalism should be to intensify its reign: "[T]he general lesson we are supposed to draw from it is that capitalist globalization is an irresistible force and that opposition to what is practically a law of nature is futile and counterproductive" (61–62). For Wood, Hardt and Negri, through their embrace of globalization, pronounce the end of the nation-state and the concentration of power (against the historical evidence), and insist on the contingent infiltration of capital into every aspect of life. Rather than freeing up an oppositional culture as they forecast, these elements of Hardt and Negri's prophecies guarantee, for Wood, the end of resistance: "[F]or all its insistence on the possibilities of insurrection..., it is much less persuasive as a call to opposition than as an argument for the futility of oppositional politics" (63).

The criticisms of Hardt and Negri do not stop at challenging their descriptions of capitalism, highlighting the ethical implications, or disputing the limitations to their thinking on resistance. Also, Hardt and Negri are frequently and often vehemently disparaged for misapplying theoretical ideas in ways that distort the historical context, often with dangerous consequences. Timothy Brennan has reproached Hardt and Negri for combining Marxist orthodoxy with a contradictory embrace of Deleuzian and other poststructuralist theory that allows for a picking-and-choosing between convenient (even if contradictory) fragments of historical events and a reading history "as a shop window filled with texts of glossy revolutionary allure" (114). The risks in this theoretical stance play out mostly in the context of the Italian workerist movement of the 1970's, with its Catholic overtones in themes of redemptive return and spiritual unification attributable, claims Brennan, to Negri's training in Italian Catholic Universities of the 1950's. The affiliation with workerism (*operaismo*) meant that the "will to be against"—to refuse work—that Hardt and Negri develop at the moment of revolutionary rupture "was poised not only against the state but also the traditional trade unions" (103), and the concept of "immaterial labor" that they see as opening the formation of a "general intellect" "signal[s] nothing more than a reference to the symbolic analysts of the information economy" (103) that calls upon millennial convictions of US economic primacy. Alex Callinicos, meanwhile, has called Negri's projections about workers' movements and wage independence "among the most foolish and irresponsible statements to be produced by a social theorist with the kind of reputation now enjoyed by Negri "(188). Callinicos disagrees vehemently with Negri's reducing economic relations to politicized domination as well as with his celebration of a "general intellect" or a "collective worker," interpreting such misunderstandings of Marx as, in part, contributing to the tragic defeat of the unions and the splintering of the left in Italy. The list of shattering criticism goes on.

Despite such debates over the accuracy of Hardt and Negri's work in empirically describing this new phase of capitalism, or the controversies over how well Hardt and Negri have understood the potentials for unification and resistance among a rising working class, or the disagreements about their readings of the philosophical or historical record, I believe that feminism has an interest in working through Hardt and Negri's texts. In fact, some part of the critics' objections may take on different appearances, stresses, and faultlines (though do not disappear) if the gender of Hardt and Negri's critique of capitalism is taken into account. Hardt and Negri want to tease out of political and philosophical traditions a way of conceiving of a resistance born out of the present but not beholden, for its definition and its character, to its abstraction through the wage and its reliance on the existing means of production: in other words, as autonomous from capital's current configuration. In this, they read "women's work" as an empiricism that breaks the hold of the empirically present.

Like Hardt and Negri, feminism has long been interested in understanding the production of subjectivities at the limits of current cultures of production, as valued and constituted differently. Hardt and Negri's focus on "women's work" as offering the descriptive vocabulary for neoliberal economic relations leads to the construction of a feminized subject that is, at the same time, universalizing. In other words, whereas Simone de Beauvoir defined femininity as particularity,[4] Hardt and Negri are calling attention to the universal feminine, brought to bear in response to the neoliberal privatization of labor, raising the question, then, of whether the universal is the same universal once feminized. They interpret this new sense of femininity as becoming visible in many of neoliberalism's emphases, stresses, and developing global cartographies: biopolitics and life, use value, immaterial labor, the split between surplus labor and necessary labor, an ontology that is at the same time transitional and generative, living labor, socialization and cooperation.[5] In all these areas, Hardt and Negri understand neoliberalism's privatizing functions as marking out a collective horizon, both as social capital and then as the collective worker. Through this analytic, they envision women's immaterial labor or labor of reproduction as universal or disembodied consciousness that, in as much as it has become central to production, leads to a break with capital.

The question for feminism remains: in what sense do Hardt and Negri augur the realization of feminist aspirations in the freeing up of women and their bodies from their symbolic relegation to private life and reproductive work outside of production? Or rather, in what sense does the universalization of the feminine symbolic promote the intensification of worker exploitation grounded in the further alienation, marginalization, and domestication of women? How does Hardt and Negri's rendition of capital's subsumption of reproduction into production differ, in degree and in kind, from the appropriation of women's labor into industrialization that Marx portrayed? In what sense does the general tendency toward making all work into "women's work" provide an opportunity for more dense exploitation than ever before imaginable, and in what sense does it outline the conditions for a transition to something other than the current unacceptable social relations? As neoliberalism seems to answer to some of feminism's most radical claims toward the abolition of the private sphere and the merging of reproduction into production, do Hardt and Negri expose feminism's failings and force its repositionings, or do they indicate that feminism all along was predicting the turn to "women's work" as fundamentally reconfiguring the capitalist playing field in ways integral to neoliberal processes and, then, to their annihilation? As Alberto Toscano comments, "It is not impertinent to ask, for example, if the destruction of the public-private barrier, lauded by Negri, is not actually in the first instance a repressive and exploitative tool, rather than an augur of red dawns to come" (114). At the same time, Hardt and Negri demand that we ask, if the red dawns do come, what they might look like?

"Real Subsumption" and "Women's Work"

One of Negri's significant contributions to Marxist thought has been the central part played by "real subsumption" in his analysis of capitalism's current phase. In contrast to "formal subsumption," which imagines capital accumulation as a progressive abstraction of diverse working forms as it grasps at the multiple branches of production, "real subsumption" is "socially constituted surplus value, the exploitation of society under the control of capital" (1991: 92), where profit "is determined by its essential capacity to be measured against the social working day" (1991: 92). "Real subsumption" is the form capital takes when production absorbs reproduction. It is therefore the setting for "the so-called feminization of work," that is, where "women's work" integrates into capital as an internal antagonism, marking a split. (In sections that follow, I show, as well, how this equivalency between capital and "women's work" influences how Hardt and Negri formulate their analysis of "biopolitics" and "immaterial labor" within their vision of life, power, and resistance, and ask what this means for feminism.)

"Real subsumption" is not an historical moment or an endpoint toward which capitalism has evolved; instead, "real subsumption" is a descriptor of capitalism as it is now which has always been part of its social inside even if now it is more fully realized. Yet, neither is "real subsumption" a telos; rather, it is a definition—the force that capital has, by definition, to turn everything into itself. "Real subsumption" is a transitional figure that depends on capital's push to reduce necessary labor time (the time that remains outside of productive time, or reproductive time) to zero and the expansion of surplus value, or profitability, over everything: "Real subsumption means the complete realization of the law of value... [I]n real subsumption... all labour is reduced to mere quantity, to time. Before us we have only quantities of time. Use-value, which in *Capital* was still given as separation from, and irreducible to, value *tout court,* is here absorbed by capital" (2003: 27).

Once exchange value has taken over the entire social field, or all social life has become the "social factory," the forces of primitive accumulation find no external spaces for expansion, and all labor is socialized by capital as the whole of social life: "it no longer produces through factories alone, but makes the whole of society work for its own enrichment; it no longer exploits only workers, but all citizens; it does not pay, but makes others pay it to command and order society. Capitalism has invested the whole of life" (2003: 136). "Real subsumption" is based on the idea of the factory once it is no longer spatially enclosed. The "social factory," Hardt and Negri later say, where the forces of discipline break out beyond the factory walls and move into the totality of the social,[6] demands a different formation of labor that slips away from the gendering implicit in factory work: "The dictatorship of the factory over society, its position at the crossroads of all processes of the formation of value, and therefore the objective centrality of directly productive (male, manual, and waged) labor are all disappearing" (1994: 280). Such a formulation raises this question: what elements in Negri's philosophical-political system require that "real subsumption" passes into history in the guise of the "so-called feminization of work"—that is, why is the "so-called feminization of work" the carrier of the historical construction of "real subsumption"?

"Real subsumption" signifies the development, within certain aspects and movements of the system, of a present crisis through which the future is setting its course, most notably: (1) politics has redrawn the field of economic transactions of time (labor power) into a system of unified or collective command (money) beyond time-measure.[7] Money turns time into collective capital, or *command*; (2) *use-value* (or labor before the exchange of labor power measured by time, that is, labor that factory time does not yet but eventually will count and appropriate) is no longer independent from capital, and in its immeasurability, also takes collective form[8]; (3) constant capital, technology, fixed capital, or the State has a decreasing need for variable capital or *living labor*, freeing up living labor (which has become collective and multiple). This is related to the break-down in the division between manual and mental labor, the first class division remarked by Marx, as the body and the imagination merge into the productive process, meaning that ideas become productive, corporeal and concrete at the same time. As knowledge and the expansion of knowledge returns to the worker, the imagination cannot be captured in the time-analysis of older forms of labor power;[9] (4) *circulation* (reproduction) is no longer distinguishable from production.[10] Whereas Marx theorized circulation as the cessation or temporal pause between cycles of production, in "real subsumption," the time lag of circulation is reduced to zero[11]; (5) therefore, production and reproduction (or the social) become interchangeable (use-value and circulation have taken on the role of the social from within production). Productivity is, for Negri, ontological like God (or, like Spinoza's God) but also at the same time material (both rational and empirical), as the human mind that expands eternally through the ability of the human body (labor) to create reality, in part by reproducing itself, by self-generating as its own cause (origin); and 6) this creates antagonism, war, or crisis, where two different, nonmediating, irreducible, asymmetrical and opposing conceptions of time, or class formations, separate (rather than unify or synthesize): "To me it seems that, in the history of thought, the hypothesis of a collective constitution of time as an operation antagonistic to the spatial and mediatory conception of time, becomes an increasingly observable element—one that is always characteristic of revolutionary thought" (2003: 56). In other words, the difference between integrated productive time (measured time) and reproductive time ("women's work," "use value," social time, or collective time) becomes an antagonism that figures as class conflict within production.

Negri's reconfiguration of time in "real subsumption" does not only break down the division between work and the social (between production and consumption) but also develops social time, with its connection to reproduction and socialization, as the time of production (one might think of the dominance, in political discussions on economic issues, of thematic of health care, education, insurance, and reproductive rights). Overall, by reducing the time of circulation to zero, production extends over the entire social field, so that the distinction between spaces of consumption-circulation and spaces of production disappears, and exploitation enters into all relations and levels of socialization. "In real subsumption," Negri explains, "capital presents itself as capitalist society, and hence as tautology of life and value, of time and labour. The relations of magnitude between the constitutive parts of the working day are imperceptible" (2003: 67). Production and life coincide (2003: 42).[12] Examples abound, from new professional standards making it easier to work from home and thus blurring the line between the time of work and the time of leisure, to the commodification of formerly social functions, from child care and elderly care to house cleaning and food preparation. As well, as Hardt and Negri never tire of pointing out, life itself has become a primary target for the creation of new markets, from life cycle promotions and nutrition to vitamins, sexual enhancers, muscle enhancers, fertility technologies, psychotropics (both legal and illegal), energy drinks, genomes, cell tissue, chromosomes, amino acids, and pharmaceuticals (both legal and illegal), health care and other health management, insurance and other risk-management, and body forms, including cosmetic surgery, exercise regimes, and prosthetics. In addition, work itself has in some instances entered a commoditified life-cycle, through the selling of business trip planning, career advising, and five-star elite services for temporary care and entertainment in urban financial centers as well as the privatization of many professional training certification functions, teaching and nursing most notably. What is more, the instruments of production have changed from the large-scale machinery of industrialization through which Marx marked history to cognitive innovations that can be traded and exchanged: know-how, communications, language processes, symbols, and imaginings, often given shape in cooperative networks of information. This movement of capital into life itself is highly politicized.

The replication of production as reproduction in Negri's sense of "real subsumption" means not only that capital begins to take on a metaphoric shape that resembles what women do but also that capital does what women do—the generation, socialization, and production of subjects—in their place. This approximation between reproduction and production—that is, between capital and "women's work"—means that as capital moves increasingly toward privatizing the social (e.g., measuring it, counting it, turning it into value and exchange), the social is increasingly excessive to it, a tendency increasingly resistant to the measure of the private.[13] Life refuses systems and systematicity. Though politics is reorganized for the purpose of controlling life, life itself escapes total subsumption, never quite stabilized within capital's categorical measurements. Just as a constitution can never capture in code and abstraction the energies that founded it and that continually surge up to overtake its limits, life itself poses the force of its multiplicity against the unifying constraints of profit's calculations. Capital's self-reinvention in "real subsumption," that brings it closer to the structural and symbolic form of "women's work" means that capital dons women's narratives as life-forms; this becoming-reproduction of production accounts for capital's separations from itself, its antagonisms, shifts, and schisms.

I read Negri as describing, in "real subsumption," a concept of capital saturated by a form of "women's work" based on industrialism's structural and symbolic placement of domestic labor in the "autonomous" private sphere, separated from production. As I detail in chapter 1, Marx explained capital as always in the process of integrating into production a domestic sphere that could never, in the final analysis, be integrated completely. This taking-up of capital as "women's work" generates the "so-called feminization of work" that Hardt and Negri interpret as underlying neoliberalism, and its excess—its resistance to capitalization—as what catapults the transition. "Real subsumption," in short, is the final universalization of capitalism that occurs with production overtaken by reproductive processes, when production assumes the shape, movement, cooperation, and creativity that permeate the totality of social life, becoming the equivalent of life (and therefore the equivalent of "women's work"): "all commodities have become services, all services have become relations, all relations have become brains, and all brains form part of the common" (2003: 177). That is, as the means of production assume the form of the social, social relations are themselves commodities. Yet, this transformation of capital's organization along the lines of "women's work" challenges, from the inside, capital's simultaneous demand for measuring, quantifying, and exchanging everything, creating destructive antagonisms.

"Real subsumption" actually *needs* "women's work"—the work of socialization and the socialization of production—to make sense as Negri renders it. This is because Negri's treatment of the issue depends on a fundamental separation between aspects of capital, a separation that tends to rely on the increasing feminization of its modes and operations. Linked to antagonism, this separation is adapted from Jean Baudrillard's descriptions of contemporary society as simulation—that is, that reproduction, copy and consumption have merged into production and overtaken it, that the objects of production have become immaterial images or symbols of a social reality that is divided off [14]: "The spark of production, the violence of its stake no longer exists. Everybody still produces, and more and more, but work has subtly become something else:...A demand exactly proportional to the loss of stake in the work process" (47). Negri sees this separation of production from work and workers in terms of generation: that is, the rupture between capital and labor forms into a new instance of working subjectivity that cannot be synthesized, appearing as an innovation. Generation is, above all, "women's work": "Thus creating is not something at the limits of being; rather it is something which gives birth. Can one say that generating is not the same as creating?" (2011: 93). The separation (transition) hinges on "women's work": it understands capital as involved in direct production of human beings, but human beings as lives that are transforming into new types of potentials and values that escape total appropriation in capital's socialization processes and measurement systems.

As reproduction *merged into* production, separation complicates Negri's analysis of the State under neoliberalism. He does not advocate, assume, or predict the end of the nation-state in the "free market's" presumption of the sovereign governing role, as Timothy Brennan and Ellen Meiksins Wood (among others) interpret it, as a "freeing up" of desire and autonomous subjectivity (though this reading of the "multitude" is certainly possible). The State is also, for Negri, composed of a set of simulations[15]: juridical and procedural functions, functions of business enterprise and social accumulation, that reference other simulations of civil society through legal abstractions in order to create a sense of balance, while no longer recognizing in themselves the contradictions, instabilities, and play "from below," nor the explosion of worker creativity as the social real. "[I]n no case," writes Negri, "does the constituent subject submit itself to the static and constricting permanence of constitutional life" (1999: 324–325). As the State devolves toward an antidemocratic symbolic of self-representation (or, command), the economy delinks from effective demand, as we can witness in policies that cut away at workers' spending power—cuts to salaries, benefits, and supports as well as global austerity measures. The juridical stimulation that composes the State ensures stability "by avoiding or excluding any external inputs" (Hardt and Negri, 1994: 233), managing exploitation, circulation, and the extraction of surplus value through command rather than through incorporating, inte-grating, absorbing, and synthesizing. As the landscape of the "social factory," the State extends over the whole field of accumulation by posing itself as an unmediated unity.[16] The State is a totality and the social is the same totality, in the same time and space, instigating a divide. Separation means that the gap between capital (or the State, which amounts to the same) and labor is no longer a space of communication, negotiation, compromise, or synthesis (like a labor union or a welfare system) but instead irresolvable, that nothing remains in common, and that the only recourse for independent labor is to pose itself as a total alternative to the total constituted machinery (the "dead labor" or simulation) of the State.

"Real subsumption" is not dialectical, says Negri's account of separa-tion: capital no longer functions by incorporating external forms of labor (as in the type of primitive accumulation described by Marx) but rather "labor processes themselves are born within capital" (Hardt and Negri, 1994: 224). With the end of the dialectic, workers are also less necessary to capital—necessary labor time (the time of the worker's reproduction) is reduced toward zero, "labor becomes invisible in the system" (Hardt and Negri, 1994: 259)—because of the expansion of technology, financializa-tion, and the "deficit of politics" (Hardt and Negri, 2994: 237). At the same time, capital represents itself as less connected to them:

In the *specifically* capitalist mode of production, in the real subsumption, labor—or even production in general—no longer appears as the pillar that defines and sustains capitalist social organization. Production is given an objective quality, as if the capitalist system were a machine that marched forward of its own accord, a capitalist automaton. To a certain extent, this image is the fulfillment of a long-standing dream of capital— to present itself as separate from labor, to present a capitalist society that does not look to labor as its dynamic foundation, and thereby to break the social dialectic characterized by the continual conflict between capital and labor. (1994: 226)

For Negri, the State, its apparatuses, and its ideologies are not so much diminished to give place to the market. Rather, they are formalized and abstracted as capital itself so that together they become an envelope, excluding from the State's constitution the active creative subjectivities from which it builds its regimes of profitability. This is less about the disappearance or "withering away" of the State than about the devolution of its representational powers, as it maintains rule through violence and command. The split between the State and civil society, or the end "of negotiation between capital and labor" (Hardt and Negri, 1994: 240), or the displacement of the social contract, takes form, for Negri, in reference to a reconstitution of industrialism's historic split between men's and women's labor spheres within the future plane of production. "Men's work" takes the guise of the symbolic constitution of the State, whereas "women's work" assumes the separation:

[T]he production and reproduction of the world have always been separate. Man produced and woman reproduced. The sector of the economy that concerned production was the prerogative of men; the one that concerned reproduction was the prerogative of women. It is only in postmodernity, when work becomes intellectual and affective, that production and reproduction cease to be divided and come to constitute a circular whole. Living labour belongs to everyone. It is in order to signal this metamorphosis that becomes manifest in the becoming-common of labour, that one laconically says: living labour has become-woman. (2003: 224–22)

As labor is relegated to the State's outside and takes on features of cooperative organization and the social, that is, as production integrates reproduction and the collective creativity of its work, the "becoming woman" of living labor underlies its refusal, its separation, and its autonomy.

Use-Value, Constituent Power, Ideology, and the Time of Innovation

Hardt and Negri's accounts of neoliberalism as "real subsumption" show that gender does not disappear under neoliberalism. On the contrary, neoliberalism needs gender to substantiate its values in production and, in fact, to organize production as a whole. Additionally, gender as production performs a type of ontological function: "women's work" is what gives production a multiplying force, a constituent power that capital needs for self-valorization but cannot fully reduce to its own temporal measure (cannot reduce to its representations of equivalency: to money, calculation, and the like). This reading seems to depend on an essentialism, as "women's work" is tied to a corporealization, and women's bodies seem to symbolize as biologically productive, as generative. Yet, underlying this seeming essentialism is an antifoundational ontology of production. Though production is usually seen as objectified, as an empirical situation materialized and congealed through repetitions and technologies (as dead labor), Negri contests that it must be understood as subjective, and, as a subjective structure, production is neither definable nor containable within a particular historical frame or a historicized body: it is neither singular nor can it be generalized. As Negri cites Marx in the *Grundrisse*: "production also is not only a particular production. Rather, it is always a certain social body, a social subject, which is active in a greater or sparser totality of branches of production" (1991: 44; *Grundrisse,* 86). Production is a social idea. *"The category of production,"* concludes Negri, "in the essential terms which distinguish it, and with the totality which characterizes it—a veritable social articulation of reality—*can only be constituted as a category of difference,* as a totality of subjects, of differences, of antagonism" (1991: 44; Negri's emphasis). Inflected through history and connected in particular to a history of changing social relations and changing material realities, production—even generation (reproduction)— is mobile and multiple, partial, and total, and the identities called in to inhabit the symbolic of the generative form are themselves transitional. As production becomes real in relation to the production of subjects and bodies, it acts and mobilizes through the material production of gender. In this, Negri's ontologies of production resemble Judith Butler's theory of gendered performativity that I analyzed in chapter 3, in that production is always the production of gender *and* the production of the social through gender. In Negri's neoliberal/postmodern world of "real subsumption," all work is on its way to becoming "women's work."

This formulation of all production as reproduction explains capital's intensification at the same time as the unsustainability of capitalist methods of exploitation: its implosion. Critics have been divided about Hardt and Negri's stance that this hardening of capital's systems conditions the forms of its dissolution. Eugene Holland, for example, wants to divide Hardt and Negri's philosophical modeling of capital onto two planes: the virtual or potential concepts and the historical actualization. The virtual concepts "provide a certain way of addressing the problem, with the aim of eventually solving it" (126) particularly by "the role of (nonlabor) markets" (125) (e.g., unemployment) as a challenge to the sovereignty of imperialist orders.

Less appealing and less likely for Holland is its realization, for which there is no evidence.[17] On the other hand, Timothy Brennan and Ellen Meiksins Wood adamantly scold Hardt and Negri for envisioning the potential for radical challenge as nothing less than a deeper immersion in the most heinous aspects of appropriation, accumulation, and control. The ambiguities and shiftiness of Hardt and Negri's depictions of capital's work could be seen as reflecting neoliberalism's own ambiguities about the role of gender in production, particularly in the way neoliberalism simulates gender as *the* ideal that structures its system of exploitation from within.

"The so-called feminization of work" appears as "real subsumption" in the following ways: the overtaking of productive process by reproductive organization, the suppression of independent "use value," the need for capital to diminish "necessary labor time" (reproductive time) to zero, the conversion of the bulk of production toward social relations and life-forms, the appropriation of social time as the time of production, and the transformation of commodity-objects into circulating symbolic forms exchanged as value (commodity production as ideological (immaterial) production, or as the production of affective social relations). To take "use value" as an example: "use value" was the standpoint of separation from the dominant tendencies of productive capital as Marx describes primitive accumulation and then industrialization. It usually pointed to a traditional or pre-technological form of life prior to capitalism, often centered on domestic life, with a division of labor organized in accordance with familial hierarchies. Knowledge, including technological knowledge, was traditional and belonged to the worker. This separation or temporal autonomy can even be seen, Negri notes, in Kant's Critiques, where the "private" interior of the subject, governed by time, has no correspondence with the exterior defined through space, extension, and measurement. In industrial capitalism, too, the "time of life" can be seen as outside the spatialization of commodity circulation, as "autonomous," domestic, private, or familial life where subjects are made. However, in "real subsumption," "use value" cannot be exteriorized because production is identical with social time, and social time is the means of extraction of social value.[18] Instead of being measured in terms of the time-units extractable through the productive process—for example, measured as a quantity of objects manipulated through an assembly line—, "use value" appears as a quality: an idea, form of life, language, affectivity, relationship that production needs to valorize itself. "Use value," Negri says, "is creative" (1991: 73); it constitutes the solid subjectivity of the worker, its [the worker's] autonomous ability to extend its needs and desires—its reproduction—against capital's profitability. In other words, "use value" is the collective social time within the process of production: the time of socialization, of the production of subjects. Capital absorbs "use value" as necessary for production even as "use value" tends toward autonomy.

Within Negri's analysis of "use value," "women's work"—like Kant's subjectivity—is what refuses synthesis or mediation. Negri speaks of "real subsumption" as a mode of time, a "tendency" (rather than as an empirical instance), where the "after" is already taking place as separate, without recourse to the "before," as its own constitution. Replacing the classical Marxist moment of the transition, where time is negated and overcome in its forward projection, the "tendency" is a nexus of specific features and social relations embedded in the present modes of production but antagonistic to them, and that open toward a general realignment, developing as a separation[19]: the "what is *to come*" as it gestates, a restlessness of the future that materializes in the present and resists it.

The analoguing of historical transition as a pregnancy is not just expressive or metaphoric but rather a serious dispute with Heideggerian phenomenology: Negri reads "Being towards death" as a closing down of new rationality, a negativity,[20] whereas for Negri, capital poses limits that generate autonomous subjectivities, actions to-be-born, a creativities. This orientation develops out of his reading of Spinoza, where God is ontological and total but still productive, still versatile, active, and multiple because of its connection to life—God is everything but still expanding because "the intensity of the first ontological passage has reached its maximum pregnancy" (1991A: 50). Negri explains this as "the opposite of the dialectical method" (1991A: 50) because a new ontology—or attribute (human consciousness, or method)—exists as infinite *and* as part of God but also as its own cause and its own foundation: "The attribute is the same thing as the substance, and yet its difference is stated in relation to the intellect" (1991A: 57). Two temporalities exist at once, and the fact that one has to be part of the other does not mean that they must not be separate.

Though Negri says that Spinoza abandons the "attribute" in his future work, its "pregnancy" reappears at moments when human politics, history, and reason are operating as an ontology on a separate plane from divine ontology: as an interruption or a rupture. Sometimes he'll use a different term, as when here he uses "mode" to imply the same sort of temporal hinge as "attribute": of an afterwards whose ontology is already present: "Reconstructing a general horizon that maintains and develops the ontological pregnancy of the mode, the power of the world, implies a series of completely new phenomenological and critical instruments" (1991A: 84). Talking about the imagination and its role in interpreting Scripture, Negri sees the "attribute" or the "mode" as pregnant with a future collective imagination, "The restoration of natural light [by which Scripture illuminates its own historical origins, or constitutive force] is a historical and human operation, and it is at the same time an excavation of reality that reveals the ontologically pregnant collective force of this human conquest, a conquest that renews being" (1991A: 101). Negri evokes "pregnancy" when historicity or phenomenological man is producing its own separate reality, an experience both inside the present and outside of calculable time (as a new collective time): "[I]t [politics] is an ontologically pregnant horizon of the continuous incursions of power (*potentia*) toward constitution, of the intersections and tensions and antgonisms that a physics of historicity describes" (1991A: 119).

By referencing potentiality like a pregnancy, Negri challenges temporality. This new temporality, or "living labor," brings into being a type of production based in imagination, subjectivities, and bodies rather than in repetitious processes and circulations commanded from above (from the system, or from God) whose objects are measured outcomes. It also denotes a type of historicity formed around open existence, life and its innovations that test and antagonize what is already constituted. Like the tendency, reproduction as production assumes the temporality of pregnancy: life jumps out of the deadened past, as separate (instead of living labor separating away from dead labor as profit). This reenvisioning of historical processes through the temporality of women's bodies is Negri's alternative to thinking through the dialectic and its mediations; it brings into play a positivity, an affirmation of a new life that does not require death or the negative in the movement of its emergence.[21] As the hinge of the transition, pregnancy or reproduction models the temporality that marks the crisis: the future sociality inside the present, the appropriation of the present by the future that is already inside of it. This temporality explains labor, where labor is the force of life within what-is that carries the dynamic strength of the constituting power to-come: "*Living labor is internal... to the rational constitution of dead labor*" (2003: 82; Negri's emphasis). The time of living labor, of "use value," is inside dead labor (constant capital, the eternal past, the State) but opposes it and bursts through the edge as innovation, as generation. Through labor, with its demand for the extension of reproductive time, the time of production accumulates, collects, mutates, diffuses, innovates, opens, generates—but against unification. The social time of living labor is not just a "continuous—reproduction of itself" (2003: 153) but rather "presents itself as a new being" (2003: 154) so that the future is already an active experience within the present and separate from it.

The combination of the centrality of labor and the rise of reproduction into production, saturating it, make productive femininity or "women's work" into the core of productive capital. The collective time of social coordination (of generation, of socialization, of reproduction) is necessary for production at the same time as it is antagonistic to the measured-time of exploitation. The structuring of production and historical time through the time of pregnancy—or reproduction—is more than metaphoric: the idea of constant generation is, for Negri, fundamental to his central concern with "constituent power." Negri developed the concept of "constituent power" in order to move beyond debates among leftist intellectuals of the 1960's over the relational definitions of base and superstructure. In parallel, he wanted to overcome the problem of structure in Foucaultian thinking, where institutions, force, and power in the system precede the emergence of subjects and act on them.[22] This compromises thinking on resistance. Negri attributes the ethics of "constituent power" to the questioning of teleology that "militant feminism" developed in 1968 (2003: 229). "Constituent power" is an open eruption from below, a potential in human labor, a productivity: "Constituent power is defined emerging from the vortex of the void, from the abyss of the absence of determinations, as a totally open need... Constituent power is this force that, on the absence of finalities, is projected out as an all-powerful and always more expansive tendency" (1999: 14). "Constituent power" is the ontological force of production that assumes the constancy of revolution, the demand of constant renewal. Though "constituent power" cannot be reduced to a particular content, to a past or future constitution, it exists always as "the social order of labor" (1999: 247), or rather, in the generation and socialization of beings that, as collectivity, cannot be synthesized. Negri's understanding of constituent power makes production appear as reproduction through equating the production of time and system to pregnant women's bodies. He de-natures women's bodies by invoking them as machines of productivity. As, through reproduction, capital takes on the collective form of the social, the social can project itself into a separate existence, an autonomous, socializing, and affirmative life-form that actively creates reality as a new foundation. As "women's work," constitutive power is oriented toward difference in the future.

In other words: in the classical Marxist view, labor evolves through a series of historical stages, each succeeding the other through negation: living labor is forced into the factory after capital imposes a violent separation between labor and its old means of production, and capital socializes labor through factory-time. In "real subsumption," the present is pregnant with the future: the factory extends over the entirety of social life, generating social cooperation ("the common") and a social subjectivity saturated by the time of need (reproduction) that escapes from the measured time-space of exploitation (the extraction of surplus). Capital then expropriates "the common," subjects it to a regime of privatization, but social cooperation and the desire to constitute revive elsewhere, through different narratives, in autonomous places, "creatively modeling, *ex novo,* the materials that it touches" (1999: 326). In capitalism, the juridical system (the constitution), too, needs "constituent power" to maintain itself, but "constituent power" is always escaping, taking leave, metamorphosing, and producing new, living being on another horizon that cannot be written into a constitution or a set of representational laws, of simulations. On one level, "constituent power" closes down into juridical power as law is codified into the constitution and the representational State, or becomes congealed in dead labor, turned into measure; on another, it—as pure desire, or ontology, as singularity—cannot assume symbolic form, is socialized, collectivized, and therefore resists synthesis and subordination to the present system.

Integrated within both ideological apparatuses of the law and the State as well as in the material relations of laboring processes, "constituent power" responds to the inconsistencies in the classical Marxist account of base and superstructure by turning production into reproduction, that is, by transforming all production—ideological and material, reproductive and productive—simultaneously into the socialization of subjects. Negri's description of "real subsumption" infuses the field of capitalist production with a social life that appears as the extension of reproduction, or "women's work," over everything. Ideology is no longer separated from production in a position of reproductive "relative autonomy" as Althusser would formulate it, creating the conditions of temporal displacement that open toward the transition to the next social stage. Neither is ideology charted, as Gayle Rubin and other feminists have charted it (and I analyze in chapter 1), as the circulation and exchange of women as symbols outside of the history of production. Rather, capital's products are themselves circulating ideas, communications, and social relations ("general intellect") made and exchanged as value. Women that in structural anthropology and psychoanalysis were circulating symbols of exchange are now internal to production (what Hardt and Negri call "immaterial production"[23]), as affect, ideas, sensibilities, and relationships now figure as capital's very substance: "The collective time...of symbolic transvaluation that functions as superstructure—is here brought completely back to, and rediscovered within reality, and is all the more unyielding the more it fluctuates across and within the determinations of production" (2003: 63). The extension of "women's work" over the entire productive field is what allows Hardt and Negri to get beyond the problem posed by ideology as a reflection of reality, as relatively autonomous, as an ideal outside of material interactions, or as a tension with the base, making ideology coextensive with reality and politics coextensive with the social.

This "postmodern" absorption[24] of superstructure and circulation into production means that production now takes shape as social cooperation, as an integration of social and communicational life in a totality—like a family but "beyond individuality, beyond the family, toward ever more complex and ever more versatile communities" (2003: 98). Production *is* the reproduction of social life. The class struggle, in Marx's *Capital,* over the parts of the working-day is transformed, in Negri, into an internal, integral antagonism between the temporalities of life and socialization (reproduction), on the one hand, and, on the other, the valorization of capital (production), or capital's drive to measure "use value" as time (or labor power) and turn it into "surplus value." In other words, for Negri the principle antagonism of production, the class antagonism, takes place in the mutation of "women's labor" as primary production and source of profit. Through the mystified form of the wage, capital divides the time of the working-day between "necessary time," or the time it takes for the worker to produce enough to reproduce himself (and the next generation), and "surplus time," or time that the worker works for the capitalist for free, subsumed by capital in the exchange of labor power. As "free time," "socially average necessary time" (or reproductive time for labor, "use value") struggles to expand against "surplus," or time that capital uses without exchanging anything for it.[25] For Negri, even as capital tries to minimize the time of reproduction to the barest minimum or to nonexistence, it still needs "necessary time," or creativity, in order to increase surplus.[26] The subsumption of this exterior space of reproduction (domestic space; traditionally, the time of "mothering") within the temporal analytic of capital creates the possibility of revolt for Negri: revolt happens when "women's work" as "use value" becomes capital (so that capital can become social) and yet is separate from capital, subsumed but irreducible and therefore antagonistic. "Surplus value" itself is an internally antagonistic operation.

In classical Marxism, there is a "before" in which "use value" is independent, both temporally and spatially exterior, and then an after, where "use value" becomes a limit to the system, a point of resistance. In "real subsumption," on the other hand, there is no time, space, or type of organization exogenous to the system. Capital has turned time and space into collective constituent time, the time of reproduction or "women's time," that it aims to codify and exploit. Here, "use value" is the horizon of a constitutive internal antagonism—a plural and collective antagonism inherent in capital—, impossible to reduce to an equivalence with exchange value or measured time. No longer exogenous, "use value" is "an element of crisis within the process" (1991: 55). "Use value" is the worker's ability to expand socially average necessary labor time, or reproduction, indefinitely; it puts a limit on capital's ability to accumulate and to realize its surplus: "This is the hypothesis that the quantity of value of the necessary part of the working day is *not only* more and more rigid but also tends toward higher values and therefore tends to diminish—subjectively, actively—the surplus value that can be extorted... Necessary labor can valorize itself autonomously, the world of needs can and must expand" (1991: 101; Negri's emphasis). Unlike in classical dialectics, where the antagonism can be resolved in a synthesis, mediation, compromise, negotiation, or combination, and the greater use of machines leads at first to greater amounts of accumulated labor power, Negri projects "use value" as separable from capital, as an opposing, independent, collective subject—as he says, quoting Marx: "the *separation* between these inorganic conditions of human existence and their active existence" (1991: 109; Marx's emphasis). "Real subsumption" depends both on the expansion of reproduction (as creativity and social relations) and on the reduction of its necessary labor time ("use value") to zero, the turning of all time into productive time. As capital pushes ever harder toward liberating itself from living labor and reducing its time of reproduction, Negri predicts greater antagonism and endless crisis.

"Women's labor" of reproduction, socialization, and production of subjects is therefore, for Negri, the crux of the transition. As necessary time (or "use value," or labor's reproductive time), it comes to represent that what capital needs for its own reproduction is also, simultaneously, its limit, or its internal block to its own self-valorization. "Women's labor" is necessary for capital's reproduction of itself because it socializes subjectivity, producing the collective subjectivities that anticipate capital's future: capital finds value in the present production of its future collective sociality—ideas, relationships, affects. Yet, "women's labor" as reproduction or necessary labor, once it is internal to capital, stands as a limit to capital's self-realization for the very reason that it, in its social organization, resists capital's drive to expand by expanding its time-measure, or quantity: there is a part of it that is excessive to capital, uncontainable, or untranslatable by it.[27] "Communism," says Negri, "is the negation of all measure, the affirmation of the most exasperated plurality—creativity" (1991: 33). The idea that "women's work" is a target for capital's drive to count everything in its place for the sake of police logic, or privatization—this idea is one that Negri shares with Jacques Rancière, as is the simultaneous sense that "women's work" is constituted as uncountable because of its relationship to morality, socialization, education, equality, and community.[28] However, Rancière goes on to attribute this incommensurability to the continuation of debate necessary for the possibility of politics,[29] and thinks of it as formative and unremitting. Negri, rather, thinks of the uncountability of women's labor of socialization, ultimately, as destructive and at the same time constitutive of an anticapitalist, productive force. In response to Negri, Rancière rejects his idea of communism, based on what he reads as a production of subjects from inside the "failure of the capitalist utopia" (2010: 174), and upholds instead a democracy created by "the free association of men and women implementing the egalitarian principle" (2010: 176), though he sees this "principle" as perennially and continually embattled by the unassailable, relentless logic of the police, or privatization, and the count. For Rancière, there is no way for the police to stop policing or privatizing (including, privatizing "women's work" in one form or another). This insistence that everything is accounted for and everything in its place is crucial, for the "dis-agreement" that is politics, against the cry of "the common," or the part that cannot be counted.

In contrast, Negri sees "women's work"—"use value," the work of reproduction, "necessary labor," or free labor—through the split that constitutes the irreducible subject: a metamorphosis, an insurrection, a refusal. "Women's work" constitutes subjects in the break from production, as a separation. "Women's work" is both constituted as the current face of capital and escapes from that constitution by always constituting anew. The revolutionary strength of "women's work" is in its destructive opposition to the forces of privatization that try to reduce it to the count—that is, to a quantity of exchange, to measure. Negri's placement of "women's work" confronts feminism as a predicament: on the one hand, women and their work exist only as capital, in its logic of privatization through the measure, and capital only exists as "women's work." Yet, women and their work are central not only to capitalism and its socialization but also to a transition. "Real subsumption" seems to fulfill the dreams of feminism, eclipsing gender difference by putting everyone inside production as "women at work": "[T]here is no difference between production and reproduction, between man and woman" (2003: 227), Negri recognizes. On the other hand, as "women's work," capital no longer needs women.[30] This recreates women as autonomous, that is, as radical, subversive potential.

"Biopolitics"

A terminology revealing "women's work" as the ontological substrata of productivity, "biopolitics" is when the processes of governance are oriented toward the production and management of life rather than the infliction of death, meaning that politics merges with the social. The body is the source of both joy and potential. Life is always resistance. "Biopolitics" is the term Hardt and Negri use to describe this production of social relations and life itself that "*exceed* all quantitative measurement" (2009: 135). "Biopolitics" indicates that women and feminism must be integral to any analysis of labor, productivity, and class struggle because "women's work" indicates that corporeal experience must be restored to the socialization of subjects (which is increasingly the dominant mode of production).

A force "from below" particularly developed from second-wave feminism's "move toward a standpoint of bodies" (2009: 26), "biopolitics" returns power to bodies, the creative power to produce through labor: "[T]he concept of biopolitics for me," says Negri, "ultimately need to confront and address the question of labor" (Casarino and Negri, 2008: 148). "Biopolitics" therefore gets its substance from the productive forces in general that Hardt and Negri term "biopower": "The paradox, though, is that even in the moment of capital's triumph in the 1960's, when bodies are directly invested in the mode of production and the commodification of life has rendered their relations entirely abstract, that is the point when, immediately within the processes of industrial and social production, bodies spring back onto center stage in the form of revolt" (2009: 27). As "when it is the body that produces" (2003: 164), "biopolitics" allows Hardt and Negri to talk about the general turn of production toward the production of bodies in action (rather than material commodities) as a resistance from within and from below.[31]

Often evoked through the female body or allusions to "women's work," the use of "biopolitics" links up the Marxist interest in reproduction, particularly the reproduction of labor power, with a focus on sexuality and its production of life: "In the biopolitical sphere of life," Hardt and Negri begin, "life is made to work for production and production is made to work for life. It is a great hive in which the queen bee continuously oversees production and reproduction" (2000: 32). "Women's work" frames the "biopolitical" because women's bodies are the entryway for the diversity of life and the "general hybridization of being" (2003: 206), the contamination of races and languages that compose the new being of living labor. Situating the body as the point of contact with the "to come," "biopolitics" also opens up the field of production to a diversity of forms, energies, and reactions—what Hardt and Negri call "the multitude," or "the ensemble of sensorial, perceptive, and mental mutations that the bodies themselves produce" (2003: 235). Though seemingly attributable to organic cause, these birthing bodies are not naturalized, corresponding instead, in their ontology, to the productive machine.

For Hardt and Negri, "biopolitics" thus shows ontology in movement, that is, as always—like living labor—recognizably effective even while assuming different materialities historically. "Biopolitics" makes visible that history is acted on "from below," and that oppressive force is a reaction to the historical momentum that constitutes living labor and its socialization. Hardt and Negri understand the problem of corporeality in contemporary formation is that bodies disappear, eclipsed into a "transcendent realm" (2009: 33).

In religious fundamentalisms, for example, bodies vanish as simply pathways to the soul, as a woman under a veil or the material of dietary restrictions, whereas in nationalisms and economisms, the body appears as a central target of discipline and command, as a container of value. Yet these fundamentalisms, as well, ultimately must consider the body as militant in its revolt, that is, as needing controls.[32] In contrast, "biopolitics" provides an analysis of bodies as woven into a critique of transcendence as property: "When he [Foucault] insists that there is no central, transcendent locus of power but only a myriad of micropowers that are exercised in capillary forms across the surfaces of bodies in their practices and disciplinary regimes,... Foucault's analyses of bodies and power... really make good on some of the intuitions that the young Marx could not completely grasp about the need to bring the critique of property, along with all transcendental structures of capitalist society, back to the phenomenology of bodies" (2009: 31).

Though "biopolitics" is a set of symptoms of contemporary power mostly analyzed in reference to Foucault, Negri has also indicated its indebtedness to feminism: "Sexuality, rather, is the fundamental element of human reproduction. I intend reproduction here in its strict Marxian sense: labor power reproduces itself above all through sexuality... I don't think I'm adding anything new to what contemporary feminism has been saying for a while, namely, that the choice of different styles of life and different styles of sexual play is overdetermined by the structuring of reproduction, which is as important as production itself" (Casarino, 2004: 166). The allusion to women's bodies and "women's work" within Hardt and Negri's thoughts on "biopolitics" poses problems to the philosophical project that would be of interest to feminism. For one, the ontological aspect of "biopolitics" flattens out productivity, identities, and situations: the body as the focal point of production tends to void out time as measure (e.g., as the division between necessary labor time (reproduction) and surplus (production), or between "use value" and exchange), drawing all temporality indistinguishably into the production process as a whole: as productivity powers everything, there is no difference from it. Thus, the "biopolitical" has similar concrete strategies to the "biopower" that opposes it and tries to dominate it. As Alberto Toscano has noted, this philosophical perspective marginalizes a central element of Foucault's thinking on "biopolitics," that is, that it is an "'anti-universal' concept" (111). Whereas Foucault's disciplined bodies are meant to cast doubt on stabilizing, transcendent concepts of political theory like state, sovereignty, and labor, localizing the institutional networks of their subjectification and showing capitalism to be penetrating deeper into the micro-levels of existence, Hardt and Negri's collapse of "biopolitics" into an ontology shifts "biopolitics" "from a localized analytical register to that of a global totality" (125): living labor in general. Particularity is lost. The effect, says Toscano, is a blurring of fields, forces, and categories where it becomes impossible to distinguish oppressive power from the "biopolitical" living labor that antagonizes it from within: the biopolitical force "from below"— no longer local, historically disassociated (as "traditional"), or spatially exterior (as "domestic")—inhabits the same collective temporal register as capital and its biopower. Additionally, the ambiguities in the periodization of "biopolitics"—that it appears as the current phase of history under "real subsumption" at the same time as merging all phases of production congruently into the now—makes it difficult to know what separation from the oppressive power of capital would entail.

What Toscano does not consider is that the move from the micro-levels of Foucaultain "biopolitics" to the universalizing grand-scheme of "real subsumption" or living labor that Hardt and Negri espouse passes through a regendering of the analytic of power. The fact that the universal of productive ontology has been feminized means that the universal is constantly coming upon its own internal limits: the limits of a returning particularity, of needs. Whereas Foucault's notions of sexuality in the first volume of *The History of Sexuality* only include women inasmuch as they are locked into the conjugal pair or hysterical, Hardt and Negri's "biopolitics" treats femininity as the underlying, even the definitional force of all production. Yet, in its capacity of transforming production into reproduction, "women's work" is also the maker of living labor with expanding needs and desires that put limits on the extraction of surplus.

The concerns this should raise for feminism include: (1) capitalist hegemony is primarily a sexual process in this view, meaning that its intensification entails its firmer expression through sexual practices, particularly violent ones; (2) the practices of sexuality developing through their integration with capitalism are not different in form from the ones that would separate themselves, though these later ones would be excessive to systemization, challenging the system to sexualize more, and beyond the law. Sexuality has become both a structure for wielding power, instituting command, and subordinating labor on the one hand and, on the other, an energy from below blended into the machine of production. As Cesare Casarino has remarked, this sexualization of power and production is not, for Negri, linked to pleasure;[33] (3) sexual difference or gender orientation are no longer a terminology around which critique or complaint can be developed; (4) since bodies are always bodies-in-revolt, differential capacities are expected equally to celebrate strength, without regard to ability or injury. Mutation is always seen as increased vitality; (5) though, through "biopolitics," "women's work" has been abstracted into productivity so that all production takes shape in reference to the female labor of socialization in the domestic sphere of industrialization, productivity still translates into "the so-called feminization of work," meaning that femininity has not been completely de-essentialized and decoupled from the meanings of private life even as it has morphed into the productive machine; (6) not only do Hardt and Negri reenvision capital as the so-called feminization of work but they also invest "women's work" with the constituent refusal, antagonism, or separation from work. Such a framing of "women's work" as a break or rupture from capital—as the transition—on the one hand endows "women's work" with radical optimism and potential while, on the other hand, marking it as a setup for under- and unemployment, under-remuneration, and the like; and (7) the flattening out of production and reproduction—between gendered times—translates into a flattening out of the time-distance between what Hardt and Negri call "biopolitical" centers. With the economic stress moving from commodities to social relations, "confusing, as we have said, the division between production and reproduction" (2009: 135), "Third World labor" enters domestic spaces, service sectors, and low-skilled manufacturing in First World contexts: "This shift goes hand in hand with the 'feminization' of work, often combined with the racial stereotype of the 'nimble fingers' of women in the global South" (2009: 135). Though Hardt and Negri interpret this migration as potentially subversive, it has also intensified exploitation (see chapter 3), and it tends to wish away any acknowledgement that national borders matter in cultural terms, in the production of value, or in relations of inequality.

Another problem in Hardt and Negri's adoption of feminism is that the ontological program substitutes production for agency. Agency is the heart-of-the-matter, particularly agency "from below," and much of the texts' energy and excitement resides in this optimism over the possibility of change, so welcome after poststructuralism's depersonalized and objectified dominance of structure, narratives, language, and the image. As well, agency, even the agency of "women's work," is always a relation to class struggle. Hardt and Negri reconceive ontology through materialism in order to formulate ontology through movement, and historical movement in particular. Yet, events (e.g., constitutions, revolutions) arise only when reproduction, the force of constituent power, or the relentless push toward revolt, emerges from the belly of the ontology of production and disturbs it from within, like an alien embryo. Often (though not necessarily) proceeding from a crowd mentality or the logic of the "swarm," the ontological grip of production is persistent, where living labor appropriates surplus *because* it falls under capital's control. True: Hardt and Negri are interested in solving the problem of structure by constituting force "from below," as decision, and insist on the primacy of resistance over repression, and true: they acknowledge that part of poststructuralism's or Foucault's failure in theorizing "from below" was a failure in theorizing the connections between intentions (or potentials) and acts—or the place of the decision without sovereignty.[34] Yet, the subject, its creativity and imagination, is nascent most strenuously through its reproductions, assimilations, and affirmations of the system of the productive machine. Women's bodies have agency because they merge with the machine.

"Immaterial Labor"

Some of these problems for feminism and its connections to "biopolitics" become visible in Hardt and Negri's treatment of "immaterial labor," or the turn of production toward ideas, aesthetics, information, knowledge, emotions, symbols, and languages. "Immaterial labor" is affective, cognitive, and relational. It can be defined as when object commodities give way to the production of the "human brain" or what Marx called the "general intellect," that is, the entire field of social interactions and imagination, and of life in all its corporeality: "the producer," emphasizes Negri, "(the worker or proletarian, intellectual or material labour-power) reappropriated the tool of production, which increasingly is called the brain" (2003: 136). Whereas Marx posed the separation of manual and mental labor as the first class division, in the current social relations of neoliberalism, "use value"—or an organization of production where workers had decisive knowledge of production, and capital is outside to the activity—has reasserted itself, and work has thereby reacquired its autonomy. Often associated with computer technologies in particular, "immaterial labor" means that actions and engagements outside of the conventional workplace or the factory feed into production, making all spaces and times potentially a source of value. Though clearly a scenario for super-exploitation, where capital has its tentacles reaching out into the capillaries of human action as well as into every node of nature and there is never a time or space free from work, "immaterial labor" also is the form of production of "the common," abstractions and temporalities like language that belong to everybody, that cannot be privatized, enclosed, or named as property (despite attempts on that score) or commanded by capital.[35] "Immaterial labor" parallels, in a positive sense, what the capitalist system has designated as "externalities," or effects that enterprises and businesses have expelled from the sphere of their responsibility, pushing costs onto all others (like environmental degradation) but also denying their ownership. "Immaterial labor" is thus the condition that allows Hardt and Negri to claim that "biopolitical labor-power is becoming more and more autonomous, with capital simply hovering over it parasitically with its disciplinary regimes, apparatuses of capture, mechanisms of expropriation, financial networks, and the like" (2009: 142). Because "immaterial labor" projects a limit beyond capital's capture and control, Hardt and Negri see it as a tendency of crisis, a function of "the common," an organic organization of labor that is antagonistic toward privatized production.

Scholars have adopted a spectrum of positions on the specific historical changes that "immaterial labor" inaugurates. Though some critics have idealistically concluded that the means of production can never be separated from the worker in creative labor, and so creative labor is ushering in greater freedom in the workplace, others have understood "immaterial labor" to be implicated in new neoliberal class relations and "the so-called feminization of work" in ways not necessarily directing toward revolutionary outcomes. Tiziana Terranova, for example, lauds creative labor as an exciting, "pioneering" (76) "high-tech gift economy" (77) because it channels "excess productive activities that are pleasurably embraced" (78) though, she continues, at the same time they are "often shamelessly exploited" (78): people are willing to work for free, she argues, to make profits for others because they consider the provision of content to be enjoyable. In a similarly positive vein, Carlo Vercellone understands "immaterial labor" as representing a phase in capitalist production where the worker has reappropriated time and knowledge in ways that emancipate her from the wage relation. He then confidently asserts that the loss of such worker autonomy could only happen with a "lowering of the general level of education of the workforce" (33) resulting from the demise of a public education system, a historical change that he (idealistically) finds unimaginable. For Vercellone, following Marx, the development of a public education system was "a central site of the crisis of the Fordist wage relation" (27) because it allowed the worker to accumulate knowledge and a "diffuse intellectuality" that furthered market interests but still went "beyond the logic of the market" (27). However, this conclusion does not take into account that the public education system is under attack in the US and worldwide, and that the ever-strengthening struggle to defeat public education in the United States and elsewhere partly has to do with an ideological struggle where knowledge is being redefined as *knowledge for the workforce,* commodifiable and transmittable as objects, and schools themselves are being redesigned as private, for-profit businesses. (As I show in chapter 4, part of this ideological struggle has to do with an appropriation of women's bodies as endowed with the productive capacities and knowledges of private accumulation, evident in the public discourse about gender segregation in public schools.)

Others, however, are less celebratory about how users provide free content or reconnect working bodies with creative knowledge. "Immaterial labor," such critics forewarn, represents a repetition of certain forms of class control and imperialist expropriation in a newly feminized form. Laikwan Pang, for example, has criticized utopian interpretations of "immaterial labor," the "information society," or the "creative economy" for insisting that creative labor is democratically accessible ("diffuses the boundaries between manual and intellectual labor" (56)) and marks the end of exploitation because it puts the means of production—the human brain—into the control of workers. Actually, says Pang, it reinforces an unequal division of labor, often between nations: "The migration of monotonous assembly-line work is in part willed by the citizens of wealthy nations, so that they—and particularly members of the younger generation—can partake in more 'innovative' and 'rewarding' careers" (56).

"Immaterial labor" has also been interpreted as a response to crisis. Christian Marazzi, for example, has linked "immaterial labor" and the information economy with "the intensification of information flows; industrial dislocation and concentration; the internalization of the goods and services markets ('global village'); the financialization of process of accumulation (the multiplication of securities markets); the dismantling of the welfare state, and the redefinition of the specific weights of the various economic powers" (87). In particular, Marazzi sees "immaterial labor" as arising in conjunction with the financialization of public sector spending, when workers' savings (e.g., pension funds) are corralled into securities investments (in the early seventies, starting with the bailout of New York City) to fill in for the dwindling public resources resulting from the deinflationary policies of the Federal Reserve. Workers' household savings got diverted into global investments. Such a change meant that workers' interests dovetailed with the interests of those who had been their wage-payers. Workers in the industrialized North would support expansionist policies at the expense of solidarity with the working-classes elsewhere. This "democratization" of securities investments required that new labor initiatives be oriented toward language, or the building of consensus and public opinion around stock trends and liquidity. Marazzi understands this overproduction of language, following Kristeva (although Marazzi does not cite her), as "the passage (the so-called 'thetic cut') from the intrauterine semiotic sphere to the symbolic sphere, from communication inside the mother's womb to the completely symbolic language of the historically determined world" (31). In other words, the rise of a productive sphere of communication means the final victory of the Symbolic over the Semiotic. This demands the sacrifice of women's work of socialization which is overtaken by a patriarchal appropriation and circulation of language commodities and symbols (or brands).

The feminization of "immaterial labor" is seen by some critics as a pitfall, a cue where Hardt and Negri don their rose-colored blinders and shroud the tendency in invented potentials instead of recognizing the grim reality of work in some sectors of technology and electronics, particularly for immigrant and other workers outside of the industrial centers, and particularly for women. For example, even as he acknowledges how Negri's interest in the "social worker" over the "mass worker" was influenced by "the emergence of the feminist component" (138) as part of 1960s social movements, Nick Dyer-Witheford notes that "immaterial labor" is often more exploitive of women than Fordism was because "the social costs of convulsive industrialization are relentlessly offloaded onto unpaid female housework" (149). He goes on to remark: "If 'general intellect' is strongly associated with digital networked processes, then how does it take account of the traditional, and in many areas persisting, patterns, of masculine predominance and female exclusion that have characterized high-tech development?" (147–148). Because it exacerbates the relations of exploitation in manufacturing by importing them, unequally, into service locations between areas of the global North and the global South, "immaterial labor" does not seem capable of assuming revolutionary potential in Hardt and Negri's terms.

Even among the so-called "white collar" classes of the creative labor workforce, "immaterial labor" has been seen as prejudicial to women. As Melissa Gregg shows in ethnographic detail, with the personalization of computers and communications systems, the space of work has become more flexible, some of it taking place in homes and often encouraging extended working hours and requiring workers to constantly be "on call" through technological devices. This "function creep" has made women able to enter the professional workplace in increasing numbers but has also led to more time spent at work in all its forms: "The refusal to mount a sustained critique of long hours culture, and the gendered assumptions underpinning it, had the effect of making women feel grateful for so-called 'flexible' work arrangements. These were conditions that allowed women to maintain traditional childcare and home maintenance expectations but only in addition to paid work" (4).

Hardt and Negri do attribute to empirical forms of "immaterial labor" "intense forms of violation and alienation" (2004: 66) connected to the precarity, mobility, and flexibility in forms of labor that "blur the distinction between work time and nonwork time" (2004: 66). Yet, they also see that capital's insufficiencies in turning ideas into property—with intellectual property rights, for example, or genetic information—have created a certain unraveling of the concept of property itself as "the common" asserts its antagonism. The productions of the imagination, of socialization, and of language—music, texts, ideas, information, education, care, financial devices, communications, and journalism, for example—do not always easily fit into capital's traditional methods of calculation, even as they are becoming a greater proportion of what capitalism is producing. Capital's failure to bring the creativity and innovation that its economic development and growth require into its legal structures of ownership and profit crashes it up against its own limits. For example, "The privatization of the electronic 'commons' has become an obstacle to further innovation. When communication is the basis of production, then privatization immediately hinders creativity and productivity" (2004: 185). The future of social coordination through "the commons" is already inside the crisis of property within the "immaterial labor" regime. "The rising biopolitical productivity of the multitude is being undercut and blocked," they conclude, "by the processes of private appropriation" (2004: 186). Envisioning "the way things are" as entrenched and unimpeachable, the critics of Hardt and Negri's consideration of "immaterial" and "biopolitical" labor do not give credence to signs in the present that could attribute "women's work"—and its sense of social coordination and affective productivity—with introducing a different future form of social organization that would break apart the domination of property. Hardt and Negri's interpretation of the new forms of "immaterial labor" considers how the tendency of "women's work" in the present breaks through into forms of social organization at the limits of capital's future.

Alberto Toscano's ruminations should be remembered here. "Women's work" is the complicated site, in Hardt and Negri's assessment, where the particularities of "biopolitics" merges into the universalism of living labor, often antagonistically. Dialectic thinking, from Hegel to Habermas, often traces the origin of the dialectic to the primitive and infantile—immediate sensations, pretechnological traditionalism, and domestic experience—that the movement of history and subjectivity absorbs and appropriates. Hardt and Negri, on the other hand, attribute dialectical thinking to bourgeois thinking, as nonidentical or autonomous forms of social organization—or, "use value" or "women's work"—compromise themselves into a resistance to the system produced within the system itself by the system's normal operations of production and accumulation. As "real subsumption" makes capital's profitability dependent on social coordination, collective cognition, and imagination, "women's work" as universal stands inside capital as what capitalism cannot absorb, particularizing it, exposing its limits. "Capital," Hardt and Negri explain, "—although it may constrict biopolitical labor, expropriate its products, even in some cases provide necessary instruments of production—does not organize *productive cooperation*... In biopolitical production,... capital does not determine the cooperative arrangement, or at least not to the same extent. Cognitive labor and affective labor generally produce cooperation autonomously from capitalist command" (2009: 140). In "immaterial" and "biopolitical" labor regimes of "women's work," capital is external to productivity.

Conclusion

In Hardt and Negri's account of neoliberalism, gender is not disappearing as a form of economic or cultural organization, nor can it be relegated to noncorporeal, purely symbolic, ideal, or ideological existence, since its concrete bodies are needed by capital to produce value and command over social relations. This does not mean that Hardt and Negri reduce gender to biology but rather that capital works through gender, endowing the body with gender as value to exploit. Arguing that production and reproduction have merged, they demonstrate that under neoliberalism, the exploitation of "women's work" *is* the exploitation of labor, and the alienation of "women's work" *is* a more extreme version of the alienation of labor described by Marx. As capitalist domination takes on the functions of industrialism's autonomous private sphere—the functions related to socialization, reproduction, and the production of subjects—, "women's work" has become increasingly a mechanism through which capitalist exploitation intensifies. Feminism's wariness of class from the late sixties till now, its search for its own autonomous understanding of women's oppression and liberation (as I analyzed in chapter 1), has paralleled capital's increased capacities to manipulate class through manipulating the work of gender. Yet, Hardt and Negri understand that capital's endowments of gender onto bodies also grants power to those bodies, the power of creation and generation. Hardt and Negri see women as other than their construction through work, as potentially outside of capital's claims on them, as an autonomous form of productivity, because of their status as carriers of value under neoliberal capitalism, because reproduction has spread over production. The autonomy of "women's work" demands the expansion of needs and worker time. Though capital realizes value by gendering bodies, gender itself exceeds capital's command. For Hardt and Negri, as much as gender is capital's need, it is also capitalism's limit: capital's demand for gender anticipates an increasingly unmanageable crisis.

Hardt and Negri's descriptions of contemporary capitalism as "the so-called feminization of work" therefore highlight a particularly salient point for feminism: as women become the bearers of surplus and value for capital's exploitation (as I analyze in chapters 1, 2, 3, and 4), "women's work" shows the fault-lines of a capitalism in crisis—"women's work" is what forces freedom to surface. While feminism was exploring the possibilities of feminist liberation through work, Hardt and Negri would show that through "women's work" considered as production, the creativity of the social explodes. One can easily shake one's head at this, call it romantic, impossible, silly, liken it to a dirty version of Cinderella, to children's tales gone wild. Or, one could judge it as cynical, as insisting that only as they sink into the harshest levels of neoliberal deprivation (read, feminization) will workers understand that they are blessed because they have nothing, not even a wage. Yet, one could also read Hardt and Negri to be saying that we *are already* in the most severe conditions of exploitation and economic polarization imaginable, with labor losing its organization, its political force, and its safety nets, but that these conditions are themselves creating types of social coordination that are the potential of something different. Hardt and Negri's optimism is tempting, especially after postmodern theories like Baudrillard's have made the present of production seem like a mechanized, bureaucratized field of disassociated symbols, no longer accessible to human manipulation or change. Linking up what women do or have done, their creative action, to a break in the present's deep structures of domination (as Hardt and Negri do), reveals a necessary connection between women and freedom that is embedded in thinking gender as a marker of class struggle and class struggle as gendered through and through in neoliberalism. For Hardt and Negri, gender is the realization that the ontology of production must take into account the autonomy, affirmation, and independent creativity of its producers: their generativity of a new, multiple, and different reality. Hardt and Negri offer an invitation to feminism: they hold out the possibility that neoliberalism projects its limit onto women and, by appropriating "women's work," leaves its present constantly open to a new foundation.

What feminism does with this identification of "women's work" as transition is, of course, an open question. Nevertheless, Hardt and Negri present ideas with which to work and develop in a feminist direction. For one, the difference between essence and construction is no longer valid: essence is by its very nature productiveness; people are what they do and what they construct and so are human nature and the world. Second, gender is not an ideal or an external symbolic or linguistic structure that subjects appropriate, embody, perform, and transform, or that makes sense by alienating the nonreferential, the unrepresentable, the sensory, and the "real": gender is not a contract or an exchange with an exterior form of power, a sacrifice made for the purpose of assuming power and subjectivity, a trade-off, a negotiation, a synthesis, or a compromise. Instead, gender is invention and innovation—it is the power to constitute itself. Third, gender is not given but multiple and multiplying; it is what elicits capital's drive to privatize it but, connected to life, it is what capital cannot count. Fourth, "women's work" and women's bodies are no longer mired in particularisms that limit and determine their sphere, bog them down in nature, and remove them from history. Though the universalizing of femininity seems to head toward a cheapening of everything and a privatizing of work as well as a forgetting of inequalities, it also extends the cooperative social relations of the factory over the entire social field, remaking "women's work" as "the commons." Fifth, Hardt and Negri resuture class and gender without reducing either one to the other. Sixth, gender is power, that is, the power of self-creation and the creation of life: of imagination. Seventh, gender is action. Unlike the orientation toward "identity" in many of the poststructuralist theories that Hardt and Negri criticize, action does not only imply a set of power relations inflected from institutional structures, languages, and the apparatuses of power, and expressed onto bodies through a "call," but also indicates the intentions of those who invent it and produce it in their bodies by working and creating. Ideology is less of an ideal or a reflection of exchange than in other Marxist or semiotic-inspired analyses because the production of its symbols, materials, social relations, and communications is riven with the intentions of its producers, and particularly of its exploited producers. As productivity, gender's being is the work of those who are life and being with it. Thus, gender is permanent revolution.

Notes

Introduction

1. Kathi Weeks has made a distinction between "work" and "labor." For her, the problem of class analysis is in its "relative disempowerment that is registered in the economic outcomes the categories of class are often used to map and measure" (19). "Work," on the other hand, is "a matter of creative activity" or "sensuous activity," assuming "the capacity not only to make commodities but to remake the world" (19). She goes on: "work is one politically promising way of approaching class—because it is so expansive, because it is such a significant part of everyday life, because it is something we do rather than a category to which we are assigned, and because for all these reasons it can be raised as a political issue" (20). Though I am certainly sympathetic to the idea that work builds consciousness by creating not just things but worlds, I do not think that it is necessary to divide labor from work in order to achieve that understanding. A reason not to make such a distinction is to realize the importance of that creative aspect of work in the development of labor unions and related social movements. I also do not agree with Weeks when she writes that class is something you "are assigned" whereas work is something you "do"—I believe there is much more overlap between these two than Weeks is willing to concede.

2. "It shall be an unlawful employment practice for an employer (1) to fail or refuse to hire or to discharge any individual, or otherwise to discriminate against any individual with respect to his compensation, terms, conditions, or privileges of employment, because of such individual's race, color, religion, sex, or national origin; or (2) to limit, segregate, or classify his employees or applicants for employment in any way which would deprive or tend to deprive any individual of employment opportunities or otherwise adversely affect his status as an employee, because of such individual's race, color, religion, sex, or national origin,"

3. As Mariarosa Dalla Costa proclaimed: "The oppression of women, after all, did not begin with capitalism. What began with capitalism was the more intense exploitation of women *as* women and the possibility at last of their liberation" (23).

4. Unfortunately, Dalla Costa identifies the division of labor as the homosexualization of capital: "But homosexuality generally is at the same time rooted in the

framework of capitalist society itself: women at home and men in factories and offices, separated one from the other the whole day; a typical factory of 1,000 women with 10 foremen; or a typing pool (of women, of course) which works for 50 professional men" (32). Her reason for making this claim is to criticize the separatist lesbian cultures of the early seventies as being not as oppositional or disengaged as their politics would warrant.

5. Selma James: "It is not that women don't want to be wives and mothers. They want and need men to share their lives with and every woman wants children. But they feel that if they can't have a human relationship they will have no relationship at all. Women go from being married to being divorced, from being housewives to working out, but nowhere do women see the kind of life that they want for themselves and their families" (79).

6. Ironically perhaps, Slaughter's model for flexible work time is the Jew: "I have worked with many Orthodox Jewish men who observed the Sabbath from sundown on Friday until sundown on Saturday" (97). Unlike women who leave work to spend time with their families, she contends, such Jews garnered admiration from colleagues for their commitment to their faith. The example is odd for the way it dismisses anti-Semitism, suggesting that gender is the most fervent or the only cause of inequality, and that inequality is just a matter of attitude.

1   The Gender of Working Time: Revisiting Feminist/Marxist Debates

1. "[I]t can be said with some certainty that part of the explanation for the decline in socialist debate on the subject lies not only in the real historical processes, but in the original weaknesses in the traditional discussion of the subject in the classics" (1966: 12).

2. Hester Eisenstein makes a related observation. Chronicling the trajectory of her own scholarly thinking when poststructuralism was gaining acceptance, she notes : "[S]omething important had shifted in the 1970s, and...this change, a restricting of the global economy, had consequences for politics, culture, and, most especially, the situation of women. The period of 'Fordism,' the expansive industrialization of the United States and other Western countries during the Golden Age of the Long Boom from 1945 to the 1970s, had been replaced by 'post-Fordism': deindustrialization, and an end to the Keynsian welfare state... Was it an unfortunate coincidence that women had been drawn into the economy in a productive capacity at precisely the historical moment when there was going to be such a dramatic slowdown? Or was it... that the slowdown caused women to become the cheap workforce of choice?... There seemed to be insufficient attention to the link between the massive increase in women's workforce participation, as the U.S. economy shed manufacturing for service jobs, and the rise of feminist consciousness and activism" (11–12). Though this is a useful observation, Eisenstein seems to conflate poststructuralist and mainstream feminism, often oversimplifying both, and she

overabstracts neoliberalism to the point where it acquires overarching agency and determinism.

3. BBC journalist Paul Mason and others have calculated a "doubling of the world's workers" with new zones of industrial labor rising up next to shantytowns in Kenya and China, "reviving the first phase of industrialization." The categories of labor and production are still holding explanatory power, he says, even as "hidden stories."

4. "This is a book about unemployment: its conceptual climax is reached with this proposition that industrial capitalism generates an overwhelming mass of potentially uninvestible capital on one hand, and an ever-increasing mass of unemployed people on the other: a situation we see fully corroborated today in the current crisis of third-stage of finance capital" (2010: 5).

5. Further, Marx writes, "The positing of a specific portion of labour capacities as superfluous, i.e., of the labour required for their reproduction as superfluous, is therefore a necessary consequence of the growth of surplus labour relative to necessary" (609).

6. I find a particularly egregious example of this to be David Harvey's recent *Rebel Cities*. I use the word "egregious" not because the example is atypical, but because David Harvey is more often than not sensitive to gender issues and a friend of feminism. David Harvey is reappropriating the ideas of Henri Lefebvre to argue that the city has replaced the factory as the primary place of production, and the urban dweller, though his/her various uses of space, makes the city into a product: "If capitalism often recovers from crises, as we saw earlier, by 'building houses and filling them with things,'" Harvey explains, "then clearly everyone engaged in that urbanizing activity has a central role to play in the macroeconomic dynamics of capital accumulation. And if maintenance, repairs, and replacements (often difficult to distinguish in practice) are all part of the value-producing stream (as Marx avers), then the vast army of workers involved in these activities in our cities is also contributing to value and surplus value production" (2012: 130–131). The focus on construction as what is driving surplus value production minimizes the role of "women's work," which is foremost in the designing of dwelling. Though Harvey does note that the dominance of construction makes labor "temporary, insecure, itinerant and precarious" and that it "fudges the supposed boundary between production and reproduction," he never mentions "women's work" as playing a particular part in that. Instead, the classical proletariat subject has taken over the role of reproduction in the service of production.

7. As Marx elaborates, for example, in the *Grundrisse*, "Labour as mere performance of services for the satisfaction of immediate needs has nothing whatever to do with capital, since that is not capital's concern. If a capitalist hires a woodcutter to chop wood to roast his mutton over, then not only does the woodcutter relate to the capitalist, but also the capitalist to the woodcutter, in the relations of simple exchange. The Woodcutter gives him his service, a use value, which does not increase capital; rather, capital consumes itself in it; and the capitalist gives him another commodity for it in the form of money. The same relation holds for all services which workers exchange directly for the money of other persons, and which are consumed by these persons" (272).

8. This seems to be a common theme. Here, Martha Gimenez makes a similar point: "I believe that Marx's most important potential contributions to feminist theory and politics reside precisely in the aspect of his work that most feminists ignored: his methodology. Exclusive focus on what he said or did not say about women kept feminist theorists from exploring the potential of his methodological insights to deepen our understanding of the phenomena called 'the oppression of women' or, in earlier times, the 'woman question'" (2005: 15). One could make a parallel point that feminist theory—particularly in the postmodern phase— appreciated what Marx might offer to metatheoretical practices, imperatives to historical and cultural contextualization, and identity construction that changes over time, so much so that they might have neglected the complexities of the relationship Marx poses between women and work, between women's work and capital, between women and time, as well as between women and profit.

9. "Marx himself has most brilliantly shown that natural propagation cannot keep up with the sudden expansive needs of capital... [Accumulation] requires an unlimited freedom of movement in respect of the growth of variable capital equal to that which it enjoys with regard to the elements of constant capital— that is to say it must needs dispose over the supply of labour power without restriction. Marx considers that this can be achieved by an 'industrial reserve army of workers'... Labour for this army is recruited from social reservoirs out-side the dominion of capital—it is drawn into the wage proletariat only if need arises. Only the existence of non-capitalist groups and countries can guarantee such a supply of additional labour power for capitalist production" (341–342).

10. Spivak here is addressing the relationship between Marxism and deconstruc-tion, particularly in the work of Derrida. I am convinced of Spivak's reading here of an important and useful overlap between use-value (linked to women's work) in Marx and Derrida's construction of aporia.

11. Biographical analyses have suggested that the women in Marx's life often suffered on account of his work: "Jenny cursed the fates that condemned her children to a life of indigence in a miserable flat full of someone else's broken furniture. But as bas as it was, she was also terrified that one more missed payment to the landlord might force the family onto the street below. There was but a vapor of income, a vacuum of savings... The Marx family sacrificed everything for that ignored masterwork [*Capital*]. Jenny buried four of her seven children, saw her three sur-viving daughters robbed of anything approaching a proper girlhood, had her once lovely face ravaged by disease, and suffered the ultimate betrayal when Karl fathered a child by another woman. She did not live to see her daughters' final sad chapters—two of the three committed suicide" (Gabriel, 7). The women in this account, though, believed in and supported Marx's ideas. Living as they did in a revolutionary intellectual culture of Victorian times, they had opportunities and contributed to the political momentum, and certainly Marx encouraged these efforts. Marx's attitude toward women in his biography is neither simple nor easily explainable in terms of his theoretical work

12. Roy cites a staffer in the USAID Women in Development office who says that "while microfinance has brought attention to the issue of women's poverty,

it has bypassed many other issues related to gender equality and empowerment—from women's participation in global labor forces to the legal rights of women" (28).

13. As Keating, Rasmussen, and Rishi point out, "In addition to bringing women into the realm of the financial services industry, the feminization of credit provisioning also engenders an increase in loan monitoring capabilities and a broadening of the industry's material base... [M]icrocredit facilitates an intensification of surveillance and regulation" (162).

14. In the first volume of *Capital,* Marx presents an algebraic equation for the relation between, on the one hand, the salaried time that the laborer works to reproduce himself and capital (variable capital) and, on the other, the unpaid time that drops profits directly into Mr. Moneybags's pocketbooks (surplus value)—the time that the worker works for free and the capitalist accumulates the value of the work. "We have seen that the labourer, during one portion of the labour-process, produces only the value of his labour-power, that is, the value of his means of subsistence... That portion of the working-day, then, during which this reproduction takes place, I call *'necessary'* labour-time... During the second period of the labour-process, that in which his labour is no longer necessary labour, the workman, it is true, labours, expends labour-power; but his labour, being no longer necessary labour, creates no value for himself. He creates surplus-value which, for the capitalist, has all the charms of a creation out of nothing" (208–209).

15. Jameson disagrees with this chronological division in the Marxian opus. For him, *Capital* proceeds out of the analysis of alienation in the early work by calling attention to the moment of separation: the peasant from his land, the community from its traditions, the craftsmen from his tools, the individual from the collective: "only capitalism constitutes a social formation—that is, an organized multiplicity of people—united by the absence of community, by separation and by individuality" (2011: 16). Or: "Where Hegelian *Entäusserung* externalized the product only to enrich itself by way of its reappropriation (and return into itself), the Marxian system posits an increasing separation which necessitates its own enlargement" (2011: 135). Jameson uses this reading to argue that contrary to standard interpretations, *Capital* is less production-determinist than about "the fundamental structural centrality of unemployment in the text of *Capital* itself" (2011: 149). This makes *Capital* relevant to understanding contemporary phenomena like displacement due to natural or human-made disaster, "failed states," and ethnic wars.

16. "That the abolition of individual economy is inseparable from the abolition of the family is self-evident" (*The German Ideology,* 157).

17. Engels borrowed the term Mother Right from Johann Jakob Bachofen who wrote a book in 1861 called *Mutterrecht,* or *Mother Right: An Investigation of the Religious and Juridical Character of Matriarchy in the Ancient World.* Using examples like the death of Agamemnon in Aeschylus' tragic trilogy *The Oresteia,* Bachofen's book describes how in the Ancient World, women's rule was overthrown by men in order to secure paternity. Engels says that Bachofen

did not need to give evidence from religion in order to support his thesis about the passage from Mother Right to Father Right (or, monogamy), but rather plenty of evidence was available in "the development of men's actual conditions of life" (7). For an analysis of how the Mother Right thesis countered feminist interests—because it is "used to inculcate in them [women] an ideology of moral failure" and because it "constantly reiterate[d] that women did not know how to handle power when they had it" (280), see Bamberger's canonical "The Myth of Matriarchy: Why Men Rule in Primitive Society."

18. "Division of labour only becomes truly such from the moment when a division of material and mental labour appears. From this moment onwards consciousness *can* really flatter itself that it is something other than consciousness of existing practice, that it *really* represents something without representing something real; from now on consciousness is in a position to emancipate itself from the world and to proceed to the formation of 'pure' theory, theology, philosophy, ethics, etc." ("The German Ideology": 159).

19. I take seriously Judith Butler's contentions against such critiques that lament that a turn away from Marxism has led to a reliance on the "merely cultural": "These are some of the forms that this kind of argument has taken in the last year: that the cultural focus of leftist politics has abandoned the materialist project of Marxism, failing to address questions of economic equity and redistribution, and failing as well to situate culture in terms of a *systematic* understanding of social and economic modes of production; that the cultural focus of leftist politics has splintered the Left into identitarian sects, and that we have thus lost a set of common ideals and goals, a sense of a common history, a common set of values, a common language, and even an objective and universal mode of rationality; that the cultural focus of leftist politics substitutes a self-centered and trivial form of politics that focuses on transient events, practices, and objects for a more robust, serious, and comprehensive vision of the systematic interrelatedness of social and economic conditions" (1997: 265). I am, however, arguing something different: I am suggesting that the turn away from class created certain discursive openings. The way arguments had to be constructed in order for feminism to step out of class critique led to the development of new analytical tools that affected new constructions of gender. As I show in chapters 2 and 3, I do think that poststructuralist critics have maintained a sense of production integral to how they are constructing new theories of language and identity.

20. As Marx says in the *Grundrisse*, "Wage labor consists of paid and unpaid labour" (574).

21. "In the traditional peasant farm economy, the family produces a large part of the goods which it consumes... The product which is consumed by the family, and thereby has a use-value, also has an exchange value, since it could have been sold on the market" (1984: 63–64).

22. Revisiting the article some 15 years later, Mohanty admits that the ascendance of the particular in her initial argument posed a problem for a "common feminist political project" (224), particularly as "an anticapitalist transnational feminist practice" (230) where "activism around antiglobalization has to be the key

focus for feminists" (230). The absence of the universalizing and homogenizing gesture of theory made the prior study less equipped for an encounter with the universalizing and homogenizing formations and effects of late capital.

23. For example, one of the current ways that capital currently profits by expanding unpaid work time is in the way it exteriorizes the environmental repercussions of production. The time and money for "clean-up" is the responsibility often of the state, or the workers, or others affected.

24. As Leopoldina Fortunati puts it, "Everything that is not strictly necessary for the reproduction that continually replenishes their capacity to work is now deemed superfluous...Now that the worker was reduced to a commodity, capital was interested in making him/her be like any other commodity, and be reproduced in the shortest possible time" (162).

25. Leopoldina Fortunati: "During the first phase then, capital shortens the working day and underdevelops the process of production within the sphere of reproduction. It has to do this because it has to lengthen the time of surplus labor within the process of commodity production. So it shortens the houseworking day, even though this latter is all posited as time of 'surplus labor.' For capital, it is a tactical and not a strategic choice. Capital usurps not only free time, but also that part of necessary reproduction work time that appears as non-work time" (159).

26. As Cesare Casarino reads in Marx: "[T]he thinker who wrote many pages on the relation between socially necessary labor time and surplus labor time...is a thinker who found it indispensable to grapple explicitly and directly with the possibility of another temporality that would be qualitatively different from, as well as antagonistic to, that homogeneous temporality of quantifiable and measurable units that during capitalist modernity found its perfected historical form par excellence in the temporality of the wage" (224).

2 Julia Kristeva's Murders: Neoliberalism and the Labor of the Semiotic

1. For example, "[The advent of the remarkable space of representation] orients the visible towards a way of thinking of the flesh that engenders *and* kills. Decapitation creeps into it as inscription of a void that gives birth" (2012: 55).

2. Kristeva's critique of Marxism on the left was part of a larger intellectual critique that she shared with other members of the *Tel Quel* group of which she was a founding member, leading toward deconstruction. As Rosemary Hennessy remarks, "[A]mong other major doctrines of this new consensus were the contention that marxism is responsible for the Gulag, that reason is inherently totalitarian, and that seizure of state power is dangerous and vain." Kristeva's analysis of Fascism in Celine puts a bit of ambiguity in the contention that she believes reason to be inherently totalitarian, as Celine turns to Fascism as a Symbolic defense against the terrors of an unleashed Semiotic sensibility expressed in the avant-garde.

3. Bataille also understands this burst of beauty from the anus through the head as worker liberation: "Communist workers appear to the bourgeois to be as ugly and dirty as hairy sexual organs, or lower parts; sooner or later there will be a scandalous eruption in the course of which the asexual noble heads of the bourgeois will be chopped off" (1985: 8).

4. Kristeva's theory does not use the maternal body only in order to explore the Semiotic as a case of linguistic disruption, a lost origin, or a heterogeneity that the Symbolic cannot contain. Gloria's decapitation—resulting from her over-possessiveness of her son Jerry, her inability to disassociate—can be seen as a metaphor as well for abjection, the space of exclusion against which the subject and the social emerge into language, experienced "only if an Other has settled in place and stead of what will be 'me.' Not at all an other with whom I identify and incorporate, but an Other who precedes and possesses me, and through such possession causes me to be" (1982: 10). Kristeva's theories of abjection are commonly interpreted as part of a later stage in her thinking because they revise the role of the paternal prohibition in maturity narratives. In the early work on revolt in *Revolution in Poetic Language,* the paternal prohibition is a barrier to access to the Semiotic that needs to be constantly resisted but, at the same time, is continually returned, bordered off. In contrast, the problem with abjection is that the paternal function has become weak, allowing entry to unwieldy pollution and putting the symbolic, as well as subjective autonomy, at risk: "The absence, or the failure, of paternal function to establish a unitary bent between subject and object, produces this strange configuration: an encompassment that is stifling (the container compressing the ego) and, at the same time draining (the want of the other, qua object, produces nullity in the place of the subject)" (1982: 49). Kelly Oliver interprets Kristeva to be saying that the weakening and corruptibility of government and its social institutions has given rise to a "breakdown of authority": "In a no-fault society, who or what can we revolt against?" (78). She is reading Kristeva to be saying that authority resides in government and its institutions only, so if public institutions recede in power, authority also recedes. I argue later on, however, that the paternal prohibition has been bolstered rather than threatened as it is appropriated into a market society within the detective form.

5. This annoys Butler: "[Kristeva's] theory appears to depend upon the stability and reproduction of precisely the paternal law that she seeks to displace. Although she effectively exposes the limits of Lacan's efforts to universalize the paternal law in language, she nevertheless concedes that the semiotic is invariably subordinate to the Symbolic, that it assumes its specificity within the terms of a hierarchy immune to challenge" (108). Butler, though, adopts some of the structure of the Symbolic-Semiotic conflict within her theory of performativity. The difference is that Butler thinks the Symbolic iterates slightly, transforms, or mobilizes when the Semiotic inhabits it. Similarly, Lois McNay notes that Kristeva's appropriations of Lacan's structural Symbolic leads to a stagnancy in language: "Julia Kristeva's idea of the destabilizing implications of the semiotic and the abject for the symbolic structure lacks a notion of mediation to explain how such pre-Oedipal or inchoate forces may have an emancipatory impact on social practices" (140).

6. Nancy Fraser criticizes this position of the semiotic in Kristeva as not being useful for feminism because of the way social acts become but vehicles of symbolic order in Lacanian French theory: "[Kristeva's] general idea is that speakers act in socially situated, norm-governed signifying practices. In so doing, they sometimes transgress the established norms in force. Transgressive practice gives rise to discursive innovations and these in turn may lead to actual change. Innovative practice may subsequently be normalized in the form of new or modified discursive norms, thereby 'renovating' signifying practices" (1990: 95).

7. Kristeva: "In 'artistic' practices the semiotic—the precondition of the symbolic—is revealed as that which destroys the symbolic... [T]he subject must be firmly posited by castration so that drive attacks against the thetic will not give way to fantasy or to psychosis but will instead lead to a 'second-degree thetic,' i.e., a resumption of the functioning characteristic of the semiotic *chora*... This is precisely what artistic practices, and notably poetic language, demonstrate" (1984: 49–50). "Magic, shamanism, esoterism, the carnival, and 'incomprehensible' poetry all underscore the limits of socially useful discourse and attest to what it represses: the *process* that exceeds the subject and its communicative structures" (1984: 16).

8. Maria Margaroni notes, "Its function, then [the function of the semiotic *chora*] is to displace the speaking subject, (re)tracing its emergence not only 'before' *logos* but also, in returning it to the maternal body, beyond the Phallus as the structuring principle of the symbolic order" (2005: 79).

9. In fact, her prior novel, *The Samarai* (1990; English translation 1992), is a mixture of sentimental love story and intellectual treatise, a continual interruption of conventions with other conventions, broken dialogues, transgressions, multiple narratives, intertextual citations from the traditions of the left, and subjective characters crossing through one another and moving in temporalities through the revolutionary culture of the sixties into a later analytic culture.

10. Fredric Jameson has characterized the modern detective novel as exploring the "places occupied by faceless people" (1995: 70). Raymond Williams points out that the detective novel evolved in the twentieth century as the quintessential urban novel expressing feelings of "strangeness or 'mystery'" (16) arising from increased immigration and the growing presence of inscrutable masses of workers in cities. Richard Sennett elaborates: "As the cities grew, and developed networks of sociability independent of direct royal control, places where strangers might regularly meet grew up. This was the era of the building of massive urban parks, of the first attempts at making streets fit for the special purpose of pedestrian strolling as a form of relaxation... Industrial capitalism was equally and directly at work on the material life of the public realm itself. For instance, the mass-production of clothes, and the use of mass-production patterns by individual tailors or seamstresses, meant that many diverse segments of the cosmopolitan public began in gross to take on a similar appearance, that public markings were losing distinctive forms. Yet virtually no one believed that society was becoming thereby homogenized; the machine meant

that social differences—important differences, necessary to know if one were to survive in a rapidly expanding milieu of strangers—were becoming hidden, and the stranger more intractably a mystery" (17–20). I have explored the relationship between neoliberalism and detective fiction more in depth in *Policing Narratives and the State of Terror.*

11. Kristeva: "The questions we will ask about literary practice will be aimed at the political horizon from which this practice is inseparable" (1984: 17).

12. Iris Marion Young interprets the anticollectivist thesis in Kristeva's thought as presenting a way of getting beyond what Derrida might call "metaphysics of presence" or Adorno might call "identity thinking," where an ideal of unity is projected. Kristeva, she says, offers a politics of difference that takes into account social alienation, violence, and contradictions. Kristeva, she continues, belies "[a]ll these formulation [that] seek to understand community as a unification of particular persons through the sharing of subjectivities: persons will cease to be opaque, other, not understood, and instead become fused, mutually sympathetic, understanding one another as they understand themselves" (10). Ewa Plonowska Ziarek also understands Kristeva's politics of radical difference as pointing to sexual difference as the model for the antagonism which builds into radical democracy: "For Laclau and Mouffe, the split subject of psychoanalysis reflects the constitutive contradictions of democracy between equality and conflict, diversity and equivalence, particularity and universality, antagonism and consensus. As we have seen, Kristeva...radicalized this thesis by emphasizing the limits of sociosymbolic identification" (2001: 138). The problem with such perspectives is that they do not consider that what Kristeva omits is any possibility of acting politically through any type of association. Not all group identifications lead to Fascism. Though it may be important to think about how communities surrender differences, it is also important to think about possible communities that would form out of difference. Kristeva's total autonomy of the subject, moreover, as Nancy Fraser say, works "to valorize transgression and innovation *per se* irrespective of content" and to inflect "norm-conforming practice as negative *tout court,* irrespective of the content of the norms" (95).

13. "The 'second phase' women, who are primarily interested in the specificity of feminine psychology and its symbolic manifestations, seek a language for their corporeal and intersubjective experiences" (2000: 187).

14. "When the women's movement began as the struggle of suffragists and existential feminists, it sought to stake out its place in the linear time of planning and history. As a result, although the movement was universalist from the start, it was deeply rooted in the sociopolitical life of nations" (2000: 186).

15. Alexandre Kojève interpreted Hegel's lord-bondsman interaction through a Marxist Master-Slave lens, and this became a dominant reading of Hegel for many French intellectuals. The role of the Slave is defined as reaching some sort of transcendence through work, where the made object is what registers the transformative consciousness of the slave: "But—still thanks to the Master—the

Slave has another advantage, conditioned by the fact that he works... Generally speaking, it is the Slave, and only he, who can realize *progress,* who can go beyond the *given* and—in particular—the given that he himself is. On the one hand, as I just said, possessing the *idea* of Freedom and *not being* free, he is led to transform the given (social) conditions of his existence—that is, to realize historical progress" (48–50). Others besides Kristeva—most notably Georges Bataille—have taken up the inherent eroticism in this relationship as part of what constitutes the dialectic.

16. The three novels that compose Kristeva's detective series—*The Old Man and the Wolves, Possessions,* and *Murder in Byzantium*—all take place in the city of Santa Varvara, a city not in France but not totally outside of it either, a city coextensive with Eastern Europe but not necessarily either absorbed in it or bordering it on the outside, a city trapped in its present but that has not escaped its history and in some senses carries living traces of its Middle Ages. Santa Varvara *is* Kristeva's biography, the spatialization of the subject. It is also Stephanie's birthplace, and she associates it with her mother's language. It is, as well, like the relationship with the mother, archaic and filled with signs of its recent "primitivism," local identities, and particularized associations, but it is also newly industrialized, with increasing influences and corruptions from abroad, growing crime rates, illegal trade, arms deals, terrorist cells, and increasing involvements with global interests.

17. In France, racial, ethnic, or immigrant violence.

18. Kristeva's account of autism links it to the insufficient repression of the mother's sensuousness (an inability to behead the mother properly). Contrasting it with the depression that analysts have observed in infants first acquiring language, she notes, "The depressive stage reveals that language comes out of the loss of the sensory satisfactions obtained through maternal contact. Grieving for tactile, olfactory, auditory, and visual symbiosis is replaced first by hallucinations of the maternal face, and then by its verbal designation. Inversely, autism demonstrates the failure of this system. Whatever the neurological props, these take form in troubling symptoms: the human being's sensory attachment to the maternal medium seems so strong that no other bond to the other is possible" (2012: 15–16).

19. "Day after day the little optical glutton eats up the various shapes of her lips, imprinting them on an almost inaudible voice... He needs Pauline in order to trace the strange paths from lips to eyes and vocal cords and then, using this mute map, to utter words. Before a word can come forth, Jerry has to capture an incredible number of contours made by Pauline's lips, together with landscapes made by her throat, and then reproduce them in his own body" (1998: 197).

20. Gloria "was forever nursing an invisible wound. Perhaps 'nursing' wasn't the right word, but she couldn't think of a better" (1998: 54).

21. Kristeva notes that care represents the moment of ontological articulation, what "raises to the level of the concept" what has already been disclosed in Dasein's wanderings. In this, she says that Heidegger aims to put care in the place of an

ontological a priori. It is not within the scope of this paper to discuss to what extent Kristeva's reading of Heidegger resembles Heidegger.

22. As Fiona Barclay observes about *Strangers to Ourselves,* "Her [Kristeva's] appeal to psychoanalysis, which illuminates the otherness within each of us and so transforms us all into strangers, neglects the lived realities of today's migrants, exiles and refugees. By directly comparing the situations of 'a Maghrebian streetsweeper riveted to his broom [and] an Asiatic princess writing her memoirs in a borrowed tongue', she elides the economic differences which historians of immigration have argued are a major factor in the violence experienced by migrant workers, and glosses over diversity in favour of the argument that, since Freud's discovery of the unconscious, we are all foreigners now" (10).

23. This does not only apply to national borders. Because Kristeva is focused here on "foreignness" and therefore relations with the nation-state, the idea of other types of otherness is under-theorized. See, for example, Fiona Barclay's critique: "Kristeva's definition...neglects the reality that the most bitterly contested ground in recent debate is not immigration *per se,* but concerns the second- and third- generation descendants of North African immigrants, who hold French citizenship but are rejected by sections of the majority population" (2).

24. "Since, as Marx notes, it lies outside the sphere of material production per se, the signifying process, as it is practiced by texts—those 'truly free works'—transforms the opaque and impenetrable subject of social relations and struggles into a subject in process/on trial. Within this apparent asociality, however, lies the social function of texts: the production of a different kind of subject, one capable of bringing about new social relations" (1984: 105).

25. Not all critics have agreed that Kristeva's assessment of the subject is an avoidance of politics or an isolation of the subject. Ewa Ziarek, for example, understands the interiorization of semiotic dissonance and disparity to be an opening to a cosmopolitan recognition that otherness is the stranger inside. "[T]his difficult recognition," she summarizes, "of the irreconcilable alterity within the self is precisely what enables a non-violent relation to the other...Kristeva's reading suggests an 'improper' parallel between the strangeness disrupting the intimacy of the self from within and the irreducible exteriority of the other eluding any form of internalization" (1995: 12). For her, Kristeva's radical splitting of the subject is a resolution for a fundamental destructuring of the social, the upsurge in immigration, the constant encounters with inscrutable strangers. Ziarek's analysis, however, cannot solve the problem of power.

26. This does not seem quite to be the case in Kristeva's earlier work where she is still struggling with Marxism. There, the Symbolic does not take shape as particularly authoritarian or repressive, but rather as a type of ordering that is other to an idealist imposition from the exterior: "One may say, then, that what semiotics had discovered is the fact that there is a general social law, that this law is the symbolic dimension which is given in language and that every social practice offers a specific expression of that law" (1986: 25).

3 Feminist Theory's Itinerant Legacy: From Language Feminism to Labor Feminism

1. Rey Chow: "Linguistic opacity, obscurity, impenetrability—these qualities that are characteristic of high modernist works of art and literature, with their aversion to realist and mimetic representation—are also characteristic of much deconstructive and critical writing" (49).

2. I have not been the first to remark on this decline, nor to lament it. See, for example, Elizabeth Grosz: "Why, at precisely the moment when the demise of theory more generally is lamented (or celebrated), does feminist theory still matter? Or is this merely an anachronism, the last dying breath of a discipline destined to a past but no future? . . . These days it has become increasingly common for academics, especially feminist academics, to say, 'I want to return to my original field of research,' whether it is literature, early childhood education, sociology, archaeology, or politics. This means: I no longer want to be distracted by those abstract, irresolvable, aporetic concepts, ideas, frameworks that once took me away from the real things in the world that fascinated me. It implies that the politicization of knowledge that occurred in university from the 1960s onward is now coming to an end and that we can get back to texts, social groups, or specifiable behavior—the objects of disciplinary and interdisciplinary study—without the interminable and irresolvable questions that theory, philosophy, always entails" (2010: 95). Also, see Wendy Brown, who worries not only about the end of thinking sex and gender in a feminist way, even after feminist theory made it clear that theorizing about sex and gender was also participating in its construction, but also about how to think about a future for feminism after the question of revolution has been set aside: "So we are compelled, now that we know the impossibility of circumscribing gender without participating in its construction and regulation, and now that we know the indissociability of sex and gender from race, caste, class, nation, and culture, to think feminism and women's studies in this condition of afterness, in this temporal condition of 'knowing better' . . . I want to turn the question of the future of women's studies a bit, to ask not whether feminism and feminist scholarship can live without sex or gender, but how it lives, and will continue to live, without a revolutionary horizon" (98–99). This perspective that feminism is over frequently also pops up in the popular media. See, for example, Jessica Bennett in *Newsweek*: "So for all the talk about feminism as passé, mine wasn't a generation that rejected it for its militant, man-hating connotation—but also because of its success. Women were equal—*duh*—so why did we need feminism?" The argument here is that there is a need for feminism, after all, that "my generation" did not notice at first, but this argument only gets raised by foregrounding that the need only becomes visible after feminism's funeral oration has been delivered.

3. By "language," I am referencing the tradition of Sassurian linguistics as it moves through Lacan and, as a critique of Hegel through Derrida, into poststructuralist

theory. Language speaks through us—it allows us entry into the social but bars access to referents, including the subject. Language is arbitrary, and because it is arbitrary, it slides through a chain of signification that gains its meanings through difference. Butler appropriates this tradition, in part, in order to show language as productive of worlds.

4. Butler is here picking up on a significant aspect of second-wave feminism. One might look, for example, to Simone de Beauvoir's 1943 novel *She Came to Stay*, where artistic production—theater, novel writing, and so on—travel, passions, conversations, outings to nightclubs and cafes, and amorous intrigues structure plot and character, but allusions to everyday work, manufacturing, service, wage labor, and so on, do not quite appear, at least among the main characters, even when the men go off into military service. In this instance as in Butler, self-production substitutes for production in the strictly industrial sense of commodity production.

5. Elizabeth Wilson also identifies this trend in feminist theory after the sixties: "In the decades after this declaration, [Gayle] Rubin's political gesture (*for* the social and *away* from the biological) became second nature to feminist and queer critique, and the act of peeling biological influence away from social principles became critically habitual. Indeed, without such action, it has often been difficult to see how any argument can lay claim to being feminist or queer or, more broadly, political" (196). Wilson goes on to contend that biological reference is not always thought of in socially determinist ways. Toril Moi also criticizes the theoretical impulse to reject references to the body as always deterministic. She argues that feminist theory is reacting against a picture of "biological sex as something that seeps out from the ovaries and the testicles into every cell in the body until it has saturated the whole person" (11). I believe that Moi overstates the position (perhaps purposefully, as irony), in favor of a description of language as acquiring meaning through ordinary use.

6. A similar line of thinking was developed by a tradition of second-wave feminism in conversation with political economy. Nancy Hartsock, for example, criticizes a feminism that built out of the philosophical perspectives of Simone de Beauvoir and Gayle Rubin. Hartsock suggested that all thinking about the exchange and circulation of symbols, when posed as outside of the standpoint of production in a separate sphere of exchange, is an offshoot of "abstract masculinity." She borrows "abstract masculinity" from the rational subject in neoclassical economic theory as it came to inform Lévi-Strauss; such a subject, according to Hartsock, was socialized to combat its connection with the mother and her cooperative reproductive labor in a struggle to the death. She notes, "From a feminist standpoint, in which the self is understood as relationally defined, as constituted by a complex web of interactions with others, it seems perverse to deny a real connection with others and to argue that community can be constituted only indirectly, that men relate only through the mediation of things, that social relations are intentionally created by the act of passing things (most significantly, words and women) back and forth" (1983:

277). Hartsock sees the cultural symbolic as the rational head that breaks ranks with the sensory body: "Intellectual activity does not reflect the social organization of society; rather, it emanates from the intellect, the human mind ever the same and located outside history" (1983: 278). In Hartsock's analysis, there is no room for ideology. Though Ong does come to an understanding of how culture works within the circulation of capital, her critique depends similarly on capital and its biopolitical institutions setting the agenda and work as the "last instance" of experience.

7. Hester Eisenstein has analyzed this tendency in Ong's work as a legacy of an earlier feminism. In the seventies and eighties, Eisenstein says, feminist thinking maintained that any kind of work outside the home would be liberating for women: "I have been arguing that the central idea of US feminism, that paid work represents liberation for women, was deeply useful to capital [...] Aihwa Ong pointed out that the village girls [*maquiladoras*] hired might be exploited workers, fired as soon as their keen young eyesight began to require the use of eyeglasses. But they were also being modernized, abandoning the peasant sarongs of their villages for blue jeans, and winning the right to choose their own husbands" (503–504).

8. As one example of a critique of agency in Butler (there are many), Lois McNay points out, "In Butler, agency remains an abstract structural potentiality which is sufficiently undifferentiated that it becomes difficult, for example, to distinguish whether an act is politically effective or not given that all identity is performatively constructed [...Butler's concept of agency] lacks [...] a sufficient understanding of how the performative aspects of gender identity are lived by individuals in relation to the web of social practices in which they are enmeshed [...] In so far as it appears to be primarily a capacity of symbolic structures rather than of individuals, Butler's idea of agency lacks social and historical specificity" (46).

9. "[R]igid gender boundaries inevitably work to conceal the loss of an original love that, unacknowledged, fails to be resolved" (1990: 86).

10. For example, "The subject is not *determined* by the rules through which it is generated because signification is *not a founding act, but rather a regulated process of repetition* that both conceals itself and enforces its rules precisely through the production of substantializing effects" (1990: 198).

11. "But there are also great riches for feminists in explicitly embracing the possibilities inherent in the breakdown of clean distinctions between organism and machine and similar distinctions structuring the Western self. It is the simultaneity of breakdowns that cracks the matrices of domination and opens geometric possibilities. What might be learned from personal and political 'technological' pollution?" (174).

12. Or at least to acknowledge that constructions of identity could be explained in economic terms, as Lukacs insists is the case in his analysis of realism. One might suggest, as Toril Moi does, that Butler has absorbed Modernist practice that vilifies realism because it assumes realism, like the body, can only be deterministic (Moi disagrees with this reading of Lukacs).

13. "In the experience of losing another human being whom one has loved, Freud argues, the ego is said to incorporate that other into the very structure of the ego, taking on attributes of the other and 'sustaining' the other through magical acts of imitation... This process of internalizing lost loves becomes pertinent to gender formation when we realize that the incest taboo, among other functions, initiates a loss of a lobe-object for the ego and that this ego recuperates from this loss through the internalization of the tabooed object of desire" (1990: 78–79).

14. "The 'biopolitical' concerns of the more well-off nation to secure middle-class entitlements depends on the availability of foreign others, creating an environment of class privilege and bias that tolerates slavelike conditions for poor female migrants. Thus, in addition to the 'biopolitical' fracture, ruptures between racial and moral economies further complicate notions about who can or cannot be considered morally worthy human beings" (2009: 160).

15. For example, "NGOs foster a moral connection between free choice in seeking overseas employment and the young woman's sense of moral indebtedness and desire to sacrifice for their families" (2009: 162).

16. Butler is borrowing this idea of identity failure from Jacqueline Rose. Rose reads the failure of identity as the locus of the unconscious in psychoanalysis, the Freudian observation that the unconscious is always saying "no" to its social construction in the ego. She writes, "What distinguishes psychoanalysis from sociological accounts of gender [...] is that whereas for the latter, the internalization of norms is assumed roughly to work, the basic premise and indeed starting-point of psychoanalysis is that it does not. The unconscious constantly reveals the 'failure' of identity. Because there is no continuity of psychic life, so there is no stability of sexual identity, no position for women (or for men) which is very simply achieved" (90–91). Rose understands the Freudian woman needs to pass through impossible hurdles and treacherous pathways in order to develop fully and successfully as a "woman." Rose sees the negativity of identity—precisely the unconscious in its relationship to the social expectations of femininity—as a heretofore under-recognized point of intersection between feminism and Marxism.

17. For example, "If the notion of an abiding substance is a fictive construction produced through the compulsory ordering of attributes into coherent gender sequences, then it seems that gender as substance, the viability of *man* and *woman* as nouns, is called into question by the dissonant play of attributes that fail to conform to sequential or causal models of intelligibility" (1990: 33).

18. As Lois McNay notes, Butler's formulation of gender performativity through constitutive failure assumes too much uniformity in recognizable gender symbolics and "a rather exaggerated notion of the internal uniformity of gender norms" (45). In this, says McNay, Butler underestimates the multiple forms of social mediation between working life, economic need, and symbolic content: "A more active notion of agency emerges, however, once its [agency's] key role in the mediation of symbolic and material relations is understood. In other words, by conceptualizing the relation between the material and symbolic as generative of variable patterns of autonomy and dependence then a more determinate sense of agency emerges" (65).

19. The implication here is that norms are coterminous expressions of the system that forms those "persons" as in some relation to those norms. There is no way to judge the system because one is always inside of it, no way not to be submerged in it. For Butler, gender is a set of citations of power; the citing of gender norms affirms the system of power to which they lay hold; yet, the citation also always misses its mark. The problem of identity as a form of citationality of power parallels a problem in Foucault, where identities—like the "homosexual"—sustain their existence from the same networks, discourses, and institutions that subordinate them. Nancy Fraser interprets this tendency in Foucault as what makes the positing of ethical norms impossible. Foucault, she says, suspends the question of normative validity because he sees it as attached to the liberal tradition that provides, through its concept of rights, a sovereign, grounded context for distinguishing between legitimacy and illegitimacy. This position raises the issue, for Fraser, of whether Foucault is denying the positing of normativity altogether or only in reference to liberalism as a political philosophy based in the exercise of sovereign power. Fraser asks, "[D]oes Foucault's bracketing of the normative represent a substantive, principled commitment to ethical cultural relativism, to the impossibility of normative justification across power/knowledge retimes?" (1989: 21–22). Similarly, Butler relegates gender normativity to the same symbolic system that resists it.

20. For example, to the Abu Ghraib torture photographs Butler responds, "When, for instance, Rumsfeld claimed that publishing the photos of torture and humiliation and rape would allow them 'to define us as Americans,' he attributed to photography an enormous power to construct national identity itself. The photographs would not just show something atrocious, but would make our capacity to commit atrocity into a defining concept of American identity" (2009: 72).

21. For example, "[T]he neoliberal stress on economic borderlessness has induced the creation of multiple political spaces and techniques for differentiated governing within the national terrain [. . . W]hat is distinctive about Asian post-developmentalism is a checkered geography of governing resulting not from an anemic state apparatus but from a deliberative neoliberal calculation as to which areas and which populations are advantageous or not advantageous in appealing to global markets. The deployment of such postdevelopmental logic in effect produces a postdevelopmental geography—the multiplication of differentiated zones of governing across the national territory—that has specific political effects" (2006: 76–78).

22. "Emerging articulations of neoliberal forms, sovereign experiments, and regimes of citizenship have radically changed the political and spatial possibilities of being actualized and of being human . . . Myriad disarticulations and rearticulations occasioned by the logic of the exception transform the elements we used to associate with a unified concept of citizenship into values placed on humanity that are increasingly varied, fragmented, contingent, and ambiguous, but permanently subject to ethicopolitical critique" (2006: 27).

4 Girls in School: The "Girls' School" Genre at the New Frontier

1. Defending himself in an interview cited by the *New York Times,* Mortenson counters that the details may have been altered but the main story was not "the time about our final days on K2 and ongoing journey to Korphe village and Skardu is a compressed version of events that took place," he said, and a Pentagon spokesperson agrees, adding that: "We continue to believe in the logic of what Greg is trying to accomplish in Afghanistan and Pakistan because we know the powerful effects that education can have on eroding the root causes of extremism" (Bosman and Strom).

2. Some of these allegations are detailed on the American Institute of Philanthropy's website at www.charitywatch.org/articles/CentralAsiaInstitute.html (Accessed: October 7, 2011). Though the investigation by the Montana attorney general found only that Mortenson "had little aptitude for record keeping or personnel management," according to *The New York Times* and the Associated Press (April 5, 2012), he was required to pay back hundreds of thousands of dollars to his charity and was banned from serving on the board or as executive director (what was not reported were any investigative conclusions about the money that was *not* spent in Afghanistan or Pakistan nor about the projects there that did not come to fruition).

3. "Reena," a 19-year-old member of the Revolutionary Association of the Women of Afghanistan, who uses this pseudo-name to travel undercover, mentions these aspects of girls' education in an interview with Amy Goodman on *Democracy Now!* "Ten Years after U.S. Invasion, Afghan War Rages on with No End in Sight" (October 7, 2011). Available at: www.democracynow.org/. Accessed: October 7, 2011. Annie Kelly reports in *The Guardian,* "A new report [by 16 NGOs] is warning that hard-won progress in girls' education in Afghanistan, heralded as one of few success stories of the last nine years, is increasingly under threat as international interest in reconstruction efforts ebbs away." Though expanding girls' education was originally seen as a "shining example" of the success of intervention, approximately one quarter never attend, many (especially in rural areas) have no access, and, according to the Afghan Ministry of Education, 47 percent have no actual building while 61 percent in some provinces remain closed, and there is little investment in female teachers ("Afghan Girls' Education Backsliding as Donors Shift Focus to Withdrawal." *The Guardian* (February 24, 2011). Available at: www.guardian.co.uk/global-development/2011/feb/24/afghanistan-girls-education-report. Accessed: October 7, 2011.

4. The girls' school is not always the place where the colonizer succeeds in "destroying the cultural resistance of a colonized country" (fn. 39) as Fanon diagnoses it. Often, postcolonial writers frame the girls' school as where the power struggle of colonial culture is played out, as nationalist culture asserts its agenda. Partha Chatterjee, for example, interprets the "feminine curriculum" of the nationalists as a way to project "superiority over the Western woman for whom [there was...] a loss of feminine (spiritual) virtues" (254). He goes on: "The real threat was seen to lie in the fact that the early schools, and arrangements for teaching women at

home, were organized by Christian missionaries; there was thus the fear of both proselytization and the exposure of women to harmful Western influences. The threat was removed when in the 1850s Indians themselves began to open schools for girls" (253). In her "primal scenes" of her childhood in Algeria, *Reveries of the Wild Woman,* Helene Cixous understands the French girls' school that she attends as where she suspects a different Algeria arising when Muslim girls begin to enroll: "they were future and necessary, but my life alone was aware of it, I didn't have a language...I looked all my Algerias in the face. I saw in bright glimmers how I will never gleam for them. They were headed for their lives, their turn is coming I guessed" (85).

5. *Stones Into Schools:* "I also came away with the conclusion that the military is probably doing a better job than any other institution in the United States government—including the State Department, Congress, and the White House—of developing a meaningful understanding of the complex dynamics on the ground in Pakistan and Afghanistan" (257).

6. This does not exhaust the list. Girls' schools are a frequent motif in Modernist literature, often introducing transgressive themes, partly because of their sexualization, partly because they tend to be a disruption of the Symbolic, often tragically. In *Olivia* by Olivia (1949), Olivia goes to school at Les Avons and falls in love with her teach Mademoiselle Julie, only to incur the jealousy of the other teacher, Mademoiselle Clara, to tragic end. In Christa Winsloe's *The Child Manuela* (first published as *Das Madchen Manuela* in 1933), Manuela is sent off to boarding school upon the death of her mother, only to fall in love with her teacher Fraulein von Bernburg. In a drunken confession, Manuela publically boasts of her love. "Manuela is sexually abnormal" (285), declares the Head. The school authorities isolate and punish her; she responds by jumping out a window to her death. Elizabeth Bowen's 1963 *The Little Girls* tells of three girls who bury in the yard of their girls' school a "time capsule" of objects in 1914, before the war. Nearly 50 years later, they respond to a mysterious personal ad and set out to retrieve the buried secret only to discover the school yard bombed out and the objects missing. The discovery of the missing objects parallels the unravelling and deterioration of the women's lives, families, health, and sanity. In Ivy Compton-Burnett's 1933 *More Women Than Men,* the protagonist and headmistress Josephine raises her homosexual brother Jonathan Swift's son Gabriel. When he falls in love and gets married to one of the teachers (Ruth) and they move to another part of town, Josephine grows jealous and lets Ruth, sick with pneumonia, get exposed to a draught and die, virtually murdering her. A 2004 Belgian film by director Lucile Hadzihalilovic, *Innocence,* plays on these tropes of the girls' school as transgression. The young girl arrives to her boarding school in a coffin, the music is ominous, the girls keep disappearing into the old, gothic-like house at the end of the woods, only to return come morning. The girls are focused on closely, playing in their white dresses. Expectations are aroused that something sinister is being planned, but as the plot unwinds, nothing ends up happening, the girls are safe, the old house is the location for their ballet classes and performances, and the graduating girls are released into a blissful scene of a flowing water fountain.

7. Title IX is a section of the 9172 Civil Rights Act that makes illegal acts of discrimination or exclusion based on sex from any educational institution receiving federal funding.

8. *The Guardian* reported that the perceived lower performance of girls in math and science is due to environmental factors. *The Guardian* cites a 2013 study by the Organization for Economic Cooperation and Development (OECD) as well as an earlier finding by the Program for International Student Assessment (Pisa). The OECD report said that "15-year-old girls around the world outperform boys in science—except for in the United States, Britain and Canada" (Keller).

9. "Whereas their male classmates yelled out or snapped the fingers of their raised hands when they wanted to speak, these girls seemed, for the most part, to recede from class proceedings, a charge they didn't deny" (11). Orenstein interprets these experiences as promising "a loss of confidence in herself" as well as "a scathingly critical attitude toward her body" (xvi) leading to hopelessness and depression. Orenstein acknowledges the limitations of self-esteem as a categorical goal: "I was suspicious of any movement that stressed personal transformation over structural change, especially for women. Self-esteem sounded to me like another way to blame the victim, warm fuzzy style" (xviii). Self-esteem seemed to her to be a product of corporate advertising, where promotional campaigns could convince girls of their lacks and deficiencies only to sell them items that would fix them. Though Orenstein does try to redefine self-esteem, it still seems to operate as a mechanism that would allow better adaption to the current system and ideology. In Orenstein's case, self-esteem is "having a sense of their potential, their competence" (xix) leading to, as she says, these girls' entering the professional labor force (perhaps as the advertisers that create the self-esteem product ads?).

10. Leonard Sax, MD, PhD, for example, finds that same-sex schooling is necessary because gendered brain differences and brain activity cause boys and girls to have different learning needs. Because of their brain organization, girls talk more and are more skilled at coordinating with others. "The gender difference in brain organization," Dr. Sax reports, "has clear implications for education. In particular, questions of the form 'How would you *feel* if...'" don't work well for most boys. That question requires boys to link *emotional* information in the amygdala with *language* information in the cerebral cortex. It's like trying to recite poetry and juggle bowling pins at the same time" (106). Such science that explains how girls learn differently often draws on feminist research—like the work of Carol Gilligan, Nancy Chodorow, and Nel Noddings—to illustrate that girls respond to situations by relating to others rather than through abstract principles, even though both Gilligan and Chodorow have made it clear that their analyses are based in socialization processes rather than essential gender types.

11. Meanwhile, single-sex state schools in the United Kingdom have fallen from 2500 to 400 over the last 40 years (Jackson, 227).

12. The research on test scores as a measure of predictability is inconclusive, at best. As Kenneth J. Saltman concludes from reviewing the research, "[H]igh stakes testing regimes do not achieve what they are designed to achieve. However, to think beyond efficacy to the underlying assumptions about 'achievement,' it is necessary to raise theoretical concerns. Theoretically, at the very least, the enforcement-oriented assumptions [...] fail to consider the limitations of defining 'achievement' through high-stakes tests, fail to question what knowledge and whose knowledge constitute legitimate or official curricula that students are expected to master, and fail to interrogate the problematic assumptions of learning modeled on digestion or commodity acquisition" (128).

13. The case law record is much longer than this historical abbreviation reveals. Other relevant cases include: *Brown v. the Board of Education of Topeka* (1954), outlawing racial segregation in schools; *Vorchheimer v. School District of Philadelphia* (1973), where the Court upheld publically funded single-sex education on the basis of the freedom to choose; *Mississippi University for Women v. Hogan* (1982), declaring unconstitutional the female-only admissions policy at a public university nursing school because of the use of stereotypes in the definition of the career choice; *Newberg v. Board of Public Education* (1983), which denounced single-sex publically funded schooling as "inherently unequal" under the Fourteenth Amendment of the US Constitution; *Wygant v. Jackson Board of Education* (1986), prohibiting the use of race and gender as a factor in faculty hiring and retention.

14. For example, Teresa A. Hughes: "In coeducational classrooms, boys and girls are easily distracted by one another. They want to impress each other and often act out in ways that are detrimental to individual learning" (9). The reason Hughes gives for this "acting out" is a preoccupation with a "dating and rating" culture that makes students obsessed with how they look. "By separating the sexes into different classes or schools," Hughes speculates, "the students would be free of distractions from the opposite sex and would be better able to concentrate on academic pursuits" (9). The *New York Times'* coverage identifies the problems of coeducation with too much sexual interest getting in the way of "focus," student-teacher bonding, "independence," a "sense of community," or "participation" (Medina).

15. Though her most famous novel, *Jane Eyre* (1847), presents the girls' school Lowood as a storehouse of poverty and disease, the school in Charlotte Bronte's 1853 novel *Villette* trains middle-class girls in the arts of conjugality. Q. D. Leavis' famous introduction to *Villette* mentions Lucy Snowe's arrival at the girls' school in Belgium, where she is hired to teach English, as an enactment of the contrast between English Protestant values and Belgian Catholic superstitions, that is, between English "probity" and Catholic "intrigue" (xxxvi), between English "trust" and French "*surveillance*" (xxxvi–xxxvii), between English "sensibility" and Belgian "callous self-interest" (xxxvii). The school at first expresses national character, and then foregrounds Lucy's mood, but never

does Leavis make explicit the particular role of the school in setting in place symbolic frames of cultural conflict over women's roles.

16. Comparing herself to Mlle. St. Pierre, one of the teachers from the region, Lucy ruminates, "She was of little use as far as the communication of knowledge went, but for strict surveillance and maintenance of rules she was invaluable" (140).

17. Lauren Goodlad also understood Victorian schooling narratives as caught between a "materialist objectification" (190) of calculation and surveillance, on the one hand, and, on the other, a sense of "character"—outside of social hierarchy—that resisted bureaucratization: "character as a manifestation of the potential for humanist or Christian development" (190). Schooling narratives were conflicted "by the prospect of a world unable to distinguish between exchange-value, a value measured in relation between things, and the value of nurturing human potential" (191), a value, that is, that could not be calculated. Goodlad, however, is less concerned with how this quandary is caught in a struggle over what counts as labor, and how this affects gender. Goodlad's concern is, rather, the construction of a particular culture of liberalism in Britain.

18. Krakauer explains that Mortenson built the schools in Afghanistan in places that were not riveted by violence or populated by the Taliban: "Only a small fraction of his schools are found in locales that might be characterized as breeding grounds for terrorists. In Afghanistan, the majority of schools CAI has established are in areas where the Taliban has little influence or is simply non-existent" (44). Krakauer labels Mortenson's claims to be directly confronting the Taliban as "fear-mongering" (46).

19. None other than "friend and hero" of feminism and die-hard supporter of female intellectuals, Larry Summers, agrees: "[A]n extensive body of recent research...has convinced me that once its benefits are recognized, investment in girls' education may well be the highest return investment available in the developing world...Expenditures on increasing the education of girls do not just meet the seemingly easy test of being more socially productive than military outlays. They appear to be far more productive than many other valuable categories of investment" (as cited in Herz and Sperling, 38). Lawrence H. Summers—who formerly filled various roles in the Clinton Administration's Treasury, Chief Economist of the World Bank, and then President Barack Obama's economic advisor—famously said, while he was president of Harvard University, that the reason there were so few professional women in science and engineering fields was because women had lower aptitudes. Mortenson cites a book on international promotion of girls' schools where this Larry Summers quote appears.

5 Gender Work: Feminism after Neoliberalism

1. In my prior work, I have called this: the "re-privatization" of women's work. For example: "I show the tendencies of a 're-privatization' of women's labor within

current formations of capitalism: That is, I show how the current organization of corporate power seeks to bypass the regulatory state by reframing labor according to the conventions of work in the industrialized home, and then directly capitalizing on this type of work, for example, a status of legal exceptionalism, of existing beyond the law and public interventions, as submissive, as under-remunerated and unprotected, and the like" (*Feminist Theory in Pursuit of the Public,* 16).

2. In this formulation, Hardt and Negri are not insensitive to race and the way it creates inequalities in the workforce. The basest forms of service, care, and "Third World" labor are exactly what they are talking about by the terminology of "the so-called feminization of work." However, because all work tends toward these forms, Hardt and Negri treat all work as equally abstractable, and this is what makes it so difficult to locate in their work ways of addressing inequalities in income distributions along the North-South divide.

3. There have been a few noteworthy exceptions. See, for example, Federici (2004), Federici (2012), Weeks (2011), Fortunati (1995), Quinby (2004), Del Re (2005), Dalla Costa and Dalla Costa, eds. (1999), McRobbie (2010), Sassen (2004), Parvulescu (2012), Corsani and Murphy (2007), and Dyer-Witherford (2005).

4. "A man would never get the notion of writing a book on the peculiar situation of the human male. But if I wish to define myself, I must first of all say: 'I am a woman'; on this truth must be based all further discussion...Woman has ovaries, a uterus; these peculiarities imprison her in her subjectivity, circumscribe her within the limits of her own nature. It is often said that she thinks with her glands" (xxi).

5. Oftentimes, even while using these terms to reconceptualize the capital/labor relationship in ways that look like "women's work," Hardt and Negri need to disqualify women from the tendency. For example, taking on the issue of "absolute surplus value," Negri notes, in parentheses: "A specific exception, which takes the definition of absolute surplus value back to its origins as an individual measure of exploitation, concerns female labour—housework and the reproduction of the species, with its unlimited extension of the working day" (2003: 62). At this point in the analysis, "absolute surplus value" has been defined as when capital captures the entire social field, turning production into reproduction. Marking his uncertainty with parentheses, Negri defensively portrays women's labor as "*exogenous* to the system" (2003: 54), a possibility that he earlier denies by showing how the exogenous is always internal in this period of "real subsumption." In fact, in many of their workings-through of the terms of contemporary capitalism, women's work is assumed as the frame of capital's complete socialization without women being imagined as the actors.

6. For Negri, "the social factory" moves beyond Michel Foucault's "disciplinary society." He picks up this idea from Gilles Deleuze's descriptions of the "Society of Control": "nineteenth-century capitalism is a capitalism of concentration, for production and for property. It therefore erects a factory as a space of enclosure,...but also...other spaces conceived through analogy (the worker's familial

house, the school)...But in the present situation,...[t]his is no longer a capitalism for production but for the product, which is to say, for being sold or mar-
keted...[T]he factory has given way to the corporation...The conquests of the
market are made by grabbing control and no longer by disciplinary training, by
fixing the exchange rate much more than by lowering costs, by transformation of
the product more than by specialization of production...Marketing has become
the center or the "soul" of the corporation. We are taught that corporations have
a soul, which is the most terrifying news in the world. The operation of markets
is now the instrument of social control and forms the impudent breed of our
masters. Control is short-term and of rapid rates of turnover, but also continuous
and without limit, while discipline was of long duration, infinite and discontinu-
ous. Man is no longer man enclosed, but man in debt" (6).

7. Negri: "Here the assumption of the command in all the intensity of its general
political functioning is...primary...Here in Marx...money is taken as the form
of bourgeois hegemony—as the monetary horizon of command" (1991: 61).
Negri's idea that the field of economic transactions has been taken over by politics and, in particular, is controlled by command—this idea is one than rankles
Callinicos most fervently. In Negri's view, says Callinicos, "The politicization
and socialization of the relations of production implies their reduction to straight-
forward relations of force, and capitalist domination is reduced to 'pure command'" (176). Callinicos believes that economic processes are still governed by
competition rather than politicization, and that economic relations have been
depoliticized rather than politicized under neoliberalism. Negri, however, like
Althusser, would not agree that either politics or command would need to reside
in the state, although he would see that as one place (not the strongest) where
command resides. Additionally, Negri would see "command" and "politicization"
as a tendency within the present rather than as a totalizing descriptor. As capital
consolidates, its movements are less governed by open market fluctuations than
by decisions, and many if not most of these decisions are political.

8. Negri: "In destroying time-as-measure *capital constitutes time as collective substance*. But for capital this temporal collectivity cannot show itself as such; it
must rather be reduced to an analytic collectivity, to a collectivity without time.
It is here that the *antagonism* erupts. The time of cooperation constitutes itself as
a subject against capital. It is *use-value*" (2003: 59; Negri's emphasis).

9. As Carlo Vercellone explains, "In the activities in which the cognitive and immaterial dimension of labour is dominant, we witness a destabilization of one of the
structuring conditions of the wage relation, that is to say, the renunciation—compensated by the wage—by the workers to any claim on the property of the product of their labour. In cognitive-labour-producing knowledge, the result of labour
remains incorporated in the brain of the worker and is thus inseparable from her
person. That helps explain, together with other factors, the pressure exercised by the
enterprises in order to attain a strengthening of the rights of intellectual property
and to re-enclose, in a new phase of the primitive accumulation of capital, the social
mechanisms at the base of the circulation of knowledge" (33).

10. As Cesare Casarino describes it: "if the real subsumption of society by capital has entailed that there is no longer virtually any aspect and indeed any time of our lives that is not productive for capital, time then—Negri seems to suggest—is that which capital needs now more than ever and yet that which capital always hopes against all hope to reduce to zero. The impossible dream of capital, after all, has always been to have production and circulation in no time and without time" (2003: 190).

11. Negri: "*Capitalist production, when it takes over society, renders inextricable the linkage of production and circulation*" (1991: 180; Negri's emphasis).

12. "Real subsumption" did not just happen one day, did not just begin. In "real subsumption," there is no before and after, no progress from one to the other, no break between phases of the working-day, no division between a time of rest and a time of work, no lag-time when capital waits for goods and equipment to arrive so the next cycle can start, because everything is production: production is "being," so time is restlessness, like the collision of falling atoms, a living force (e.g., Negri: "[T]he common appears as the product of an eternal agglomeration of elements, as a great shower of matter" [2003: 194]). Different temporal speeds coordinate in a singular process as different phases of production and the working-day overflow into each other. I find the naturalistic metaphors taken from physics less compelling and more theological than the ones that connect capital with birth and socialization. They come out of Negri's reading of Spinoza and feed some of the criticisms that say that Negri reduces resistance to a spontaneous reaction. The idea of materialist ontology—where this movement of time is historicized—would seem to me to be trying to block this naturalization.

13. Hardt and Negri (1994): "All privatistic alternatives that single capitalists could express are negated, not by the laws of development but by the directly expressed and directly effective political law of collective capital" (62).

14. Baudrillard, for example, "What society seeks through production, and over-production, is the restoration of the real which escapes it" (44).

15. Hardt and Negri: "The sites delegated to popular representation and the continuous production of constitutional ordering are impiously permeated by these constricting logics of command, and what remains of them is only an empty carcass that the communicative simulation of the 'democratic media' tires to camouflage in aesthetic garb" (1994: 299).

16. "The entire machine of the State is seen developing on the basis of the necessity to control this socialization of the capitalist relationship of exploitation" (Hardt and Negri, 1994: 160).

17. "It would be one thing to claim that the *potential* for such exists in the virtual Empire being forged in the ongoing passage from colonialism to neo-colonialism, from formal subsumption to real subsumption, from modernity to postmodernity: with that I would willingly agree. It is quite different to claim that such potential is actually being realized, or even that it is likely to be realized. This is a probability assessment for which they provide very little evidence—but for

which they need provide no further evidence, as long as Empire is understood primarily as a philosophical concept" (129).

18. "The remainder of the use value of workers' labor is completely subsumed by capital and by virtue of that produces surplus value" (Negri, 1991: 74).

19. Negri: "The tendency: it is not simply what permits a passive construction of the categories on the basis of a sum of historical acquisitions; it is above all what permits a reading of the present in light of the future, in order to make projects to illuminate the future. To take risks, to struggle. A science should adhere to that. And if occasionally one is an ape, it is only in order to be more agile" (1991: 49).

20. Negri: "The time of constituent power, in the void of determinations to which it has been reduced, is conceived as a negative substance. It becomes time of 'being for death'—the implacable perspective and totalitarian reduction of the being of the world to the negative... In what sense? In the sense of death... This is constituent power formally assumed and posed as the dark appearance of a will to power—certainly fully untouched by the ghosts of modernity—but at the same time absolutely inimical to any determination of the strength of the multitude" (1999: 317). And with Casarino: "The limit is creative to the extent to which you have been able to overcome it qua death: the limit is creative because you have overcome death... And while Spinoza tell us to free ourselves from the presence of death, Heidegger tells us the contrary" (2004: 175).

21. Pierre Macherey reads Negri's challenges to dialectical thinking as an affirmation of the independent development of freedom for the purposes of constitution. The elements of the social body "are deployed in the extensiveness of an expanding body, in the conquest of its own domain" (26). Macherey's depictions of Negri's dismissal of the dialectic are constantly embedded in such language of human development and birthing in order to outline the terms of Negri's notion of autonomy: for example, "Thus, by projecting itself onto the terrain of liberation, the constitutive power of Being undergoes a veritable mutation: it becomes precisely practice, subjectivity, an opening onto a world of possibilities or an ethical world in which it tends consciously and voluntarily to be realized" (22).

22. In an interview with Cesare Casarino (2004), Negri remarks, "I felt that in the end Foucault's archeology was unable to turn into an effective process of power: the archeological project always moved from above in order to reach below, while what concerned me most was precisely the opposite movement from below. For me, this was his project's main limitation" (152).

23. "This common is not only the earth we share but also the languages we create, the social practices we establish, the modes of sociality that define our relationships, and so forth" (Hardt and Negri, 2009: 139).

24. Negri: "Now, postmodernism... poses citizenship (Man) and market (society) in a relation of uninterrupted circulation, almost as an equivalent tautology,... going so far as to speak of an 'end of history'" (2003: 202).

25. Negri: *"The fundamental law of crisis lies therefore in the contradictory relation between necessary labor and surplus labor, that is, in the functioning of the law of surplus value"* (1991: 97; Negri's emphasis).

26. Negri: "The more surplus value is developed, the less one can compress necessary labor, and less is the quantity and the quality of the creative activity which capital can subsume in the labor process" (1991: 83).

27. Negri's ideas about excess evolve from the concept developed by Georges Bataille in *The Accursed Share*. Bataille unconventionally believes that marriage is set up originally as a social control on "a kind of inner revolution whose intensity must have been excessive" (48), or eroticism, rather than as an institution to protect rights of property and inheritance. According to Bataille, marriage systematized the prohibition against this excess alongside the periodic letting-up of the prohibition by, for one, restricting the understanding of women to "their fecundity and their labor" (49). Sometimes the excess had to do with women's bodies or with women as objects that circulate and are exchanged. Negri's treatment of excess relies on a similar construction of an excess internal to women's labor and visible in bodies, only for Negri, as a post-Hegelian thinker, excess does not grant transcendence but rather introduces antagonism. Negri faults Bataille for being a "technician of urbanism" and "rather shallow" (Casarino, 2004: 162).

28. Rancière: "The familiar police logic that…militant feminists are strangers to their sex, is, all in all, justified. Any subjectification is a disidentification, removal from the naturalness of place, the opening up of a subject space where anyone can be counted since it is the space where those of no account are counted, where a connection is made between having a part and having no part" (1999: 36).

29. Rancière: "Politics ceases wherever this gap no longer has any place, wherever the whole of the community is reduced to the sum of its parts with nothing left over" (1999: 123).

30. In its affiliations with Freudian psychoanalysis, second-wave feminism has been concerned foundationally with the relationship between the development of a full-fledged, socially adapted, appropriately sexed adult female and a symbolics of femininity that does not necessarily connect to that psychic formation. In his lecture on "Femininity," Freud himself did not only make it seem nearly impossible for an infant child to progress toward becoming a woman, but he also mystified the symbolic itself, concluding "that what constitutes masculinity and femininity is an unknown characteristic which anatomy cannot lay hold of" (114). Though, he continues, "when you say 'masculine', you usually mean 'active', and when you say 'feminine', you usually mean 'passive'" (114), there is no concrete biological determination or causal factor and, what is more, femininity often contains a fair amount of aggressivity, according to Freud, as in lactation. This break between femininity's experiences and its symbolic codings has been an important one in feminist thinking, even as it passes through Lacan (e.g., "There is an antinomy here that is internal to the

assumption [assumption] by man (*Mensch*) of his sex: why must he assume the attributes of that sex only through a threat or even in the guise of a deprivation?" [575]). We see it as well in Simone de Beauvoir's famous dictum that one is not born a woman but becomes one: "It would appear, then, that every female human being is not necessarily a woman; to be so considered she must share in that mysterious and threatened reality known as femininity" (xix). It plays out further in Julia Kristeva's split between the Semiotic and the Symbolic, where the Semiotic operates separately but still feeds into the Symbolic to boost it up, and then in Judith Butler's performativity, where the Symbolic calls the subject into being but the subject never quite fits the expectations of its Symbolic constitution, producing the Symbolic anew by answering the call. Reading this split from the Symbolic of femininity as, finally, a total rupture of the subject or failure of identity, Jacqueline Rose notes, "[P]sychoanalysis is no longer best understood as an account of how women are fitted into place (even this, note, is the charitable reading of Freud). Instead, psychoanalysis becomes one of the few places in our culture where it is recognized as more than a fact of individual pathology that most women do not painlessly slip into their roles as women" (91). Negri takes this disassociation, or alienation, to a new level.

31. "[B]iopolitical production," they emphasize, "particularly in the ways it exceeds the bounds of capitalist relations and constantly refers to the common, grants labor increasing autonomy and provides the tools or weapons that could be wielded in a project of liberation" (2009: 137).

32. "On the biopolitical terrain … where powers are continually made and unmade, bodies resist. They have to resist in order to exist" (2009: 31).

33. Casarino faults Negri for not substantially distinguishing pleasure from desire (the time of productivity, the time of consumer capitalism). In contrast, Casarino sees in Marx's *Grundrisse* a doubling of pleasure, where it is both attached to the commodity and attached to a refusal of capital's demand for "self-denial" in the worker. Pleasure serves to "broaden *the sphere of non-work,* that is, the sphere of their own needs, the value of necessary labor" (2003: 200–201) in ways that Negri fails to recognize. It gets in the way of surplus value. Additionally, "[a]s the sphere of pleasures widens, it does not disavow the present and yet also projects itself towards an undetermined future of experimentation" (2003: 202).

34. Negri: "In essence, the problem that I was struggling with—and I think Gilles [Deleuze] too was struggling with it, without nonetheless having any desire whatsoever to find a solution for it—was a classical problem of the phenomenological tradition, namely, the problem of the relation between intention and act. But if one lives this problem from a collective standpoint—that is, from the standpoint of collective subjectivities—this then becomes a fundamentally historical problem, the problem par excellence of constituent power. And this is also the fundamental problem that the main traditions with the philosophy of right—namely, juridical formalism and critical realism—repeatedly faced, without ever being able to come to terms with it adequately, because within these traditions the birth of the norm is always a transcendent act" (Casarino,

2004: 156–157). Also: "In some way or other, all I think, say, write or do is an attempt to understand…what are the mechanisms of decision that can posit the multitude as subjectivity" (Casarino and Negri, 2008: 96).

35. "The…notion of the common is dynamic, involving both the product of labor and the means of future production. This common is not only the earth we share but also the languages we create, the social practices we establish, the modes of sociality that define our relationships, and so forth" (Hardt and Negri, 2009: 139).

Works Cited

Adorno, Theodor W. *Aesthetic Theory.* Ed. and Trans. Robert Hullot-Kentor. Minneapolis: University of Minnesota Press, 1997.

Althusser, Louis. "Ideology and Ideological State Apparatuses (Notes Towards an Investigation)." In *Lenin and Philosophy and Other Essays.* Trans. Ben Brewster. London: New Left Books, 1971, pp. 123–173.

American Association of University Women. "Separated by Sex: Title IX and Single-Sex Education." *American Association of University Women.* Available at: www.aauw.org/act/issue_advocacy/actionpages/upload/single-sex_ed111.pdf. Accessed: October 6, 2011.

Arrighi, Giovanni. "Lineages of Empire." *Debating Empire.* Ed. Gopal Balakrishnan. London and New York: Verso, 2003, pp. 29–42.

Associated Press. "'Three Cups' Author to Stay With Charity He Founded." *New York Times* (April 5, 2012). Available at: www.nytimes.com/aponline/2012/04/05/us/ap-us-books-three-cups-of-tea.html?_r=2&hp. Accessed: April 6, 2012.

Bair, Jennifer. "On Difference and Capital: Gender and the Globalization of Production." *Signs* 36, 1 (Autumn 2010): 203–226.

Balibar, Etienne. "The Basic Concepts of Historical Materialism." In *Reading "Capital."* By Louis Althusser and Etienne Balibar. Trans. Ben Brewster. London: NLB, 1970.

Bamberger, Joan. "The Myth of Matriarchy: Why Men Rule in Primitive Society." *Woman Culture & Society.* Ed. Michelle Zimbalist Rosaldo and Louise Lamphere. Stanford, CA: Stanford University Press, 1974, pp. 263–280.

Barclay, Fiona. "Kristeva's Stranger Within: The Question of the Foreigner in Daniel Prévost's *Le Passé sous silence*." *Paragraph* 33, 1 (2010): 1–19.

Bataille, Georges. *The Accursed Share: An Essay on General Economy; Volume II: The History of Eroticism; Volume III: Sovereignty.* Trans. Robert Hurley. New York: Zone Books, 1993.

———. *Visions of Excess: Selected Writings, 1927–1939.* Ed. Allan Stoekl. Trans. Allan Stoekl with Carl R. Lovitt and Donald M. Leslie, Jr. Minneapolis: University of Minnesota Press, 1985.

Baudrillard, Jean. *Simulations.* Trans. Paul Foss, Paul Patton, and Philip Beitchman. New York: Semiotext(e), 1983.

Beardsworth, Sara. "From Revolution to Revolt Culture." *Revolt, Affect, Collectivity: The Unstable Boundaries of Kristeva's Polis.* Ed. Tina Chanter and Ewa Plonowska Ziarek. Albany, NY: SUNY Press, 2005, pp. 37–56.

Beauvoir, Simone de. *The Second Sex.* Ed. and Trans. H. M. Parshley. New York: Vintage Books, 1989.

Bederman, Gail. *Manliness & Civilization: A Cultural History of Gender and Race in the United States, 1880–1917.* Chicago and London: The University of Chicago Press, 1995.

Bellaigue, Christina de. *Educating Women: Schooling and Identity in England and France, 1800–1867.* Oxford, UK, and New York: Oxford University Press, 2007.

Bennett, Jessica. "Feminism or Bust." *Newsweek* (March 23, 2010). Available at: www.newsweek.com/2010/03/22/feminism-or-bust.html. Accessed: April 6, 2010.

Bosman, Julie, and Stephanie Strom. "'Three Cups of Tea' Author Defends Book." *New York Times* (April 17, 2011). Available at: www.nytimes.com/2011/04/18 /business/media/18mortenson.htm. Accessed: April 18, 2011.

Boushey, Heather. "Not Working: Unemployment among Married Couples." *Center for American Progress.* 2011. Available at: www.americanprogress.org /issues/2011/05/marital_unemployment.html. Accessed: May 6, 2011.

Bracey, Gerald W. "The Success of Single-Sex Education is Still Unproven." *The Education Digest* (February 2007): 22–26.

Brandt, Joan. "Julia Kristeva and the Revolutionary Politics of *Tel Quel.*" *Revolt, Affect, Collectivity: The Unstable Boundaries of Kristeva's Polis.* Ed. Tina Chanter and Ewa Plonowska Ziarek. Albany, NY: SUNY Press, 2005, pp. 21–36.

Brennan, Timothy. "The Italian Ideology." *Debating Empire.* Ed. Gopal Balakrishnan. London and New York: Verso, 2003, pp. 96–120.

Bronte, Charlotte. *The Professor.* London: Wordsworth Editions, 1994.

———. *Villette.* Ed. Helen M. Cooper. London and New York: Penguin Books, 2004.

Brown, Wendy. *Edgework: Critical Essays on Knowledge and Politics.* Princeton and Oxford: Princeton University Press, 2005.

Butler, Judith. *Antigone's Claim: Kinship Between Life and Death.* New York: Columbia University Press, 2000.

———. *Frames of War: When Is Life Grievable?* New York and London: Verso, 2009.

———. *Gender Trouble: Feminism and the Subversion of Identity.* New York and London: Routledge, 1990, 1999, 2006.

———. "Merely Cultural." *Social Text* 52/53 (Autumn/Winter 1997): 265–277.

———. *Subjects of Desire: Hegelian Reflections in Twentieth-Century France.* New York: Columbia University Press, 1987.

———. *Undoing Gender.* New York and London: Routledge, 2004.

Butler, Judith, and Gayatri Chakravorty Spivak. *Who Sings the Nation-State?: Language, Politics, Belonging.* London, New York, and Calcutta: Seagull Books, 2007.

Callinicos, Alex. "Antonio Negri and the Temptation of Ontology." *The Philosophy of Antonio Negri: Revolution in Theory, Volume Two*. Ed. Timothy S. Murphy and Abdul-Karim Mustapha. London and Ann Arbor, MI: Pluto Press, 2007, pp. 169–197.

Casarino, Cesare. "Time Matters: Marx, Negri, Agamben, and the Corporeal." In *In Praise of the Common: A Conversation on Philosophy and Politics*. Minneapolis and London: University of Minnesota Press, 2008.

———. "Time Matters: Marx, Negri, Agamben, and the Corporeal." *Strategies* 16, 2 (2003): 185–206.

Casarino, Cesare, and Antonio Negri. *In Praise of the Common: A Conversation on Philosophy and Politics*. Minneapolis and London: University of Minnesota Press, 2008.

———. "It's a Powerful Life: A Conversation on Contemporary Philosophy." *Cultural Critique* 57 (Spring 2004): 151–183.

Charania, Munira Moon. "Reading the Body: The Rhetoric of Sex, Identity and Discipline in Girls' Education." *International Journal of Qualitative Studies in Education* 23, 2 (May–June 2010): 305–330.

Chatterjee, Partha. "The Nation and Its Women." *A Subaltern Studies Reader*. Ed. Ranajit Guha. Minneapolis and London: University of Minnesota Press, 1997.

Chow, Rey. *The Age of the World Target: Self-Referentiality in War, Theory, and Comparative Work*. Durham and London: Duke University Press, 2006.

Cixous, Helene. *Reverie of the Wild Woman: Primary Scenes*. Trans. Beverley Bie Brahic. Evanston, IL: Northwestern University Press, 2006.

Colette. "Claudine at School." In *The Complete Claudine*. Trans. Antonia White. New York: Farrar, Straus and Giroux, 1976.

Corsani, Antonella A., and Timothy S. Murphy. "Beyond the Myth of Woman: The Becoming-Transfeminist of (Post-Marxism)." *SubStance* 36, 1 (2007): 107–138.

Covert, Bryce. "What Paul Ryan's Budget Means for Women." *The Nation* (March 12, 2013). Available at: www.thenation.com/blog/173300/what-ryans-budget-means-women. Accessed: March 12, 2013.

Dalla Costa, Mariarosa. "Women and the Subversion of the Community." *The Power of Women and the Subversion of the Community, Third Edition*. By Mariarosa Dalla Costa and Selma James. Bristol, UK: Falling Wall Press, 1972, pp. 21–56.

Dalla Costa, Mariarosa, and Giovanna F. Dalla Costa, eds. *Women, Development and Labor of Reproduction: Struggles and Movements*. Trenton, NJ, and Asmara, Eritrea: African World Press, 1999.

Del Re, Alisa. "Feminism and Autonomy: Itinerary of Struggle." *The Philosophy of Antonio Negri: Resistance in Practice*. Ed. Timothy S. Murphy and Abdul-Karim Mustapha. London and Ann Arbor, MI: Pluto Press, 2005, pp. 48–72.

Deleuze, Gilles. "Postscript on the Societies of Control." *October* 59 (Winter 1992): 3–7.

Delphy, Christine. *Close to Home: A Materialist Analysis of Women's Oppression*. Trans. Diana Leonard. London: Hutchinson, 1970.

———. "Protofeminism and Antifeminism." In *French Feminist Thought: A Reader.* Ed. Toril Moi. Oxford, UK, and New York: Wiley-Blackwell, 1987, pp. 80–109.

———. "Rethinking Sex and Gender." In *French Feminism Reader.* Ed. Kelly Oliver. Lanham, MD, and Boulder, CO: Rowman & Littlefield, 2000.

DeParle, Jason. "Two Classes, Divided by 'I Do.'" *The New York Times* (July 14, 2012). Available at: www.nytimes.com/2012/07/15/us/two-classes-in-america-divided-by-i-do.html?pagewanted=all. Accessed: July 31, 2012.

Dyer-Witherford, Nick. "Cyber-Negri: General Intellect and Immaterial Labor." *The Philosophy of Antonio Negri: Resistance in Practice.* Ed. Timothy S. Murphy and Abdul-Karim Mustapha. London and Ann Arbor, MI: Pluto Press, 2005, pp. 136–162.

Ebert, Teresa L. "Rematerializing Feminism." *Science & Society* 69, 1 (January 2005): 33–55.

Eisenstein, Hester. "A Dangerous Liaison?: Feminism and Corporate Globalization." *Science & Society* 3 (July 2005): 487–518.

———. *Feminism Seduced: How Global Elites Use Women's Labor and Ideas to Exploit the World.* Boulder, CO, and London: Paradigm Publishers, 2009.

Engels, Friedrich. *The Origin of the Family, Private Property, and the State.* Trans. Alick West (proofed and corrected by Mark Harris, 2010). Available at: www.marxists.org/archive/marx/works/download/pdf/origin_family.pdf. Accessed: April 1, 2011.

Ewing, E. Thomas. "The Repudiation of Single-Sex Education: Boys' Schools in the Soviet Union, 1943–1954." *American Educational Research Journal* 43, 4 (Winter 2006): 621–650.

Fanon, Frantz. *A Dying Colonialism.* Trans. Haaken Chevalier. New York: Grove, 1965.

Federici, Silvia. *Caliban and the Witch: Women, the Body and Primitive Accumulation.* Brooklyn, NY: Autonomedia, 2004.

———. "Reproduction and Feminist Struggle in the New International Division of Labor." *Women, Development and Labor of Reproduction: Struggles and Movements.* Ed. Mariarosa Dalla Costa and Giovanna F. Dalla Costa. Trenton, NJ, and Asmara, Eritrea: Africa World Press, 1999, pp. 47–81.

———. *Revolution at Point Zero: Housework, Reproduction, and Feminist Struggle.* Oakland, CA: PM Press; and Brooklyn, NY: Common Notions, 2012.

Felski, Rita. "Nothing to Declare: Identity, Shame, and the Lower Middle Class." *PMLA* 115 (January 2000): 33–45.

Fortunati, Leopoldina. *The Arcane of Reproduction: Housework, Prostitution, Labor and Capital.* Ed. Jim Fleming. Trans. Hilary Creek. New York: Autonomedia, 1995.

Foucault, Michel. *The Birth of Biopolitics: Lectures at the Collège de France, 1978–79.* Ed. Michel Senellart. Trans. Graham Burchell. London and New York: Palgrave Macmillan, 2008.

———. *Herculine Barbin: Being the Recently Discovered Memoirs of a Nineteenth-Century French Hermaphrodite.* Trans. Richard McDougall. New York: Pantheon Books, 1978, 1980.

Fraser, Nancy. "Feminism, Capitalism and the Cunning of History." *New Left Review* (March/April 2009): 97–117.

———. "The Uses and Abuses of French Discourse Theories for Feminist Politics." *Boundary 2* 17, 2 (Summer 1990): 82–101.

———. *Unruly Practices: Power, Discourse and Gender in Contemporary Social Theory*. Minneapolis: University of Minnesota Press, 1989.

Freud, Sigmund. "Lecture XXXIII. Femininity." *The Standard Edition of the Complete Psychological Works of Sigmund Freud*. Trans. James Strachey in collaboration with Anna Freud, assisted by Alix Strachey and Alan Tyson. London: The Hogarth Press, 1986. Volume XXII, pp. 112–135.

Friend, Jennifer. "Single-Gender Public Education and Federal Policy: Implications of Gender-Based School Reforms in Philadelphia." *American Educational History Journal* 34, 1 (2007): 55–67.

Gabriel, Mary. *Love and Capital: Karl and Jenny Marx and the Birth of a Revolution*. New York, Boston, and London: Little, Brown and Company, 2011.

Gates, Henry Louis. "'Authenticity,' or the Lesson of Little Tree." *New York Times Book Review* (November 24, 1991): 1, 26–30.

Gimenez, Martha E. "Capitalism and the Oppression of Women: Marx Revisited." *Science & Society* 69, 1 (January 2005): 11–32.

———. "Connecting Marx and Feminism in the Era of Globalization: A Preliminary Investigation." *Socialism and Democracy* 18, 1 (September 2010): 85–105.

Goodlad, Lauren M. E. *Victorian Literature and the Victorian State: Character & Governance in a Liberal Society*. Baltimore, MD, and London: The Johns Hopkins University Press, 2003.

Goodman, Amy. "Ten Years After U.S. Invasion, Afghan War Rages on With No End in Sight." *Democracy Now!* (October 7, 2011). Available at: www.democracy-now.org/. Accessed: October 7, 2011.

Goodman, Robin Truth. *Feminist Theory in Pursuit of the Public: Women and the "Re-Privatization" of Labor*. New York: Palgrave, 2010.

———. *Policing Narratives and the State of Terror*. Albany, NY: SUNY Press, 2009.

Gray, Ann. "Enterprising Femininity: New Modes of Work and Subjectivity." *European Journal of Cultural Studies* 6, 4 (2003): 489–506.

Gregg, Melissa. *Work's Intimacy*. Cambridge, UK, and Malden, MA: Polity, 2011.

Grosz, Elizabeth. *In the Nick of Time: Politics, Evolution, and the Untimely*. Durham, NC, and London: Duke University Press, 2004.

———. "The Practice of Feminist Theory." *Differences: A Journal of Feminist Cultural Studies* 21, 1 (2010): 94–108.

Halpern, Diane F. et al. "The Pseudoscience of Single-Sex Schooling." *Science* (September 23, 2011): 1706–1707.

Haraway, Donna J. *Simians, Cyborgs, and Women: The Reinvention of Nature*. New York: Routledge, 1991.

Hardt, Michael, and Antonio Negri. *Commonwealth*. Cambridge, MA: Harvard University Press, 2009.

———. *Empire*. Cambridge, MA and London: Harvard University Press, 2000.

———. *Labor of Dionysus: A Critic of the State-Form*. Minneapolis and London: University of Minnesota Press, 1994.

———. *Multitude: War and Democracy in the Age of Empire*. New York: Penguin Press, 2004.

Hartmann, Heidi. "The Unhappy Marriage of Marxism and Feminism: Towards a More Progressive Union." *Women and Revolution: A Discussion of the Unhappy Marriage of Marxism and Feminism*. Ed. Lydia Sargent. Montreal: Black Rose Books, 1981, pp. 1–41.

Hartmann, Heidi, and Ann R. Markusen. "Contemporary Marxist Theory and Practice: A Feminist Critique." *Review of Radical Political Economics* 12, 2 (Summer 1980): 87–94.

Hartsock, Nancy. *The Feminist Standpoint Revisited and Other Essays*. Boulder, CO, and Oxford, UK: Westview Press, 1998.

———. "Globalization and Primitive Accumulation: The Contributions of David Harvey's Dialectical Marxism." *David Harvey: A Critical Reader*. Ed. Noel Castree and Derek Gregory. Malden, MA, and Oxford, UK: Blackwell, 2006, pp. 167–190.

———. *Money Sex and Power: Toward a Feminist Historical Materialism*. Boston, MA: Northeastern University Press, 1983.

Harvey, David. *A Companion to Marx's Capital*. London and New York: Verso, 2010.

———. *Rebel Cities: From the Right to the City to the Urban Revolution*. London and New York: Verso, 2012.

Hegewisch, Ariane, Claudia Williams, and Angela Edwards. *Insitute for Women's Policy Research Fact Sheet: The Gender Gap: 2012*. Available at: www.iwpr.org/publications/pubs/the-gender-wage-gap-2012/. Accessed: March 8, 2013.

Hellman, Lillian. *The Children's Hour. Acting Edition*. New York: Dramatists Play Service Inc., 1934.

Hennessy, Rosemary. *Materialist Feminism and the Politics of Discourse*. London and New York: Routledge, 1993.

———. "Open Secrets: The Affective Cultures of Organizing on Mexico's Northern Border." *Feminist Theory* 10, 3 (2009): 309–322.

Herr, Kathryn, and Emily Arms. "Accountability and Single-Sex Schooling: A Collision of Reform Agendas." *American Educational Research Journal* 41, 3 (Autumn 2004): 527–555.

Herz, Barbara, and Gene B. Sperling. *What Works in Girls' Education: Evidence and Policies from the Developing World*. New York: Council on Foreign Relations, 2004.

Holland, Eugene W. "Optimism of the Intellect…" *Strategies* 16, 2 (2003): 121–131.

Hughes, Teresa A. "The Advantages of Single-Sex Education." *National Forum of Educational Administration and Supervision Journal* 23, 2 (2006–2007): 5–14.

Irigaray, Luce. "Women on the Market." In *This Sex Which Is Not One*. Trans. Catherine Porter with Carolyn Burke. Ithaca, NY: Cornell University Press, 1985.

Jackson, Janna. "'Dangerous Presumptions': How Single-Sex Schooling Reifies False Notions of Sex, Gender, and Sexuality." *Gender and Education* 22, 2 (March 2010): 227–238.

James, Selma. "Introduction" and "A Woman's Place." *The Power of Women and the Subversion of the Community, Third Edition.* By Mariarosa Dalla Costa and Selma James. Bristol, UK: Falling Wall Press, 1972, pp. 3–20 and 57–79.

Jameson, Fredric. "A New Reading of *Capital.*" *Mediations* 25, 1 (Fall 2010). Available at: www.mediationsjournal.org/articles/a-new-reading-of-capital. Access: February 28, 2011.

———. *The Political Unconscious: Narrative as a Socially Symbolic Act.* Ithaca, NY: Cornell University Press, 1981.

———. "On Raymond Chandler." *The Critical Response to Raymond Chandler.* Ed. J. K. Dover. Westport, CT, and London: Greenwood Press, 1995, pp. 65–87.

———. *Representing Capital: A Reading of Volume One.* London and New York: Verso, 2011.

Kaminer, Wendy. "The Trouble with Single-Sex Schools." *The Atlantic* (April 1998). Available at: www.theatlantic.com/doc/199804/single-sex. Accessed: October 9, 2011.

Keating, Christine, Claire Rasmussen, and Pooja Rishi. "The Rationality of Empowerment: Microcredit, Accumulation by Dispossession, and the Gendered Economy." *Signs: Journal of Women in Culture and Society* 36, 1 (2010): 153–176.

Keller, Emma G. "Girls and Science: Why the Gender Gap Exists and What to do About it." *The Guardian* (February 5, 2013). Available at: www.guardian.co.uk/world/us-news-blog/2013/feb/05/girls-science-gender-gap-fix?INTCMP=SRCH. Accessed: February 15, 2013.

Kelly, Annie. "Afghan Girls' Education Backsliding as Donors Shift Focus to Withdrawal." *The Guardian* (February 24, 2011). available at: www.guardian.co.uk/global-development/2011/feb/24/afghanistan-girls-education-report. Accessed: October 7, 2011.

Kojève, Alexandre. *Introduction to the Reading of Hegel: Lectures on the Phenomenology of Spirit.* Ed. Allan Bloom. Trans. James H. Nichols, Jr. Ithaca, NY, and London: Cornell University Press, 1969.

Krakauer, Jon. *Three Cups of Deceit.* New York: Anchor Books, 2011.

Kristeva, Julia. *Black Sun: Depression and Melancholia.* Trans. Leon S. Roudiez. New York: Columbia University Press, 1989.

———. *Desire in Language: A Semiotic Approach to Literature and Art.* Ed. Leon S. Roudiez. Trans. Thomas Gora, Alice Jardine, and Leon S. Roudiez. New York: Columbia University Press, 1980.

———. *Hannah Arendt.* Trans. Ross Guberman. New York: Columbia University Press, 2001.

———. *This Incredible Need to Believe.* Trans. Beverley Bie Brahic. New York: Columbia University Press, 2009.

———. *Possessions.* Trans. Barbara Bray. New York: Columbia University Press, 1998.

————. *Powers of Horror: An Essay on Abjection.* Trans. Leon S. Roudiez. New York: Columbia University Press, 1982.

————. *Revolution in Poetic Language.* Trans. Margaret Waller. New York: Columbia University Press, 1984.

————. *The Severed Head: Capital Visions.* Trans. Jody Gladding. New York: Columbia University Press, 2012.

————. *Strangers to Ourselves.* Trans. Leon S. Roudiez. New York: Columbia University Press, 1991.

————. "The System and the Speaking Subject." *The Kristeva Reader.* Ed. Toril Moi. Oxford, UK: Blackwell, 1986, pp. 24–33.

————. "Women's Time." In *French Feminism Reader.* Ed. Kelly Oliver. Lanham, MD: Rowman & Littlefield, 2000, pp. 181–200.

Kuhn, Annette. "Structures of Patriarchy and Capital in the Family." *Feminism and Materialism: Women and Modes of Production.* London, Henley, and Boston: Routledge and Kegan Paul, 1978, pp. 42–67.

Lacan, Jacques. "The Signification of the Phallus: *Die Bedeutung des Phallus.*" *Ecrits.* Trans. Bruce Fink with Heloise Fink and Russell Grigg. New York and London: W. W. Norton & Company, 1966, pp. 757–784.

Laclau, Ernesto, and Chantal Mouffe. *Hegemony and Socialist Strategy: Towards a Radical Democratic Politics. Second Edition.* London and New York: Verso, 1985.

Ladenson, Elisabeth. "Colette for Export Only." *Yale French Studies* 90 (1996): 25–46.

Leavis, Q. D. "Introduction." In *Villette.* By Charlotte Bronte. New York: Harper Colophon, 1972, pp. vii–xli.

Levy, Anita. "Gendered Labor, the Woman Writer and Dorothy Richardson." *NOVEL: A Forum on Fiction* 25, 1 (Autumn 1991): 50–70.

Luxemburg, Rosa. *The Accumulation of Capital.* Trans. Agnes Schwarzschild. London and New York: Routledge, 2003.

Macherey, Pierre. "Negri's Spinoza: From Mediation to Constitution, Description of a Speculative Journey." Trans. Ted Stolze. *The Philosophy of Antonio Negri: Revolution in Theory, Volume Two.* Ed. Timothy S. Murphy and Abdul-Karim Mustapha. London and Ann Arbor, MI: Pluto Press, 2007, pp. 7–27.

Marazzi, Christian. *Capital and Language: From the New Economy to the War Economy.* Trans. Gregory Conti. Los Angeles, CA: Semiotext(e), 2008.

Marcuse, Herbert. *One-Dimensional Man: Studies in the Ideology of Advanced Industrial Society.* Boston, MA: Beacon Press, 1964.

Margaroni, Maria. "Julia Kristeva's Chiasmatic Journeys: From Byzantium to the Phantom of Europe and the End of the World." *Psychoanalysis, Art, and Politics in the Work of Julia Kristeva.* Ed. Kelly Oliver and Stacy Keltner. Albany, NY: State University of New York Press, 2009, pp. 107–124.

————. "'The Lost Foundation': Kristeva's Semiotic Chora and Its Ambiguous Legacy." *Hypatia* 20, 1 (Winter 2005): 78–98.

Marx, Karl with Friedrich Engels. "The German Ideology, including Theses on Feuerbach and Introduction to the Critique of Political Economy." In *The*

Marx-Engels Reader, Second Edition. Ed. Robert C. Tucker. New York and London: W. W. Norton & Co., 1978, pp. 146–200.

Marx. Karl. *Capital Volume I: A Critical Analysis of Capitalist Production.* Ed. Frederick Engels. Trans. Samuel Moore and Edward Aveling. New York: International Publishers, 1967.

———. *Capital Volume II: A Critique of Political Economy.* Trans. David Fernbach. New York: Penguin Books in association with New Left Review, 1978.

———. *Grundrisse: Foundations of the Critique of Political Economy (Rough Draft).* Trans. Martin Nicolaus. London and New York: Penguin Books in association with *New Left Review:* 1973.

———. "Manifesto of the Communist Party." In *The Marx-Engels Reader, Second Edition.* Ed. Robert C. Tucker. New York and London: W. W. Norton & Co., 1978, pp. 469–500.

Mason, Paul. "Paul Mason on *Live Working or Die Fighting: How the Working Class Went Global.* Radio interview with Amy Goodman and Juan Gonzalez. *Democracy Now!* September 24, 2010. Available at: www.democracynow.org/2010/9/24/paul_mason_on__live_working. Accessed: May 28, 2011.

Mbembe, Achille. "Necropolitics." Trans. Libby Meintjies. *Public Culture* 15, 1 (Winter 2003): 11–40.

McCreary, Andrew J. "Public Single-Sex K-12 Education: The Renewal of Sex-Based Policy by Post-Race Politics, 1986–2006." *Journal of Law & Education* 40, 3 (July 2011): 461–497.

McDonough Roisin, and Rachel Harrison. "Patriarchy and Relations of Production." *Feminism and Materialism: Women and Modes of Production.* London, Henley and Boston: Routledge and Kegan Paul, 1978, pp. 11–41.

McNay, Lois. *Gender and Agency: Reconfiguring the Subject in Feminist and Social Theory.* Cambridge, UK and Malden, MA: Polity, 2000.

McNeil, Michele. "Singe-Sex Schooling Gets New Showcase." *Education Week* (May 7, 2008): 20–22.

McRobbie, Angela. "Reflections on Feminism, Immaterial Labour and the Post-Fordist Regime." *New Formations* (2010): 60–76.

McRobbie, Robbie. "Top Girls?" *Cultural Studies* 21, 4–5 (2007): 718–737.

Medina, Jennifer. "Boys and Girls Together, Taught Separately in Public School." *New York Times* (March 11, 2009). Available at: www.nytimes.com/2009/03/11/education/11gender.html. Accessed: October 8, 2011.

Mies, Maria. *Patriarchy & Accumulation on a World Scale: Women in the International Division of Labour.* London and New York: Zed Books, 1986, 1998.

Mitchell, Juliet. *Psychoanalysis and Feminism: A Radical Reassessment of Freudian Psychoanalysis. New Edition.* New York: Basic Books, 1974.

———. "Women: The Long Revolution." *New Left Review* 40 (November–December 1966): 11–37.

Mohanty, Chandra Talpade. "'Under Western Eyes' Revisited: Feminist Solidarity through Anticapitalist Struggles." *Feminism without Borders: Decolonizing Theory, Practicing Solidarity.* Durham, NC, and London: Duke University Press, 2003, pp. 221–251.

————. "Under Western Eyes: Feminist Scholarship and Colonial Discourses." In *Feminist Postcolonial Theory: A Reader*. Ed. Reina Lewis and Sara Mills. New York: Routledge, 2003, pp. 49–74.

Moi, Toril. "Introduction." *The Kristeva Reader*. Ed. Toril Moi. Oxford, UK: Blackwell, 1986, pp. 1–22.

————. *What Is a Woman? And Other Essays*. Oxford, UK, and New York: Oxford University Press, 1999.

Mortenson, Greg. *Stones Into Schools: Promoting Peace Through Education in Afghanistan and Pakistan*. New York: Penguin, 2009.

Mortenson, Greg with David Oliver Relin. *Three Cups of Tea: One Man's Mission to Promote Peace… One School at a Time*. New York: Penguin, 2006.

Nealon, Christopher. "Reading on the Left." *Representations* 108, 1 (Fall 2009): 22–50.

Negri, Antonio. *Art & Multitude: Nine Letters on Art, Followed by Metamorphoses: Art and Immaterial Labour*. Trans. Ed Emery. Cambridge, UK, and Malden, MA: Polity, 2011.

————. *Insurgencies: Constituent Power and the Modern State*. Trans. Maurizia Boscagli. Minneapolis and London: University of Minnesota Press, 1999.

————. *Marx Beyond Marx: Lessons on the Grundrisse*. Ed. Jim Fleming. Trans. Harry Cleaver, Michael Ryan, and Maurizio Viano. Brooklyn, NY, and London: Autonomedia/Pluto, 1991.

————. *The Savage Anomaly: The Power of Spinoza's Metaphysics and Politics*. Trans. Michael Hardt. Minneapolis and Oxford, UK: University of Minnesota Press, 1991A.

————. *Time for Revolution*. Trans. Matteo Mandarini. London and New York: Continuum, 2003.

Nicholson, Linda. "Feminism and Marx: Integrating Kinship with the Economic." In *The Second Wave: A Reader in Feminist Theory*. Ed. Linda Nicholson. London and New York: Routledge, 1997, pp. 131–145.

Oliver, Kelly. "Revolt and Forgiveness." *Revolt, Affect, Collectivity: The Unstable Boundaries of Kristeva's Polis*. Ed. Tina Chanter and Ewa Plonowska Ziarek. Albany, NY: SUNY Press, 2005, pp. 77–92.

Ong, Aihwa. "A Bio-Cartography: Maids, Neo-Slavery, and NGOs." *Migrations and Mobilities: Citizenship, Borders, and Gender*. Ed. Seyla Benhabib and Judith Resnick. New York and London: New York University Press, 2009, pp. 157–184.

————. *Flexible Citizenship: The Cultural Logics of Transnationality*. Durham and London: Duke University Press, 1999.

————. *Neoliberalism as Exception: Mutations in Citizenship and Sovereignty*. Durham and London: Duke University Press, 2006.

Orenstein, Peggy, in association with the American Association of University Women. *SchoolGirls: Young Women, Self-Esteem, and the Confidence Gap*. New York: Anchor Books, 1994.

Pang, Laikwan. "The Labor Factor in the Creative Economy: A Marxist Reading." *Social Text 99*, 27, 2 (Summer 2009): 55–76.

Parker, Andrew. "Unthinking Sex: Marx, Engels, and the Scene of Writing." *Fear of a Queer Planet: Queer Politics and Social Theory.* Ed. Michael Warner. Minneapolis and London: University of Minnesota Press, 1993, pp. 19–41.

Parvulescu, Anca. "Import/Export: Housework in an International Frame." *PMLA* 127, 4 (October 2012): 845–862.

Pelletier, Madeleine. *L'éducation féministe des filles.* Ed. Claude Maignien, Paris: Syros, 1978.

Policy and Program Studies Service of the US Department of Education's Office of Planning, Evaluation and Policy Development. "Single-Sex Versus Coeducational Schooling: A Systematic Review." Washington, DC: US Department of Education, 2005. Available at: www.ed.gov/about/offices/list/opepd/reports.html.

Pollit, Katha. "The Bitter Tea of Greg Mortenson." *The Nation* (May 16, 2011): 9.

Poovey, Mary. *Uneven Developments: The Ideological Work of Gender in Mid-Victorian England.* Chicago and London: University of Chicago Press, 1988.

Provost, Mark. "Why the Rich Love High Unemployment." *Truthout* (May 24, 2011). Available at: www.truthout.org/why-rich-love-high-unemployment/1305061465. Accessed: July 2, 2011.

Quinby, Lee. "Taking the Millennialist Pulse of *Empire*'s Multitude: A Genealogical Feminist Diagnosis." *Empire's New Clothes: Reading Hardt and Negri.* Ed. Paul A. Passavant and Jodi Dean. New York and London: Routledge, 2004, pp. 231–252.

Rancière, Jacques. "Communists without Communism?" *The Idea of Communism.* Ed. Costas Douzinas and Slavoj Zizek. London and New York: Verso, 2010, pp. 167–178.

———. *Dis-agreement: Politics and Philosophy.* Trans. Julie Rose. Minneapolis and London: University of Minnesota Press, 1999.

Richardson, Dorothy Miller. "Backwater." In *Pilgrimage I.* By Dorothy M. Richardson. New York: Alfred A. Knopf, 1967.

———. *Pointed Roofs.* London: Duckworth & Co., 1915.

Rogers, Rebecca. *From the Salon to the Schoolroom: Educating Bourgeois Girls in Nineteenth-Century France.* University Park, PA: The Pennsylvania State University Press, 2005.

Rose, Jacqueline. *Sexuality in the Field of Vision.* London and New York: Verso, 1986.

Rousseau, Jean-Jacques. *Emile or on Education: Includes Emile and Sophie, or the Solitaries.* In *The Collected Writings of Rousseau, Vol. 13.* Ed. and Trans. Christopher Kelly and Allan Bloom. Hanover, NH, and London: University Press of New England, 2010.

Roy, Ananya. *Poverty Capital: Microfinance and the Making of Development.* New York and London: Routledge, 2010.

Rubin, Gayle. "The Traffic in Women: Notes on the 'Political Economy' of Sex." *Towards an Anthropology of Women.* Ed. Rayna R. Reiter. New York: Monthly Review Press, 1976, pp. 157–210.

Ruth, Jennifer. "Between Labor and Capital: Charlotte Brontë's Professional Professor." *Victorian Studies* 45, 2 (Winter 2003): 279–303.

Salomone, Rosemary C. *Same, Different, Equal: Rethinking Single-Sex Schooling.* New Haven, CT, and London: Yale University Press, 2003.

Saltman, Kenneth J. *Capitalizing on Disaster: Taking and Breaking Public Schools.* Boulder, CO, and London: Paradigm Publishers, 2007.

Sassen, Saskia. "The Repositioning of Citizenship: Emergent Subjects and Spaces for Politics." *Empire's New Clothes: Reading Hardt and Negri.* Ed. Paul A. Passavant and Jodi Dean. New York and London: Routledge, 2004, pp. 175–198.

Sax, Leonard. *Why Gender Matters: What Parents and Teachers Need to Know about the Emerging Science of Sex Differences.* New York and London: Doubleday, 2005.

Sayers, Dorothy L. *Gaudy Night.* New York: Harper Paperbacks, 1936.

Scott, Anna. "One-Sex Classes Bill Wins Approval." *Sun* (April 3, 2008). Available at: www.sun-sentinel.com/news/local/florida/sfl-flfxgr0403sbapr03,0,3985358. story. Accessed: April 4, 2008.

Sennett, Richard. *The Fall of the Public Man.* New York and London: W. W. Norton & Co., 1974.

Shah, Saeeda, and Conchar, Catherine. "Why Single-Sex Schools? Discourses of Culture/ Faith and Achievement." *Cambridge Journal of Education* 39, 2 (June 2009): 191–2004.

Sjöhom, Cecilia. *Kristeva & the Political.* London and New York: Routledge, 2005.

Slaughter, Anne-Marie. "Why Women Still Can't Have It All." *The Atlantic* (July/ August 2012): 85–102.

Spivak, Gayatri Chakravorty. *Outside in the Teaching Machine.* New York and London: Routledge, 1993.

Stein, Gertrude. "Fernhurst." In *Fernhurst, Q.E.D., and Other Early Writings.* New York: Liveright, 1971.

Sullivan, Alice, Heather Joshi, and Diana Leonard. "Single-Sex Schooling and Labour Market Outcomes." *Oxford Review of Education* 37, 3 (2011): 311–332.

Terranova, Tiziana. *Network Culture: Politics for the Information Age.* New York: Pluto Press, 2004.

Tilburg, Patricia A. *Colette's Republic: Work, Gender, and Popular Culture in France, 1870–1914.* New York and Oxford, UK: Berghahn Books, 2009.

Toscano, Alberto. "Always Already Only Now: Negri and the Biopolitical." *The Philosophy of Antonio Negri: Revolution in Theory, Volume Two.* Ed. Timothy S. Murphy and Abdul-Karim Mustapha. London and Ann Arbor, MI: Pluto Press, 2007, pp. 109–128.

Utchitelle, Louis. "From Two Breadwinners to One." *The Nation* (May 4, 2011). Available at: www.thenation.com/article/160438/two-breadwinners-one. Accessed: May 6, 2011.

Vercellone, Carlo. "From Formal Subsumption to General Intellect: Elements for a Marxist Reading of the Thesis of Cognitive Capitalism." *Historical Materialism* 15 (2007): 13–36.

Vogel, Lise. *Marxism and the Oppression of Women: Toward a Unitary Theory.* New Brunswick, NJ: Rutgers University Press, 1983.

Weber, Heloise. "The Imposition of a Global Development Architecture: The Example of Microcredit." *Review of International Studies* 28, 3 (2002): 537–555.

Weeks, Kathi. *The Problem with Work: Feminism, Marxism, Antiwork Politics, and Postwork Imaginaries.* Durham, NC, and London: Duke University Press, 2011.

Weis, Lois, and Centrie, Craig. "On the Power of Separate Spaces: Teachers and Students Writing (Righting) Selves and Future." *American Educational Research Journal* 39, 1 (Spring, 2002): 7–36.

Williams, Juliet A. "Learning Differences: Sex-Role Stereotyping in Single-Sex Public Education." *Harvard Journal of Law & Gender* 33 (2010): 555–579.

Williams, Raymond. "The Metropolis and the Emergence of Modernism." *Unreal City: Urban Experience in Modern European Literature and Art.* Ed. Edward Timms and David Kelley. Manchester, UK: Manchester University Press, 1985, pp. 13–24.

Wilson, Elizabeth A. "Underbelly." *Differences: A Journal of Feminist Cultural Studies* 21, 1 (2010): 194–208.

Winsloe, Christa. *The Child Manuela.* New York: Arno Press, 1975.

Wolf, Naomi. "The Paycheck Fairness Act's Realpolitik." *The Guardian UK* (June 8, 2012). Available at: www.guardian.co.uk/commentisfree/2012/jun/08/paycheck-fairness-act-realpolitik. Accessed: June 10, 2012.

———. "Why Women Still Can't Ask the Right Questions." *New Europe Online* (July 2, 2012). Available at: www.neurope.eu/author/naomi-wolf. Accessed: July 4, 2012.

Wood, Ellen Meiksins. "A Manifesto for Global Capitalism?" *Debating Empire.* Ed. Gopal Balakrishnan. London and New York: Verso, 2003, pp. 61–82.

Woolf, Virginia. *A Room of One's Own.* San Diego, CA, New York, and London: Harcourt Brace Jovanovich, 1929, 1957.

Wright, Melissa W. *Disposable Women and Other Myths of Global Capitalism.* New York and London: Routledge, 2006.

Young, Iris. "Beyond the Unhappy Marriage: A Critique of the Dual Systems Theory." *Women and Revolution: A Discussion of the Unhappy Marriage of Marxism and Feminism.* Ed. Lydia Sargent. Montreal: Black Rose Books, 1981, pp. 43–69.

———. "The Ideal of Community and the Politics of Difference." *Social Theory and Practice* 12, 1 (Spring 1986): 1–26.

Ziarek, Ewa Plonowska. *An Ethics of Dissensus: Postmodernity, Feminism, and the Politics of Radical Democracy.* Stanford, CA: Stanford University Press, 2001.

———. "The Uncanny Style of Kristeva's Critique of Nationalism." *Postmodern Culture* 5, 2 (1995).

Index